Tracing Homelands

T010974b

TRACING HOMELANDS

ISRAEL, PALESTINE, AND THE CLAIMS OF BELONGING

By Linda Dittmar

OLIVE
BRANCH
PRESS

An imprint of Interlink Publishing Group, Inc.
Northampton, Massachusetts

In memory of my parents

First published in 2023 by

Olive Branch Press
An imprint of Interlink Publishing Group, Inc.
46 Crosby Street, Northampton, MA 01060
www.interlinkbooks.com

Copyright © Linda Dittmar 2023
All photographs © Deborah Bright 2023
Cover photograph: Deborah Bright

Disclaimers
Village and Population numbers diverge, sometimes wildly, in both eyewitness and published reports. Those noted here are frequently cited and aim for a middle ground.

Except for named authors, historic figures, and people who participated in this work "on the ground" (Deborah, Eitan, Nurit, Amira, Judd, Anis, Donnie, and Jacoby), all names have been altered.

All rights reserved; no part of this publication may be reproduced, stored in a retrieval system, or transmitted, in any form or by any means, electronic, mechanical, photocopying, recording or otherwise, without the prior written permission of the publisher.

Library of Congress Cataloging-in-Publication Data:
Names: Dittmar, Linda, 1938– author.
Title: Tracing homelands : Israel, Palestine, and the claims of belonging / by Linda Dittmar.
Description: Northampton, Massachusetts : Olive Branch Press, an imprint of Interlink
    Publishing Group, Inc., 2023.
Identifiers: LCCN 2023017089 | ISBN 9781623717506 (paperback)
Subjects: LCSH: Dittmar, Linda, 1938– —Travel—Israel. | Dittmar, Linda, 1938– —
    Travel—Palestine. | Palestinian Nakba, 1947–1948. | Israel-Arab War, 1948–1949—
    Personal narratives, Israeli. | Israel—Description and travel. | Palestine—Description
    and travel. | BISAC: BIOGRAPHY & AUTOBIOGRAPHY / Personal Memoirs |
    BIOGRAPHY & AUTOBIOGRAPHY / Historical
Classification: LCC DS107.5 .D58 2023 | DDC 956.04/6092—dc23/eng/20230520
LC record available at https://lccn.loc.gov/2023017089

Printed and bound in the United States of America

9 8 7 6 5 4 3 2

Contents

Prologue: Points of Departure

*To recognize the "grey zones" of Israel-Palestine is to be truthful to the
many shades of reality that exist on the ground.*
—Amjad Iraqi

Trees rooting in the masonry of a hilltop ruin in the Galilee.

I was climbing up a steep village alley, writing in my notebook as I walked, when the ink ran out. I stood there, my feet unsteady on the cobblestones, trying to coax legibility out of letters that refused to yield even the barest hint of color. I no longer remember what I wanted to jot down: A date? The name of an artist whose work we'd seen a few minutes before in the gallery we had just visited? The group was moving on, some thirty or more Jewish Israelis tramping behind a Palestinian guide, strangers to me and mostly to one another. They won't notice if I go missing, I thought as the last stragglers were reaching the bend near the crest of the hill.

I hurried on. The cobblestones were slippery, smoothed by the generations of bare, sandaled, and shoed feet that had walked to and away from the village center. The houses flanking the alley rose right at its paved edge: massive stone walls, heavy wooden doors shut, small windows shuttered or barred, no garden in front. Tarshiha, this Palestinian village where I suddenly felt so alone, was sealed against me. I hardly even speak their language, I realized, not registering at that moment that they, the Palestinians, had no choice but to learn mine.

It was with relief that I saw, once I rounded the corner, the wide open door of a small neighborhood shop, a net full of colorful balls hooked by the doorjamb, a single light bulb hanging bare from an arched ceiling. Inside was a jumble of crowded shelves: toys, batteries, sewing notions, brooms, rumpled magazines, cheap electronics, cards for overseas phone calls, and ribbons of state lottery tickets.

"Shalom," I say in Hebrew to the heavy-set older man sitting behind the counter. No use in pretending to be anything but who I am, I tell myself—an Israeli passing through his Palestinian village up in the Galilee, an intruder at best, an enemy quite likely, one of "them" as far as he is concerned.

"Shalom," he answers, his tone qualified, eyes hooded, not meeting mine.

"May I buy a pen?" I ask.

He pulls a blue BIC pen from somewhere under that counter, sliding it in my direction.

"How much is it?" I ask, opening my wallet.

"Are you with the Zochrot tour?" he asks.

"Yes," I say.

"Then *t'fadali*, please, it's free." He raises his tired dark eyes. They meet mine.

"But I want to pay," I say, half sliding the pen back toward him.

"No, no … it's for you," he insists. There's new warmth in his voice.

I smile back, still tentative, my eyes searching his for something I cannot name. I am grateful for his kindness but also, in some hard-to-admit way, ashamed. Why should my coming to his village with Zochrot deserve this gift?

Zochrot ("We Remember") is an Israeli NGO dedicated to commemorating the Nakba, the Palestinian "catastrophe" of 1948, when Israel depopulated some 450 Palestinian villages and forced an estimated 750,000 men, women, and children into exile. Zochrot conducts tours to such villages, mostly destroyed, with barely a trace left. The tours are in Hebrew. Often guided by a Palestinian descendant of that village, they are meant primarily for us Israelis, who know little about that history. The assumption is that this firsthand knowledge, learned through the senses, will open up new possibilities for peace—for recognition, dialogue, and restitution.

Walking through a field or forest, you may come across the remains of a house, or perhaps a caved-in well or an oil press overrun by brambles. In some places the scent of wild thyme, za'atar, may reach you; in others it might be the scent of newly planted pine trees or the pungent dust of grass disintegrating under a harsh sun. In late summer, figs and then pomegranates ripen where nobody is left to pick them. This is what my body has registered on such tours, but also on my own, during my childhood and even now, as I keep revisiting Israel. It is the language of the land, on which is overlaid another language, that of the conscience: what do I feel about this history and what does it mean to this Tarshiha shopkeeper whose name I never thought to ask?

Speeding on Israel's paved roads, one rarely notices signs of the Nakba, even when some ruin or an abandoned tomb or a mosque comes into view, especially in built-up areas. They've been absorbed into Israel's evolving vernacular and ornamental architecture in ways that disguise what they are, let alone what they used to be. Does it matter that a lone fig tree happens to stand near a pile of stones in an empty field? Or that a lovely restaurant had once been a mosque? Or that a grocery in a small Israeli village, built of beautifully chiseled stones, used to be a Palestinian two-room schoolhouse? Once you know enough to notice this grafting of the new on the old, Israel no longer looks the same. Seen through the filter of the Nakba, both the bucolic

Ajjur: A Palestinian home, renovated as an Israeli restaurant, Hebron district.

beauty of its countryside and the dynamic effervescence of its modernity are shadowed by lives erased from the land that sustained them for centuries.

It did not come easily to me, this new way of looking that had me also question Israel's dearly held myths of origin. Yet between 2005 and 2008 that is what I did, searching the land with my photographer-partner, Deborah, aiming to record whatever evidence of the Nakba we could still find. It felt obsessive at times, this search, both the "why" of it and the "how."

Suggesting that we photograph signs of the Nakba came easily to Deborah. For her, an American, not even Jewish, it was initially a matter of professional interest, a forensic expedition and an aesthetic challenge, unmarked by personal or political attachments. A landscape photographer, she had previously located and photographed a defunct atomic reactor hidden in a forest outside Chicago and gone on to produce an impressive series of historic battlefield panoramas, American and European. All you see in these panoramas is an empty field, a torpid suburban sub-division, or a low-lying fenced-in hill, and yet thousands died there—at Antietam and Little Big Horn, at Agincourt and Waterloo, at the Ardennes and more. Somber, still, and expansive in their horizontal reach, these unpeopled black-and-white images had me thinking of my own landscape and the sabra cactuses that marked them.

Glimpsed from a passing car, you might not notice the prickly bushes that used to enclose a yard or fence in some animals. At a distance, they are just pale grayish-green patches, sometimes a whole bank of them. Such clumps dot the land. Dense with thorny pads that render them impassable, they hover at the smoggy margin of our Jewish awareness, along with remnants of demolished houses, neglected orchards, the odd minaret or Sheikh's tomb, the Arab street names that were gradually replaced by Hebrew ones, the Arabic words that entered our victorious slang. Though proof of the Nakba was everywhere, it remained unnamed among us Israeli Jews, a forbidden zone where none was to enter. "They," we were told, simply fled at the urging of their own leaders.

This narrative seeped in through the media, reassuring us of our righteousness, its truth reflexively accepted. There were recordings to prove it, we were told, though none turned up. There was no mention of the intimidation, forced deportations, or the massacres we committed to sow panic and impel flight. Victorious and aglow with accounts of Jewish heroism—our response to the Nazi atrocities that continue to sear our collective memory—we had only contempt for the people we called "the Arabs," denying their local identity. Steeped in dread of the unknown ahead of us, the pre-'48 Jewish population—the *yishuv*—and the newly arrived Jewish refugees clung together in a desperate need to ensure our own survival. The Nakba was a ghostly presence we could not afford to see.

Of course I rejected Deborah's suggestion that we document the Nakba. It took twelve years for my resistance to crumble, not because of any sudden awakening or a flash of life-changing insight, but through a slow journey into a murky territory where harsh realities kept crashing against a mythic utopian Zionism. Giving the Nakba image and voice, I hoped, would make peace and restitution possible. Photographing the residues of the Nakba would not be about hazily remote wars, as Deborah's earlier work had been, but about fighting alive within memory and continuing, in Gaza, the Golan, the Occupied Territories, and inside Israel itself.

This slow and painful process of peeling the film off my eyes is the subject of this book. Growing up in British Palestine as it became Israel (1939–1960) and born to a Zionist family that settled there in the nineteenth century, I was steeped in our narrative of national becoming: ancient expulsions and migrations, conquests and exiles; the Spanish Inquisition, ravaging pogroms and the Holocaust; the early *aliya* immigrations with women dying in childbirth and the pioneers dying of malaria; the ghetto fighters and the Jewish partisans of World War II; Hannah Senesh parachuting into Nazi-occupied Hungary to rescue Jews; Britain denying Europe's Jewish refugees shelter in Palestine, and much more. Tragedy and heroism were entwined in this story as I was taught it at school, in the neighborhood, and at home. *Bekol dor vedor*, in every generation, as the Passover Haggadah tells us, they rise to annihilate us—"they" shape-shifting from one era to the next, always against us.

Ours was not Hollywood's frothy tale of handsome, blue-eyed Paul Newman leading the ship *Exodus* to safe haven as Ari Ben Canaan, but a grim history where the rules of engagement and the supposed ethics of combat crumbled. In my young imagination this history was bound between the heroic defenders of Tel Hai in 1920 and the youths who, in 1948, risked their lives to defend the convoys to besieged Jerusalem at the narrow ravine of Bab el-Wad. For me, growing up in fledgling Israel, training through high school in the Gadna youth brigades, and then serving in Israel's Defense Forces (IDF), there was nothing more inspiring than our shared love of the land and pride in our new nation. These were, I truly believed, the only just responses to the appalling history we had inherited.

And then, so our national narrative went, after millennia of suffering and dispossession, after the Ottomans and then the British left, and after the United Nations vote confirmed our right to statehood, when the land we believed ours all along could finally become our refuge, the entire Arab world rose to destroy us, as we saw it, not giving a thought to what the Palestinians were losing through our rebirth.

For me, like so many others swept by the gales of this history, what happened to them seemed secondary to our own desperate need to survive centuries of unrelenting genocidal hate. During my school years and for decades beyond, the word "Nakba" didn't exist, let alone the historic facts it invoked. It was only our own suffering we studied at school—closely, obsessively, year after year. But by the time I visited Tarshiha, in 2006, I had changed and

Israel was changing too. By the time an unknown shopkeeper insisted on giving me a pen as a present, I was visiting his village in recognition of the Nakba, and he knew it.

Unlike most Zochrot tours, this time we were visiting a living Palestinian village in Israel's mountainous Galilee. It was also the first time I found myself inside a populated Israeli Palestinian locale that, unlike Jerusalem or Nazareth, is not a tourist destination. We were touring Tarshiha by invitation, timed to coincide with an observance of its fifty-eighth year of conquest and rebirth. The streets were empty and the houses shut only because people had assembled elsewhere, as we were soon to discover. During the tour we did learn about the devastating air raid attack Tarshiha had suffered in 1948, its fifty surviving residents' expulsion, the failed attempt to settle Jewish immigrants there, and the eventual return of a fraction of Tarshiha's residents augmented by Bedouins and other internal refugees. But the outstanding event of the day was Tarshiha's commemoration of the Nakba—to mourn the destruction and celebrate resilience.

Several small art galleries participated in this event, often showing work in which the indigenous, hard-to-eradicate prickly pear cactuses, sabras, serve as an icon of Palestinian resistance. There were landscape drawings where cactuses marked eradicated villages, and sculptures made from the plant's large succulent leaves, some "wounded" by cuts scored into their flesh. Included was also a glass book whose "pages" were transparent sheets of rough-edged glass bound with a cord—a palimpsest of receding layers of inscription whose razor-sharp edges deterred all but the brave.

Was I jotting down this artist's name when my ink ran out? The shopkeeper's welcome was no antidote to the bitter resistance inscribed in that lacerated cactus art and sharp-edged glass, a resistance that became explicit later that afternoon, when we—local Palestinians and Israeli visitors—gathered in a public hall for the screening of a new documentary, *Arous al-Jaleel.*

Made by Basel Tannous, a Tarshiha native, the film's title cites the village's affectionate nickname, "Bride of the Galilee," but it also refers to the film's protagonist, Fatma Hawari, who lost both her legs on her wedding day during the Israeli aerial attack on the village in late October of 1948. While the film celebrates both Fatma's and the village's resilience, its culminating moment occurs when, years later, she meets the pilot who bombed her village.

This combat pilot was Abie Nathan, who became notorious after I'd left Israel for the US in 1960. Having seen the carnage that aerial bombings inflicted on another nearby village, he became a peace activist, known between 1966 and 1993 for his Voice of Peace radio broadcasts from a ship he kept in international waters. At some point a CNN crew filmed him and Fatma, both of them old now, in an encounter included in Tannous's film. In this wrenching scene we see Fatma visiting Abie, who is now paralyzed by a stroke. These two old, crippled enemies, each in a wheelchair, show a certain affection for each other, like an old couple, yet they fail to reconcile, perhaps also like an old couple. Abie, slumped in his wheelchair, asks for forgiveness. Fatma, about to leave, says "no" with a bone-chilling smile I'll never forget, even as she pats his hand with consoling intimacy.

I had no sense of the audience's true feelings about the film, neither the Palestinians' nor the Jewish Israelis'. What might the storekeeper who gave me that pen think, I wondered, if he eventually closed his store and joined his neighbors at the film screening? Or what might she say, the artist who made the glass book that threatened to slice my fingers, were I to dare turn a page?

There was much applause as the credits rolled, with the smiling director present to receive the accolades. Some may have thought the woman was wrong to withhold forgiveness; many may have thought she was right. Everybody was affable, as is generally the case on such occasions. I don't recall the Jewish visitors saying anything, then or later, and what the Palestinians might have said in Arabic was opaque to me. I only remember my own paralysis and my sense of the chasm, the unhealed wounds, separating us.

And it's not one chasm. It's many, crisscrossing the landscape on which our Israeli and Palestinian claims to a homeland are being played out. The booklet Zochrot compiled for our tour includes heartbreaking eyewitness accounts of the carnage in Tarshiha. But in 1948 this hilltop village had also served, at least for a while, as headquarters for the Arab Liberation Army (ALA) and partner to an attack on a Jewish convoy at nearby Kabri. A hostile enemy village to us, Tarshiha was ultimately abandoned by the ALA, which left its poorly armed and badly trained men without protection.

Much has been written and more can be said about the military history of '48, including its global as well as local contexts, but this book heads elsewhere. Its Tarshiha stands as a parable, an account of suffering that has no symmetry and of politics that elude a simple "right" and "wrong." Each people have their own truth, their own claims to justice, never equivalent and not always spoken. What, finally, did the gift of a blue BIC pen mean that afternoon in Tarshiha? I like to think of it as a simple exchange of good-will between an Israeli Jew who felt accountable for the Nakba and a local Palestinian who acknowledged it. But surely neither he nor I could forget that, even as I walked up the alley that led me to his shop, I was intruding on contested lands.

Our silence haunts this account, his and mine, his people's and mine. It concerns what we don't say even to ourselves, within our own communities, let alone what we hold back across the national and political divide.

By the time I finally invited Deborah to join me for a two-week visit to Israel, in 2005, she had read an impressive number of books regarding the '48 war and the Nakba. Among them was Meron Benvenisti's *Sacred Landscape: The Buried History of the Holy Land Since 1948*. I'd known of Benvenisti for years as liberal deputy mayor of Jerusalem and journalist, but it was Deborah who tugged at my sleeve and made me pick up the open book. As it turned out, *Sacred Landscape* was our companion throughout our Nakba work. In a sense, it fathered it.

Benvenisti's opening words jolted me to attention: "This book is about my troubled internal landscape as much as it is about the tortured landscape of my homeland." As if to explain it, he quotes from Simon Schama: "Landscape is the work of the mind. Its scenery is built up as much from strata of memory as from layers of rock.'"

A historian, journalist, and political geographer who'd worked for years across the Jewish-Palestinian divide, Benvenisti saw us inhabiting two utterly separate yet coexisting worlds, their destinies hanging in the balance: the Jewish world of his childhood and an Arab world that is utterly apart from his own. It's a conundrum I knew well, a radical apartness in which we are joined. His words—"troubled," "tortured," "strata of memory"—could have been mine. In this state of intimate proximity we are still separated by radical apartness, he writes. "Only those who have experienced the dichotomous environments of Sarajevo, Beirut, or Belfast can truly comprehend the phenomenon of the 'white patches' on the mental maps carried around in the heads of the Jews and Arabs of Eretz Israel/Palestine, which cover the habitat of 'the other' … "

I froze, I'm not sure for how long. Benevisti was putting words to paper that I had not allowed myself to voice. And then I remembered: *Heart of Darkness*. Conrad mentions a map where territories waiting to be claimed by us westerners were drawn as "white patches," empty. I had seen such maps in my mother's schoolbooks, printed in Britain after World War I, where much of Africa was an empty pink area. A land without people! Like Conrad's conquerors, I thought, we too arrived with a sword in one hand and a torch in the other, with military force and a sacred fire.

PART I: DENIALS

From the place where we are right
Flowers will never grow
In the spring.
—Yehuda Amichai

You ask: What is the meaning of "homeland"?
They will say: The house, the mulberry tree, the chicken coop, the
beehive, the smell of bread, and the first sky.
—Mahmoud Darwish

Ruin in Kula forest, near Tel Aviv, with fine masonry removed for Israeli re-use.

1. Mount Gilboa

*T*hough *Sacred Landscape* affected each of us deeply, our plans for Deborah's first visit, in 2005, didn't change. She was to come for just two weeks and enjoy a few highlights like most tourists. There were to be no cactuses, no Nakba, no photo project. When we headed for Beit Shean's extensive Roman archaeological park a few days after her arrival, there were to be no politics. Ahead was the promise of Decapolis, as it was called in Roman times: its amphitheater, its colonnaded agora, and a mosaic floor depicting an alluring Tyche, the goddess of good fortune. I'd already been to this well-excavated site and looked forward to enjoying Deborah's pleasure at seeing it. We'd planned to arrive in the late afternoon and explore the park the next morning, except that we didn't take into account how short distances actually are in Israel. Checking our map I realized that we would arrive too early for the youth hostel where we were to spend the night and too late for the antiquities.

"Look," I said, pointing to a meandering green-marked road that snaked its way on the map though the tiny tree-shapes that signal forests. "It's marked 'scenic' and we have time."

Deborah slowed down to check the map. It took only a slight turn of the wrist, the hand coaxing the steering wheel to the right, to get us onto a narrow country road running through a lush pine forest.

In a country like Israel, parched for months on end, forests always stand for "scenic." The trees confirm that moisture is feeding them, that survival is possible and wellbeing imaginable. A sense of resolve about these forests is felt on the paths and roads that slice through them. Visibly man-made, these clearly demarcated patches of uniform pines planted by the Jewish National Fund (JNF) embody that urgency.

That June afternoon these thoughts were not on my mind. I was seeing the beauty that enveloped us through Deborah's eyes, not thinking about its geo-political meaning. The pine trees were softly lit by a sun that was slowly descending into the coastal plain we had left behind. Mild breezes swayed the pine branches, dappling the forest floor and perfuming the air with the pungent scent of sap. We had entered the Gilboa mountain range, I realized with the kind of sentimental catch in the throat that some of us Jews feel when a biblical story becomes tangible. These are the mountains where young David, in his dirge for King Saul and his beloved Jonathan, commands the skies to withhold their dew and rain in mourning for the heroes dead in battle.

We were also, I realized with dismay, near the northern border of the Occupied West Bank, the Palestinian lands Israel has been holding since 1967. In the distance, as the planted forest ends abruptly and the rolling expanse of eroded mountains opens up to view, we could see tiny Palestinian villages, maybe even the outskirts of Jenin. We were hugging the border, the Green Line that demarcates the cease-fire agreement of 1949, not far from Jenin's refugee camp, which just three years earlier, in 2002, had seen terrible fighting.

The forest felt eerily deserted. There were no houses near the road and no cars traveling on it. The lone sign that advertised boutique cheeses available at a farm down a dirt road only deepened the sense of desolation. The place felt empty, its beauty awash in melancholy—partly because of the deepening shadows but perhaps also because I sensed on some not yet articulated level that we were skirting no-man's-land. The line delineating where the forest ends and the eroded dun hills begin was strikingly clear.

Was Deborah thinking about that too? Never chatty, she drove on silently, leaving me to my own ruminations.

Trees and more trees, and after a while stone markers began to appear along the road at more or less regular intervals, perhaps a quarter of a mile apart. Shaped like tombstones, each stood facing the road with a small metal plaque affixed to it. Our curiosity piqued, we stopped by one of them and read that this segment of forest was paid for with money donated to the JNF.

I should have guessed. After all, tree planting has been a major drive for years, both for the local Jewish *yishuv* and for the diaspora. Tree purchase certificates were given as wedding and Bar Mitzvah gifts, for graduations, condolences, and prizes, for days of remembrance and days of joy. It was a special moment in my elementary school when my class would line up in our Sabbath clothes—every Friday, every year—to deposit coins in the white enamel JNF collecting box that had a map of Eretz Yisrael in its pre-'48 Mandatory borders printed on it. There'd be songs, a story or a special reading, sometimes a short puppet show for the lower grades, before our teacher would remove the JNF box from its nail for us to deposit coins. We children were each helping to redeem the land.

The forest was somber in the lengthening shadows. Glancing again at Deborah, I felt a chasm separating us. What did she know, this American gentile? She never lined up to deposit a coin in a JNF box, wearing the navy blue skirt and Yemenite embroidery blouse that marked our special occasions.

Driving on, we paused by the next marker, and the next, each a memorial: "… *planted in memory of Ida L., beloved wife and mother…* "; "… *in honor of those lost in the deportation of …* " ; "…*by members of the Beth Emunah congregation of …,* "; "… *by survivors of … living in …* "; and on it went, marker after marker: Canada, Argentina, Israel, South Africa, Italy, Australia, England … too many to count.

It was a mature forest. The pines, all of them pines, were large, the carpet of dead pine needles beneath them thick. The memorials also showed their age, with some markers coming loose from the rusting nails that pinned them into the stones, some missing altogether, the names of loved ones already gone. In the darkening afternoon a sense of mourning weighed on me, learned over years of Yizkor, the prayer of remembrance. This road, so short in actuality, suddenly felt long.

We drove on silently, each alone in her own thoughts, until Deborah suddenly slowed the car.

"Look!" she said, chin gesturing to the right, taking her hand off the steering wheel and pointing toward my open window.

"What? Just forest. Nothing there."

"The stones, there, under those trees …"

"So what? There are stones everywhere."

The hills beyond the tree line, toward Jenin, were in fact stony and bare. Stones stripped of their thin layer of earth and scattered among the trees are everywhere in mountainous Israel. Over centuries of erosion the land has been exposing its boulders and ejecting its stones.

"Yes, everywhere," she said. "But these are piled up, probably the remains of a wall."

"I don't see anything special," I said, leaning to peer in the direction she pointed to as she pulled over. "Just stones. So what?"

"No, no. This is masonry. These are house stones, chiseled."

I shrugged, settling back into my seat. "Just because you read about the Nakba doesn't mean that every stone we pass is a remnant of a Palestinian house."

If she was right, I didn't want to know it. I had already made it clear that I would not be a guide to the Nakba.

Still, by now, years after our conversation about photographing cactuses, this argument couldn't be buried. Was it the weight of experiencing Jewish suffering memorialized in the forest that made us also think about the Palestinian catastrophe? Or was it that we had each just finished reading Benvenisti's writing about Palestinian land claims and the tangles of ownership and attachments that people feel for this land? The history he describes challenges the Zionist myth of reclaiming "a land without people for a people without land." It offers a devastating account of Israel's systematic erasure of Palestinian presence, measured by the destruction of hundreds of villages. I could no longer shrug off evidence of the Nakba if that was what Deborah saw.

Deborah's supposing that the stones were once part of a house was reasonable, but so was my claim that similar stones are scattered throughout the region. Village masonry was not so uniform as to be easily identifiable, and builders often used ordinary fieldstones. But Deborah was determined. Ignoring me, she got out of the car and strode into the forest. As her faded denim shirt grew smaller in the distance, I could see her searching the forest floor, bending to lift a stone, laying it down, and moving on, while I sat glumly in the car.

When she returned she confirmed that that the stones had once been part of a house. She can't be so sure, I thought. There aren't stones fitted together, no residual mortar, let alone a standing a wall. These had to be just scattered fieldstones.

That afternoon we dropped the matter, except that now the Nakba had been named. The thought of the desolate Yizkor markers facing what may have been the remains of a Palestinian village made complacent tourism impossible. By the time we entered that scenic road we already knew too much. Tired and on edge, we let our argument fester, reminded by the darkening skies to head for the hostel.

We never made it to the end of the scenic road that afternoon. Only years later did I get to the lookout, named for Israeli soldiers fallen in battle. The sweeping views it offered of Jordan, Syria, and the Golan Heights rising in the hazy distance embraced a vast, borderless expanse, seemingly unpeopled, available for possession.

We woke up at dawn the next morning. It was a good time to explore the neighborhood, since the town, which sits at the edge of the Jordan Valley, would soon be prostrate in heat. The mountains surrounding this bowl of a valley trap the heavy air so that by midmorning everything already shimmers with refracted light. But at this early hour, the light was still limpid, pale gold, and there was still a slight breeze in the air.

"I'm going that way," Deborah said, heading to the left, her "I" making it clear that she wanted to be alone. Feeling abandoned as I stood by the large empty lot outside our hostel, I watched her head for a phalanx of cramped apartment blocks hastily built for some of Israel's poorest immigrant communities—originally North African and now, with new waves of immigration, Ethiopians and "Russians" from Georgia and Central Asia. All I could see in front of me was a flat area, two city blocks in size, strewn with fragments of stones, dead grass, and wind-tossed garbage caught on thistles and thorns, though a row of small houses at the far rim of this area intrigued me: they were nothing like the standard-issue apartment blocks where Deborah had vanished. I had noticed none of it the previous night.

I had to tread carefully as I stepped through the thorns and rubble. Just an empty lot, I was thinking when I stubbed my toe on a rusting valve attached to a piece of corroding pipe. Evidence, it occurred to me as I bent to pick it up, a fragment small enough to fit in my bag. I carried it for a while as I walked toward the low houses that edged the open space, and then changed my mind. But as I bent to lay the valve down I noticed that the fragments strewn on this lot included smashed pieces of tile, shining white in the sunlight.

The row of small houses at the rim of this lot turned out to be strung along a smashed asphalt street, their metal doors dented, their splintering window frames sunk into cinderblocks that sealed the original stone arches. The sweep of their arches, the decorative use of black volcanic stone, and fragments of ornamental wrought iron all spoke of a thriving Palestinian city that existed here before '48, before the doorways were sealed and before urban planners turned Arab Beissan into the Israeli immigrant "development town" of Beit Shean.

This was no longer a case of hard-to-decipher stones. At one time these buildings lined a busy street bustling with commerce, I realized. Later I learned that Beissan had been a provincial Ottoman capital and then a commercial Arab center under the British. Now the few remaining buildings of old Beit Shean, no longer Beissan, had been sealed, padlocks rusting on their makeshift doors, abandoned construction materials visible behind their dusty windows. One shop, its padlock new, displayed handmade crafts for which there seemed to be no buyers: candles, ceramic bowls, Jewish mezuzah door blessings. One derelict building, free standing and hugging a spacious courtyard, apparently an affluent home, stood apart, with a shredded awning dangling from a twisted metal frame. A rusting Hebrew sign still advertised a restaurant.

I don't know how long I stood there surveying this dereliction before I allowed myself to register what I had known all along, that the buildings I was staring at were not merely old but Palestinian, and that the lot I had just crossed, where I'd noticed the corroding valve, wasn't empty either. It was a demolition site where absence resonates with presence, where bits of ceramic tile, stone, and plumbing testify to people having lived there, knowing daily joys and sorrows.

Yesterday's argument returned with a rush: it is a *choice* whether to see a razed city block as empty or pause to reflect on what a rusting valve might mean. It was a choice, too, whether or not to look closely at stones strewn under the forest's canopy. It would still be some time before I'd allow myself to wonder what became of the people who used to live and work in this neighborhood of Beissan.

Most, I later learned, fled to Jordan, a few to Nazareth, but that morning I did not dwell on that. I was distracted, rather, by a strange grating-whining sound that came from inside the courtyard of the failed restaurant.

Rounding a corner, I froze in my tracks. A man, standing on a ladder in the middle of that courtyard, was pruning a lone tree with an electric saw.

"What's happening?" It was Deborah, suddenly appearing at my side.

"Look," I said, pointing to the tree, where the saw was slicing through the silver-leafed branches, letting splinters fly and cut branches fall below. Repositioning his ladder, the man was shaping the stumps into a neat topiary-like ball.

"So what? He's just pruning a tree."

"But this isn't 'just.' It's an *olive* tree! One doesn't prune olive trees into topiaries."

Deborah stared at me. After all, here was an effort to prettify a tree, perhaps open a new restaurant despite the neighborhood's gloomy economic prospects. What was wrong with that?

Of course Deborah did know something about our olive trees. In her evangelical past she had read about the dove bearing an olive branch to Noah and Jesus' lonely night in the Garden of Gethsemane. She also knew about the settlers decimating Palestinians' olive groves in the West Bank and had seen photos of stumps left by that devastation. In a year, she and I would assist in the Palestinians' olive harvest, and a year after that we would drive by a "nursery" where ancient olive trees, uprooted, awaited buyers. With their branches clipped, their roots exposed, and dry red earth still clinging to their ancient trunks, these amputees lay in a fenced enclosure, destined to be prized ornaments in Israel's urban and suburban gardens.

But that knowledge would come later. In Beit Shean, my dismay about the pruning mystified Deborah.

"I'll show you Anna Ticho's drawings when we're back in Boston," I said, painfully aware of how apart we were.

I remembered those drawings vividly: delicate pencil-and-ink sketches done in the first half of the twentieth century. Wind-battered and drought-ridden, gnarled, twisted, and lopsided, sometimes just a rough trunk with

Uprooted olive trees for sale at a roadside nursery, Hebron hills.

barely one living branch remaining, Ticho's olives are nothing like the clouds of diaphanous silver seen in romantic Jewish paintings, let alone Beit Shean's would-be topiary. Sketched against a mostly blank page, they're both grim and alive. As an adolescent I found them singularly ugly. Why would anyone want to frame and hang pictures of these arthritic trees? And yet they were iconic, hanging in many homes.

Later, in Boston, I told myself, I'd open my old book of Ticho's drawings, its soft cover fraying, its parchment wrapping crumbling at my touch. "This is what olive trees are like," I'd say, my finger tracing a line.

We didn't linger in that courtyard. The sun had risen, the air was turning into a soupy haze, and the archaeological site was now open to visitors. We paid our entrance fee and trudged along the park's colonnaded agora, gazed at its mosaics, and admired the sweep of its Roman amphitheater, but our hearts weren't in it. For the first time I was seeing my country differently. I could no longer ignore the Nakba.

And so, leaving the carefully preserved ruins of what was once Roman Decapolis, we headed back toward the few run-down Palestinian houses still standing, the gardener gone, the chainsaw silent. Now we noticed something else that escaped us earlier: rising incongruously out of the flat valley was a huge flat-topped mound, the length of a city block or more.

"Not in our guidebooks" I shrugged, resenting the question that was sure to come. Am I supposed to be the all-knowing guide? "Maybe an archaeological 'tel,' you know? A village or some such gradually turning into a hill?"

Deborah nodded. "A fort?" she ventured, scrutinizing this huge flat-top lump of earth where the outlines of massive, well-cut stones could still be visible. "And this wide ditch, a moat?"

Our eyes met and we smiled. Crusader, we agreed. It was a guess, but we were learning to cobble meaning, to read mute signs.

"And that building across the street?" she asked, pointing to a large building we also hadn't noticed earlier.

Towering above us was an impressive building, two very tall stories high, its grand entry arch topped with an elaborately carved keystone. The rooms on both floors opened into a capacious, newly whitewashed courtyard where a scallop-edged stone fountain, now dry, stood on a slim pedestal. It looked like the Koranic madrassa schools or the khans that served the caravans that traveled across central Asia. Or it could have been an administrative building, perhaps the municipality, since Beisan had been a regional Ottoman capital. A public building, its scale suggested, built to impress.

"It's beautiful," Deborah said, shading her eyes as she gazed at the bas-relief carving on the arched entrance's keystone. "What does this plaque say?"

I gestured dumbly, confessing ignorance.

"But you studied Arabic in high school, didn't you?" she protested.

"Yes," I shrugged, squinting at the keystone, "but not calligraphy. Maybe it's the name of whoever built it, and a date I can't read either. Gorgeous, though, isn't it?"

As I tried to extract meaning from the entwined curls that were letters so dense that no single letters stood out, it was the beauty of the script that arrested me—and the difficulty. I managed to identify an "a" and an "l," yet here they did not spell "Allah." "Allah" is usually the easiest to decipher, even when nesting within lush arabesque curves. That's because "a" and "l" are almost identical in Arabic, mirroring each other in "Allah" in a spellbinding sequence of vertical lines that come to an abrupt stop with an "h," except that this pattern wasn't happening in that keystone.

Gazing at that sinuous design, memories of my Arabic teacher flooded in—Hamoreh Lavie, "Teacher Lavie" as we called him—who taught with such obvious joy those of us who chose four years of high school Arabic over the easier and more prestigious two years of French. What made some of us choose Arabic at age fourteen still mystifies me. There was no practical reason for it and certainly no social cachet, except that somehow it felt right. Now, in Beit Shean, puzzling over this calligraphy, I could see Hamoreh Lavie again as he drew those chalk letters on the blackboard. I could still see his thin-rimmed eyeglasses glint in a fine-boned face, a slim brown hand reaching up to the blackboard, chalk poised, discussing a new word or explaining its arbitrary allocation of gender to the unending merriment of his adolescent students.

For me, lost in that memory, it was as if time folded on itself, hugging the past into its soft present. Like Anna Ticho's gnarled olive trees, the image of our teacher writing at the blackboard persists. I felt, and still feel, the wonder of his fingers gently pressing the soft white chalk against the blackboard, letting a sinuous line widen at a curve or taper to a slim vanishing edge with just the slightest shifting of pressure.

"Let's go in," said Deborah, quelling that memory. I now noticed some boys kicking a ball in the courtyard, weaving their way among ladders and buckets of paint. The place was being rennovated and the workers had gone on their lunch break, leaving a battered transistor radio to blare tinny Israeli pop music. Clearly the building was being reclaimed for public Israeli use.

As I paused there, surveying the imposing interior, I imagined the Arabic-speaking bureaucrats who used to work in the offices that opened into the courtyard, serving petitioners and dignitaries. They would have worn dark slacks and red fezs while self-important merchants bustled about and farmers in long galabias sat in the shade waiting their turn. The nearby market would have smelled of spices, and the muezzin's call for prayer would have been heard five times a day, swallowed in the din of the marketplace. After the Nakba, once Arab Beissan became Jewish Beit

Shean, Hebrew-speaking bureaucrats replaced the Palestinian ones—not in this building but ensconced in drab offices somewhere else in town. Now that this building is being renovated, I wondered, would Jewish officials occupy these offices? I could see them in jeans or light slacks, many wearing the kippah skullcaps of observant Jews, their speech still betraying traces of their original tongues. The din of the market would be replaced by the sound of traffic on the resurfaced road, silenced by early Friday afternoons, as Beit Shean would prepare for the Jewish Sabbath.

We were mostly silent on our way back to Tel Aviv. The traffic was heavy and we were too tired and preoccupied to talk. I was still feeling the heat that radiated from Beit Shean's baking earth, but it was more than that. Something had shifted inside me. The easy, familiar embrace of belonging to my country had started to lose its hold. All I knew, as our car sped through the Palestinian enclave of Wadi Ara, was that there was no turning back to the person I had been barely twenty-four hours earlier. I could no longer let the Nakba hover at the edge of my awareness.

"There is no getting away from this war," I heard myself say.

Deborah, silent, was waiting for me to say more.

"Not just the war of '48," I explained. "It's the Sinai War, the Six-Day War, the Yom Kippur War, the invasions of Lebanon, the attacks on Gaza, and all those other clashes inside and across our borders. It's been going on for over a century."

"If you count the '49 cease-fire line as the border," she said. "A slow, creeping Nakba," she added, and I cringed, still not wanting to hear it.

The rocky hills that stretch along the few kilometers that make up Wadi Ara, where some of Israel's Palestinians managed to stay, looked worn in the dusty heat as we headed west, toward the coastal road that would take us to Tel Aviv. Umm-el-Fahm and the smaller Palestinian villages flanking this narrow valley, all of them within that border, seemed more crowded than ever. I already knew that draconian government restrictions limit Israeli Palestinians' access to land, forcing their villages to grow upward. I'd seen new houses climb uphill over time and old ones get new stories, with tall minarets appearing among them, surveying us from above the highway we were driving on, as if to assert their presence.

Excellent perches for sharpshooters, I caught myself thinking, remembering the slim Hassan Beq minaret at the outskirts of Jaffa from which, back in '48, Palestinian sharpshooters shot into Tel Aviv.

"So much here is about war," I said, remembering the interminable lists mentioned at school and at times repeated in tourist brochures: "Egyptians, Phoenicians, Greeks, Romans, Arabs, Crusaders, and Salah a-Din, and the early Chalculiths and Canaanites and Israelites before them, and then more Arab dynasties, and the Ottomans, and the British, and now us."

Deborah nodded, intent on overtaking the fume-belching truck that was slowing us down.

"And who were those Chalculiths?" she asked, teasing me, guessing that I wasn't likely to know the answer.

Thinking of the tall minarets we'd just passed, my mind meandered back to the mound we saw earlier that morning, and then to another fort, this one officially known as Crusader: Kawkab el-Hawa, (the Star of the Wind). It was one of several forts the Crusaders built in the Holy Land.

Names mean so much here, I thought. For years I only knew this fort as Kawkab el-Hawa, not as the Belvoir it had been for its builders or the recent, less poetic, more territorial Hebrew name, Kokhav Hayarden (Star of the Jordan). Overlooking the Jordan Valley, this fort made for a famously difficult climb. Benvenisti, I remembered, published a short article in the daily *Haaretz*, recommending a day-trip and hike to this fort when it was still called Kawkab el-Hawa. He ended the article with a challenge: why are we Israelis so enamored of the Crusaders who were here so briefly while we ignore the much longer Islamic rule?

I glanced at Deborah as the last houses of Wadi Ara disappeared behind us, her eyes shielded by sunglasses against the lowering sun ahead. Yesterday's argument was still with us, even if we tamped it down. The "we" of Benvenisti's question includes me too, and her. So much is invested in what we chose to see, I thought, and what serves our interests.

2. Forests

*T*he Israeli pine forests of my childhood, before and shortly after the war of '48, were nothing like the dense, self-sowed growths covering huge swaths of North America. They never became the harvested wastelands found in the United States either, where stumps jut out of the earth like rotting teeth. Our soft Aleppo pines were meant for erosion control, we all believed, not for logging. The image I have of the forests where my family went picnicking is of young pines, always pines, forever slim and pliable, speckling the landscape with meager shade. Mere saplings, I see them still tentatively rooted in the crumbling red earth, propped up by wooden supports, waiting to grow into the green fuzz that would eventually blanket parts of Israel's eroded land.

By the time I was born, in 1938, Jewish pioneers had already drained the swamps. They were redeeming the land, we learned at school, and we children, from kindergarten on up, were to help with that redemption. The forests we were planting would reverse centuries of misuse, the legacy of marauding armies, and Arab neglect. Every Tu Bishvat (the New Year of the Trees) we would file out of the schoolyard, each child holding a small paper cup where a tiny seedling sat in a fistful of damp dirt, singing the "Planters' Song":

> *That's how the planters walk,*
> *With a song in the heart and a spade in hand,*
> *From cities and from villages,*
> *In Tu Bishva-at, in Tu Bishvat.*

We were doing our bit for the Hebrew state yet to be born. One day, we knew, our saplings would give shade. The barren, rocky hills would soon look like Europe, like Romania perhaps, or the forests drawn in our picture books—verdant places where red polka-dotted toadstools grow in moist brown earth, where witches live in candy houses and wolves converse with little girls who bring food in pretty baskets to their grandmothers.

My family had just moved from the small village of Herzeliah to a new house in what was, on a city planner's map, North Tel Aviv. During that between-wars hiatus, that house stood, a lone treeless sentinel in the empty area that was to be city center, facing the Palestinian village of Summayl, whose farmers would sow and reap their barley and wheat just outside our fence. Camel caravans would pass by, carrying sand for new Jewish construction somewhere beyond the horizon, while in nearby Tel Aviv—the First Hebrew City, as we proudly called it—the grinding noise of cement mixers and construction dust filled the air.

At seven, eight, even nine, I still yearned for the ficus trees of Herzeliah that our gaggle of neighborhood children used to climb. The newly planted pine trees were too scraggy, their brittle limbs too high, their bark too scratchy, their needles too prickly. They could never match the smooth skin, strong limbs, and leathery leaves of a ficus. Impatient for the new plantings to mature, I nonetheless looked forward to the day trips when we'd picnic among the fledgling pines we called "a forest," pretending that the dry hot air that singed our nostrils was a refreshing breeze and that the skinny young trees were already providing us with a shady canopy.

We'd arrive equipped with a blanket, water, a food hamper, and a ball if we happened to remember it. My sister and I would try to play hide-and-go-seek among trees that were too skinny to hide anyone, while our parents would try to find a perch in a clearing that promised to be slightly less stony than the others on the rugged forest floor. We acted as if these picnics were fun, though now I wonder whether they were worth the trouble. Mom would stress about the preparations, my sister and I would quarrel, and our grandmother, whom we'd detour to pick up—yet another play-hour lost—always had trouble negotiating the inhospitable land.

By the time we had parked, staked out a clearing, and opened the picnic hamper, we were hungry and grumpy. Grandma, even without the corset she'd leave at home, had a hard time finding a comfortable spot. Her body heavy, her joints stiff, her balance poor, she walked uncertainly on the stony ground. My sister and I were sullen, our resentment sharpened by hunger. After all, just getting there robbed us of a half day's playtime. "It is lovely to be jolly," Mom would sing as she laid out the food. "To be-be be, to be-be be/ To be-be jol-ly…" The song morphed into French words I didn't understand, shutting me out. Underneath the loveliness that spilled from Mom's voice I sensed something darker, belying the insistent cheer.

And yet, as the scent of grilled chicken with traces of rosemary and lemon would reach us, and as we'd bite into juice-dribbling tomatoes (so richly fragrant they seemed the essence of tomato-ness), we revived. The grownups lounged and chatted. I busied myself stringing a necklace of fallen pine needles, picking out the pliant green ones that wouldn't break when bent into loops. My sister, her blonde curls dancing as she skipped from rock to rock, was angling for a scraped knee. We'd joke that she was Izza P'zziza, "frisky goat," in homage to Alphonse Daudet's story "The Goat of Monsieur Seguin," which my grandmother read to me in its Hebrew translation. For one blissful day, before Daudet's spirited young goat met the wolf at nightfall, she escaped her fenced yard to frolic in the craggy mountains that rose above Monsieur Seguin's farmhouse.

My sister's Izza P'zizza is still vivid in my memory, though not much else is—just a hammock, a grilled chicken leg, Grandma's city hat pinned incongruously to her thinning hair, and my sister, arms spread for balance, repeating snatches of a song as she skips from rock to rock. It could have been any family enjoying the meager wellbeing that the country, still British Palestine, had to offer. The grown-ups knew though, even if we children didn't, that clouds were gathering: the "War of Independence" for us, the local Jews, but the Nakba, the catastrophe, for the Palestinians, when the forests would take over their lands.

As the sun would start its descent across the plain, behind the then still Palestinian towns of al-Lydda and al-Ramleh, we'd gather our belongings and drive Grandma home, the car straining on the climb toward Jerusalem.

"*B'tov talinu*," she'd say, her biblical Hebrew comically ornate. Nobody said "May you slumber in goodness" anymore.

"Good night, Grandma, *laila tov*" we'd chorus back, our Hebrew dodging the "*B'tov talini*" one might offer in return.

Did the others feel as letdown about these outings? I wonder, remembering how quiet we all were on the way home. A half-day, it turned out, was enough.

I forget the names of the forests where we picnicked before the war of '48, or maybe I never knew them. The trees were all alike. The clearings too. The only name I remember is Ben Shemen's. It's the forest my parents mentioned most often, occupying a special place in their hearts. For me, "forest" was simply a grove of trees seen at child-level, where even the lowest branches were above my reach.

Though nothing much happened on those early family outings, there were national sequels whose plots insinuated themselves into the familial one. They concern my country's myth of becoming: the stories we tell ourselves about "redeeming the wilderness" and "making the desert bloom."

Over the decades, larger patches of Israel's eroded lands turned green. Seen through the window of a speeding car, the green pleases the eye. There's a gratifying sense of recovery, so visible when the lush green comes to an abrupt end as it abuts eroded land. And yet within this satisfaction lurks doubt, not about the rare instance of a forest mistakenly planted on drought-ridden soil, but the sense, perhaps subliminal, that there is something unnatural about all this green. It may be the clearly drawn line that separates a forest from the brown-gray earth, or the uniform planting, so clear when one stands among the multitude of these pines. They are all of an age, all spaced at regular intervals, planted with machine-like determination.

The resolve seen in this planting inspired but also puzzled me. It was only decades later that I finally learned that these standard-issue forests had to do with much more than the proverbial redemption of the land or providing recreation for families lucky enough to own a car. The forests my family visited were, and continue to be, planted and maintained by the Jewish National Fund, a non-governmental entity whose mission is to own, improve, and manage Jewish lands in Israel. By its own charter, JNF lands are not to be sold or given to outsiders. They are for the exclusive use of the Jewish people, in perpetuity.

Visitors to our "national forests" are not likely to consider the Palestinian ownership of the land on which they were planted. There are marked scenic roads to enjoy, hiking and biking trails, children's playgrounds, picnic tables and barbecue grills, trash containers, and the occasional remains of an old irrigation system, a well, or an oil press identified as "ancient"—not "Palestinian" or "Arab." As Deborah and I discovered, the tourist brochures for the former Palestinian village of Sataf, for example—now a verdant park just outside Jerusalem—present Sataf's springs, irrigation, and agricultural terracing as "Biblical." The fact that this land had been terraced and farmed by generations of Palestinians is not mentioned, nor the fact that, after the '48 war, the JNF bought extensive absentee lands from the Israeli government that was supposed to be their custodian.

The JNF reports that by the 1990s these forests have come to exemplify the realization of the Zionist dream. Certainly the trees clear the air, prevent erosion, beautify and shade the landscape, and provide recreation. Yet Dor Guez, an Israeli artist who is Palestinian on his mother's side, tells a different story. It was 2011 or 2012 when I first chanced on his work in a small out-of-the-way gallery in the basement of Tel Aviv's art museum. At first glance, this exhibit was just a series of black-and-white photographs, modest in size, showing forest playgrounds, each with its own set of swings, climbing structures, platforms, and slides, each standing in a small clearing. They were all shot frontally and at the same distance, all denuded of people. What's the point, one might wonder, staring at this dreary repetition? Guez leaves it to us, both to notice the repetition and to name what's missing.

A large light-box transparency I saw a year later at Brandeis University, also Guez's, is only slightly more explicit. In "Two Palestinian Riders: Ben Shemen Forest," Guez named his subjects explicitly and situated them in the iconic forests my parents remembered so fondly. Despite the title, neither the riders nor their mount are anywhere to be seen. Only the forest is shown clearly, filling the frame with evenly spaced pines. Though the image is spectacular—large, backlit in glowing color, given an entire gallery wall when I saw it—it is still unpeopled. The Palestinian riders register, if at all, only as a faint, ghostly blur at the center of the frame, seemingly an accidental defect, a print gone wrong. They are "present absentees," as Israel defines the internally displaced Palestinian citizens who lost their lands and homes in 1948.

"Ben Shemen!" I registered as I read the label for this photograph. We used to be so oblivious during those picnics. It was only gradually, over several decades, that I came to know the history that turns the literal absence in Guez's photographs into a ghostly presence. These images, so devoid of human beings, say much about how all of us Israelis abstained and continue to abstain from knowing how we came by our forests. Kindergarten children cupping Tu Bishvat's pine seedlings in their hands do not account for that history, but inevitably they are part of it. After all, nobody told us off when some joker amended the refrain to the "Planters' Song" to rhyme as "*be-tu, tu, tu-tu / ha-aravim yamutu*" ("In tu, tu, tu-tu/ the Arabs will die"), which we did sing, sometimes.

The sixty years that separate my kindergarten years and Guez's art were marked by key events: the Suez war, when Israel occupied the Sinai peninsula while supporting France and Britain's attempt to retake the newly nationalized Suez Canal; Israel's building a nuclear reactor in Dimona; the Six-Day War that resulted in Israel's occupation of the West Bank, Gaza, and the Golan; the Yom Kippur War; Lebanon's Civil War and the Black September fighting in Jordan; two Palestinian intifadas; Prime Minister Rabin's assassination; Israel's two invasions of Lebanon and the massacres in Sabra and Shatila; and all the other bloodshed that was too local to be called "war" but really was.

Yet events of this kind—the ones that get recorded in history books—are not the only way to mark history's ebbs and flows, including its tragedies, changes, and the seeping in of understanding. When, I now wonder, did I first recoil from the children's reinvented ending for the "Planters' Song"? And when did Israel's forests become for me not just a place to picnic, but a record of a history I can no longer ignore?

One dreary January day, when I was in Israel on semester break, my parents took me to Jerusalem for a day trip. It must have been 1965 or 1966, after I'd left for the United States but before the Six-Day War of 1967. On a whim, we decided to stop at Ben Shemen on the way, spurred by nostalgia for outings that were rarely as good as we wished. By then my grandmother was dead, my sister was studying abroad, and I was a married student living in California. Mom, increasingly depressed and homebound, was in better spirits than usual when she proposed this detour. Dad was quiet, increasingly hard of hearing. But we were all eager to be outdoors, and he enjoyed driving and loved Mom, as her rare sparkling moods were all the more precious.

We just headed south—past Tel Aviv's grimy industrial fringe, past fragrant orange groves, past the flat-topped mountain of garbage that rose near the airport, past the former Palestinian towns of al-Lydda and al-Ramleh, now Lod and Ramle. Here and there were new Jewish villages where red-tile roofs peeked through dark avocado and citrus trees, and then, farther away from the city, cultivated fields, lush and redolent, now that the rainy season had began.

The concrete walk-up apartment blocks of the town of Beit Shemesh emerged from the morning haze as we approached the forest. Here was a "development" town for new immigrants, one of several sprinkled around the country—monotonous blocks built in haste, ugly and unwelcoming.

"Awful!" Mom said. She knew this firsthand: she had been doing community work with North African and Polish immigrants in yet another development town.

Why gaze at this dispiriting place, I thought, turning to search the landscape for the forest ahead.

It was just coming into view when I noticed a narrow brook running parallel to the road, its precious water topped with fluffy white foam islands dancing on its pink and turquoise surface, flecked with greens and shimmering gold.

"Oh, how pretty," I exclaimed.

"Uh-uh," Dad said, summoning his years of experience as an engineer. "This is industrial waste. Poisonous."

The proof soon emerged as the road curved to reveal that the ribbon of iridescence was coming from a factory whose chimneys belched thick smoke over the wasteland that separated Beit Shemesh from the forest. So much for the "development" this dreary town represented. It had been built, I'd learn years later, on the cultivated Palestinian lands that saw heavy fighting in '48, before al-Lydd, al-Ramle, and other area villages fell.

The forest had of course matured, its pines grown, its carpet of needles softer, even the rocks seemed to have shrunk. There were now the generic picnic tables, a playground, and a sign warning people that they'd be fined if caught littering. Rusty bottle caps lay on the ground near the sign, and a plastic bag, snagged on a branch, rustled in the breeze.

I have since avoided Ben Shemen and tried not to think about those family outings. New lands are still being expropriated. New roads are cut through the landscape, swaths of pines continue to be planted, and ever-new laws define who does or does not have a foothold on this land. Palestinians continue to lose their homes as newer Jewish immigrants replace the old "new" ones, with new housing and improved playgrounds that now welcome Russia's towheaded children and Ethiopia's dark curly ones. The very thought of a day "in the embrace of nature," as we call it in Hebrew, has become for me a sweet-sad memory.

My parents were in their eighties when the new Spa of Ye'arot Hacarmel (Carmel Forests) opened, a less rugged version of nature. I happened to be visiting them just as they returned from their first time there, speaking glowingly about its array of rejuvenating treatments and the expansive forests that surrounded it, but also bemused at the overflowing buffet, people's casual walking around in little more than gowns and flip-flops. For them, the standout was the forest, where one could hike or stroll or just recline in a deck chair set in a clearing, lulled by rustling branches in a grove that, in this small country, seemed vast. The view from the spa's wide terrace did not include weathered swings, trash cans, and "facilities." Undisturbed, their eyes roamed across a scrim of trees, acres covering the undulating hilltops.

As it turned out, my parents never returned to Ye'arot Hacarmel. Some time after their first stay, a huge fire decimated a large swath of the Carmel forest, and not much later my father declined and died. Mom couldn't bear the thought of sitting on the terrace, gazing at blackened tree stumps, and anyway, her health, too, was deteriorating.

Mom told me about it the minute I had arrived from the airport, barely recovered from my sixteen-hour Boston-to-Tel Aviv journey.

"Did you hear about the fire?" she asked, by way of welcome.

It was just past sunset yet a faint glow still lingered, filtering in through the lowered blinds of the window. Mom was already in bed, her hair thinning but still light brown, looking frail in her white gown.

"What fire?" I asked, still standing, my coat still on.

"On the Carmel, near the spa. Just happened," she said as I lowered my heavy shoulder bag and struggled out of my coat. Weren't we going to kiss? Say hello?

"Huge," she said. "So many trees gone. They aren't saying how it happened but it must be arson. Palestinian," she added with a prosecutor's certainty. "Just as in A. B. Yehoshua's story, you know, where a Palestinian starts a forest fire. Only it's not fiction!"

The last of the sunset glow was gone now, replaced by a faint oblique light coming in from the corridor. The air purifier was gurgling and I could hear the evening news coming from a distant radio. Mom, I could see, was not doing well.

I hadn't yet read Yehoshua's "Facing the Forests" but I recognized the know-it-all bitterness in her words. It was the familiar rush of adrenaline that sometimes infused her depression, convincing her that she knew the hidden meaning lurking under some fact where conspiracies and secrets multiplied and mutated like some primitive organism. I resented these divinations, not yet allowing myself to see the depression from which they sprang, or the painful truths and possible truths they often contained.

Mom's account of that fire had these familiar contours: conspiratorial suspicions alleging "Arab"—that is Palestinian—arson and pessimism about the future ahead, including the future of Israel, the Middle East, Western civilization, humanity, and the planet, a pessimism not without its truths. She was sure it was arson, citing Yehoshua's story as prophecy and proof.

Seeing my blank stare, she briefly summarized the story: An Israeli student, stalled in his research on the Crusaders, spends the summer as a forest-fire watchman. When he discovers that his local Palestinian assistant is amassing gasoline, he helps him burn the forest, exposing the village over which it was planted. The old "Arab" is mute (tongue cut off) and the student doesn't speak Arabic, yet he, an Israeli Jew, helps the Palestinian burn the forest.

Here Mom had to pause, coughing. The room seemed to grow even darker, though it couldn't have been. I could still see her thin hand lowered to drop a tissue into the straw wastebasket by her bed.

"It's just a story," I said. "It proves nothing about the Carmel fire. Nobody would do that!" It didn't yet occur to me that my "nobody" assumed one of "us." No Israeli Jew, I meant, though it's not far-fetched to imagine a Palestinian doing it.

My mother knew better. "No," she said and paused, coughing. "It's about how they hate us, and hate our forests, and want to burn us off this land."

Though investigation showed conclusively that this fire (and the next, much worse, in 2010) was not caused by arson, my mother had a point: the mute Palestinian had reason to set that fire. It was an act of revenge for his destroyed village but also, with the trees gone, an act of witnessing. The fire laid bare the traces of his village, the ruins mourning but also protesting a catastrophe that includes many villages beyond this one.

Mom took the story more literally than I did. She saw it as proof that her intuition about the inevitability of revenge was right. Some years later, when I finally read "Facing the Forests," I took it to be a parable about our joint Israeli-Palestinian history, and I still see it this way. Most immediately, it's about our razing of Palestine's villages and disguising their traces. But it's also about silence. Like Guez's "Two Palestinian Riders," Yehoshua's story is taut with what is not being said: the student's inability to write his thesis, the official Israeli silence about villages buried and populations gone, and an old Palestinian's mute protest.

A thick pall chokes these stories. Like the pine needles that suppress the undergrowth, the act of giving image and voice to the Nakba gets clogged in its Israeli telling. And not only in its Israeli telling. At a curatorial talk about Guez's work, held at Brandeis University in 2012, much time was given to discussing the regenerative use of forest fires, while the human subjects of Guez's work, those two Palestinian riders, were never mentioned. When I noted A.B. Yehoshua's "Facing the Forests" in this connection, my comment drew a blank. "It's a photo about absence," I offered. It felt reckless to say even those few words. Through the corner of my eye, I noticed two or three heads nodding, though nobody picked up the thread.

My mother kept returning to that conflagration during my following visits home. To her, the very prospect of such fires seemed apocalyptic, a final drama of justice, where an all-consuming blaze of near-biblical dimensions spread vengeance across the land.

I can still see that bedroom as it was during countless conversations with my mother, where the doom awaiting us at Palestinian hands seemed the logical end point for her. "Not unjustly, mind you," she'd say. In the darkened room, its shutters fastened and curtains drawn, the outlines of her body would barely be visible as she lay on the bed, pillows propped to ease her labored breathing. She was growing thin, the skin on her hands transparent, the veins showing through, her nails still carefully rounded. She was beginning to vanish, but her mind wouldn't let go. It was, as usual, razor sharp, more insightful, and more depressing, than I could bear.

3. Between Wars

*T*here was no way Deborah could truly understand what the forests meant to me, I thought, let alone what they meant to my mother. Deborah never planted a tree in Tu Bishvat, never picnicked in the stingy shade of a young forest, never dropped coins into a Jewish National Fund box, or sat around a smoldering campfire singing "Hinei ma tov u-ma na'im."

Deborah, who grew up in a tidy Maryland suburb, went to church every Sunday and attended an evangelical college, came from a world I didn't know and entered one she didn't know. The difference between us would blur in the United States, but it became sharp in Tel Aviv, which all my senses told me was my home, not hers: the mingling sounds of traffic and Hebrew speech, the pillar entrances to our walk-up apartment blocs, the dusty shriveled palm fronds waiting on the sidewalk to be removed, the afternoon breeze rising so reliably from the west, and everywhere street signs, shop signs, traffic signs, and advertisements in a language she couldn't read. Every so often I'd look at her and see a stranger: straight silver hair that still had some blonde in it, blue-gray eyes, high cheekbones in a thin face. Not one of us, I'd think.

The detour into the Gilboa forest turned out to be pivotal, drawing us to the lacerated geography that would engage and obsess us in the coming years: Jewish suffering remembered on the left side of the road, Palestinian suffering erased on the right, with the early evening lights beginning to twinkle across the 1949 Green Line armistice border, where the future was yet to be determined.

But much of Deborah's first visit to Israel was spent in Tel Aviv. My first commitment was to my mother, who was increasingly weak and reclusive, with me running errands or sitting by her bedside. That she allowed Deborah a rare short visit was her way of saying, wordlessly, that she understood that Deborah was more than a casual visitor. Mostly, it was a small transistor radio that kept her company. When not tuned to the hourly news, she'd listen to popular Israeli songs of the 1940s and 1950s, melodies of ineffable longing about sundered lovers and the beauty of our land. "Don't say 'goodbye,'" crooned Freddie Durra's silky voice. "Just say, 'Till we meet again.'" Mom, who used to dismiss all but "high" culture, now tuned into the melodies that have always nourished the gentler side of Israel's relentless self-creation. "How beautiful are the nights in Canaan," another song went, "where the doleful howl of jackals can be heard in the depths of the darkening night."

This music also defined my own coming of age in the 1950s, when we city teenagers added couple dances to our Friday night sing-alongs and folk dancing. And yet how to convey to Deborah the younger "me" that this music summoned out of a past she didn't know?

Deborah was a quiet listener. As we crisscrossed Tel Aviv, with me trying to make its call to me come alive to her, she'd nod but leave me unsure of how she'd heard me. There'd be the "then" and the "now" of my telling, the "has been" and "is" in this fast-changing city, but also, inevitably, my city and hers—a logjam of truths. Floating over the present city were scrims of faded memories: the wheat and barley fields now taken over by apartment houses, the young trees grown to shade boulevards, fallow lands that were now Tel Aviv's hub of civic, residential, and commercial activity, but also, perched above the noisy traffic of Ibn Gabirol Street, Palestinian Summayl, its few remaining houses now a shabby Jewish enclave.

"Here is where my grandparents' house used to be," I pointed at the ugly apartment tower that had replaced it as she and I threaded our way through a group of soldiers milling about, guns casually at hand, waiting for their transportation. When I was a kid, that two-story house, perched on a slight rise, seemed a mansion. After all, who had the money then to build a single-family home, let alone two-stories? Whenever strangers remarked on it to me with a mix of admiration and envy, I'd cringe. The grandfather clock chiming in the dim hallway, the long hours of "rest" stretching through the strictly observed Sabbath, the somber furniture, all of it gone, to my relief.

A few blocks away we paused by a nondescript apartment building where a small, barely noticeable plaque noted that the Hagana fighters' secret headquarters was housed there during British Mandate, when this seedling of the IDF was labeled a "terrorist" organization. An excellent disguise, I smiled to myself: a small two-room apartment in a featureless workers' housing complex, a tiny victory for the labor movement. The plaque, Deborah pointed out, was only in Hebrew, for insiders only. '48 wasn't *your* war, the missing translation said.

My sense of her as an outsider continued as we walked down the spiral ramp of Dizengoff Center's mall, overflowing with shops and food courts. I had just read Tamar Berger's book *Dionysus at Dizengoff Center*, which recounts how this mall replaced the Jewish shantytown of Nordia—a large tract of urban land owned by an Arab—where he built flimsy huts to rent to poor Jews but lost them during the war, when he escaped to Egypt. It used to be within an easy walk from my elementary school, its board and tarpaper huts sheltering people I was unlikely to ever know.

The only child I knew from Nordia was Pinchas, a skinny, sallow-faced child, his shabby schoolbag fastened with a string. When he showed up one day with a shaven head, we snickered and pointed: lice. The teachers never called on him and they didn't discourage our scorn. Clearly they too wished him away. And then I remembered, for the first time in years, our mothers gathering at the end of each school year to give our homeroom teachers a present. Pinchas's mother never showed up.

"It was a harsh country," I murmured, more to myself than to Deborah. "A survivor nation expecting the worst and preparing for war. Nobody had patience with weakness."

"Still is," she said as we passed the armed guard at the mall's exit, "All that bitterness passing for strength … "

We were heading toward the beach, just past the eucalyptuses that still marked the edge of Nordia, when another memory surfaced: the rusty, algae-covered hulk of the ship *Altalena*, half-submerged, floating on its side. It was a near civil war that sank the *Altalena* in '48, caused by a rift that divided the *yishuv* at the time and even now. At war were not just Zionist two militias—the Hagana and the Irgun—but two opposing views of our national character and destiny: the Hagana's socialist-leaning roots in Labor

Zionism and its view of the '48 war as waged to defend the fledgling nation ("*hagana*" means "defense"), and the Irgun's uncompromising nationalist "revisionism," which argued that only repressive, strong-arm violence would force the Palestinians to accept a Jewish state.

Even as a child, understanding little about the battle for the *Altalena*, I sensed that the incident was momentous. A tone of voice or lips curled in disapproval said as much whenever the ship's name was mentioned, often followed by the to-me mysterious word "fascists." The *Altalena*, I learned later, was carrying weapons and fighters for the Irgun just as it was being disbanded and absorbed into the Hagana under a tense agreement. With resentment already running high among the Irgun's members, the fighters aboard the ship refused to surrender their weapons. The fighting was fierce, and the Hagana's victory left lasting scars. In Hebrew, it occurred to me, a "civil war" is not merely "civil." It is "*milkhemet akhim,*" a "war of brothers."

The hulk of the *Altalena* bobbed on the water for a long time, lingering near the Herbert Samuel promenade, named for Britain's Jewish High Commissioner. In a photograph taken by the American war journalist Robert Capa, you can see thick, dark smoke rising from the shelled ship; in another, curious crowds stand nearby, with some people swimming near the ship. Elegant couples tea-dancing and matrons enjoying Viennese cakes *mit schlag* at the nearby Café Piltz could see *Altalena* from the café's wide balcony. We daredevil children were among the swimmers. A memory I still relish is of me climbing up the slimy metal ladder fixed to the ship's side in company with some daredevil boys. Of course it was dangerous, but daring was the call of the hour.

Walking with Deborah in Tel Aviv, I found myself pointing out places that charted my growing-up years: the cooperative Tnuva restaurant where we'd eat cheese dumplings; the cavernous Elephant Shoes where an x-ray machine measured children's feet; a flooded street corner where I had to remove my shoes to wade home from school; or the bicycle repair shop where a few years later I learned how to patch a flat tire. This memory pileup is not just my story, it occurs to me as I write. It's the story of a nation coming into being, made up of the small details of everyday life: a McDonald's replacing Café Piltz, a workers' cooperative running a restaurant, or a girl in a dripping bathing suit climbing up the slippery, algae-covered side of a sunken ship as her nation enters war.

Some day I'll take Deborah to see the village of Summayl, I thought, emptied in '48 within sight of our house without my even registering it. Some day. Not now. Our argument about the Palestinian house she may or may not have seen in the Gilboa forest was still raw. It's easier to be bemused by a café turned into a McDonald's, I thought, or even shrug off *Altalena* as a thing of the past, than to think about the Nakba. The Nakba is what we, Israelis, can't bear to name but what Deborah, in her quiet way, did not let me forget.

The war of '48 was the halfway marker of my elementary school years. Before that, during the short lull between the end of World War II and the start of the '48 war, the important event in my life was leaving the bucolic life of Herzelia for Tel Aviv. That move happened in the middle of first grade, as soon as our new Tel Aviv house was ready.

The 1942 Italian bombing of Tel Aviv and Haifa made us move to Herzelia in the first place—my parents, me, and my new infant sister. We shared a house with my uncle and aunt and their two daughters, us downstairs, them one flight up. Herzelia was a small village at the time. The paved part of our street was only some four house-lots long, turning to dirt just after the ice factory next door. The short, unpaved cross street ended at a farm owned by a towheaded family of Russians, members of the Sabbatarian sect. Nobody would bother bombing this place, my parents felt, even if it was war. With curfew at night and transportation difficult because the British requisitioned car tires and rationed fuel, they passed those long evenings with my aunt and uncle, reading *The Pickwick Papers* aloud. It was their version of the spirit that sustained London during the Blitz.

I was too young to understand why they'd leave me at night—crying for them is my earliest memory. I can still see them smiling and waving on their way upstairs. It was only in 1948, as we sat in the Tel Aviv corridor that served as our bomb shelter, that my parents mentioned those readings, and even more years would pass before I'd come to feel amused and proud of their grit.

It's easy to smile about this scene of reading Dickens under fire, though it couldn't have been easy at the time. World War II was raging in Europe, and at least some notion of what was happening to Europe's Jews was known or imagined. As Germany's General Rommel led his troops into North Africa, the *yishuv* trembled. Many volunteered for the British Army's Hebrew Brigade, including women like my mother's friend Varda. Spoken or not, everyone wondered, "Are we next?" Only later did I appreciate the extent to which history spared us: led by Field Marshal Montgomery, Britain blocked the German advance into Egypt and Palestine, defeating Rommel at El-Alamein.

We children knew nothing of that. In a small black-and-white photograph, its borders edged in white scallops, you see my cousin and me concentrating on building a tower from wooden blocks, a small, upturned toy bucket serving as its precarious base. In another, we are grinning, squeezed into the seat of the swing my father had built in the back yard. One year apart, we are obviously dressed for the shoot: ribbons in our hair, dresses smocked and gathered. In another photo taken that afternoon, my young mother is cradling my infant sister, and there is one of the entire group, including Grandmother in her best dress.

It is hard to imagine that even as this record of familial well-being was being posed, my friend Raya (also age three or four) and her parents were hiding from the Nazis in a remote Romanian village, and that by then others were perishing by the millions in ghettos, in cattle cars, in forests, and in death camps. Focused on building our wobbly block tower, my cousin and I knew nothing of Germany's advance into Egypt, let alone what was happening in Europe. For us children, Herzelia was paradise. Within the limited radius of our world, we were able to roam freely. We'd climb trees, harass the neighbors' chickens, cultivate silkworms in perforated shoeboxes, and pick narcissi in the nearby swamp, the *bassa*, from which I returned in tears one Sabbath morning, a new patent leather Mary Jane shoe lost in the oozing muck.

The war in Europe meant little to us. We sang funny songs about somebody called "Hitler" and played with a folded sheet of paper that had a picture of a pig but revealed a head with stringy black hair and a toothbrush mustache when flattened. "Hitler" was just a word to me, meaningless. Once, after overhearing worried adults talk about German spies parachuting into Palestine, we joyfully caught our own "spy"—a gangly man in shabby khakis who was measuring the interior of a packing shed in a neighbor's orange grove. *"Gey avec!"* he shouted at us in German, or possibly Yiddish, as we made faces at him through an open window. "Go away!" That he obviously knew no Hebrew was all the proof we needed for us to rush to Ami, the sole village policeman, thrilled to report our "spy." To his credit, Ami nodded and promised to act right away.

Though war was a game for us children, we sensed that it wasn't. Newly minted Sabras, we may not have known the difference between Yiddish and German, but the air was dense with foreboding. British soldiers were everywhere in sight, and certain grownup conversations would come to an abrupt silence when we children would walk into a room. Playing in the backyard, we could see my uncle's car resting on cinderblocks and knew that its tires had been requisitioned by the British army. Visiting my grandparents in Haifa, I was awed by the view of the bay spreading below their house. Suspended over the entire port, from the breakwater in the west to the oil refineries in the east, was a dense air-defense net of crisscrossing wires kept afloat by dark balloons. It was a somber scene in daytime, though it turned into a magical fairyland at nightfall, as searchlights roved across the velvety darkness that enveloped the giant cooling tanks of Haifa's oil refineries.

While I jeered at a "Hitler" I did not understand and gazed at Haifa's anti-aircraft installations, the Jewish *yishuv* was holding its breath. The allies needed the oil flowing from Iraq to Haifa's refineries and beyond. The port was crucial to the Allies, as were my uncle's tires. Yet even as World War II raged, Arab-Jewish tensions did not entirely disappear. Memories of anti-Jewish violence in 1920, the Hebron and Safed massacres of 1929, and the Arab Revolt of 1936 to 1939, just before my birth, were still rife among us, and now the Palestinian population was becaming restive again, anxious about the Jewish refugees flooding the country. Some even called for German victory, including Jerusalem's Grand Mufti, Haj Amin al-Husseini, who for a while moved to Germany and met with Hitler with an alliance in mind.

One afternoon, just before we moved back to Tel Aviv, I heard a strange clapping sound coming from the back lawn: "kap, kap, ka-pap-pap." A group of teenage girls in gym shorts, ten years older than my five, were practicing "kappap"—a mode of fighting with bats sure to be useless in case of a German invasion but perhaps could prove remotely useful in hand-to-hand combat. I can't imagine that anyone took "kappap" seriously, though it made its point: everybody from teens on upward, girls as well as boys, must be prepared to fight.

As for me, I knew little beyond the fact that the British were unwelcome and the Arabs were alien. This left me confused, as my parents spoke English among themselves (though only Hebrew with my sister and me), and my dad seemed to have cordial relations with the Palestinians near us. A first grader by 1945, now back in Tel Aviv, I walked to school through the fields that surrounded our new house, a white cube of an outpost deposited just beyond the young Hebrew city. Afternoons, I spent hours rambling in those fields, tasting the weeds, picking the tiny flowers that for a few short weeks peeked out through the heavy clay, learning to identify the stinging nettles, and recognizing the first Nachlieli bird that was to announce the rains' arrival. As the sun set, you could hear the lion roar in the nearby zoo. Later I'd lie in bed, waiting for the jackals to start their yowls, sounding and fading in the darkness.

The fields belonged to the village of Summayl, cultivated by Palestinian farmers who'd stop to chat with my father or help remove the occasional snake that entered our house. In spring and early summer their wheat and barley would turn golden as it ripened, with red poppies dotting the gold. Later, the harvested earth would harden into a black crust that would contract, leaving terrifying gashes, deep enough to swallow my foot. Snakes, scorpions, centipedes, and lizards lived in those dry clay crevices. Come winter, drivers would need Dad and local Palestinians to help extricate their cars from the thick black mud.

This was a harsher world than the one I'd known in Herzelia: no familiar neighbors, no trees, no cousins, no chickens next door, not even a mulberry tree whose leaves might feed silkworms. Instead, this new world included Bedouin nomads who would graze their sheep near us in the rainy season, camel caravans that passed carrying sand for new Jewish construction, and the Palestinian village of Summayl stretching along a rise facing us.

My parents did not discuss politics, at least not in front of me. Perhaps they wanted to protect us children, though what I heard in the streets during that inter-war hiatus was disquieting in ways I couldn't quite understand. "*Aliya Khofshit,*" people chanted in ever-growing demonstrations. "*Medina Ivrit,*" they called out. Though I did not know what this call for free immigration and a Hebrew state meant, the catchy pulse and rhyme took hold: children chanted it with gusto. It claimed "Hebrew" (*Ivrit*), not "Jewish," as the rightful name for the country's renewal, discarding the diaspora's religious-Jewish heritage.

Even the "Partisans' Hymn" of World War II said as much: "We are Hebrew partisans," its refrain claimed. "*Partisanim ivrim anakhnu.*"

There was no ignoring the Jewish underground either. Even if my parents didn't discuss it openly, I did hear them call Jabotinsky's and Begin's Irgun militia, the IZL, "fascists." But what did "fascist" mean? Snippets of radio broadcasts and talk on the street made it clear that the *yishuv* wanted the British out of Palestine, whatever our differences. I don't remember anyone commenting on what the Palestinians might want other than that they hated us Jews—for no reason, as we saw it. Somehow, the mysterious phrase "the *saison*" also flitted by in hushed tones. As I learned years later, it referred to the near civil war that was waged by our Jewish paramilitary groups, where the Hagana fought to suppress the Irgun and Lehi. The word meant "the hunting season."

In fact, the seeming inter-war calm was a tense time for both the *yishuv* and the Palestinians. The *yishuv*, still raw from the Holocaust, was desperate to allow Jewish immigrants into Palestine and establish its own state. For the Palestinians, the rising tide of Jewish immigration and, even worse, the prospect of a Jewish state, spelled the end of their world as they had known it for centuries and indeed millennia. They had rightly seen it coming even before World War II. But with the war over, smoldering antagonisms rekindled. Snippets of information ricocheted around me: reports of militias, terrorism, weapon caches, and the interminable radio commentary, all of it mysterious to me.

Inevitably, British soldiers became increasingly visible, the sight of their red berets almost routine. I could see them from our house, so near Sarona, the former German colony that had become a British camp. They'd march in full gear past our fence, stop for water from our garden faucet, speed through town in their jeeps, and check the identity papers of passersby. With the country so restive, any ordinary person might be a terrorist, any apartment could house a cache of weapons, any garden could hide ammunition under some bushes, and any closet might hold a stash of hand grenades behind neatly folded towels.

Curfews were frequent, searches too. Suddenly, usually at night, there would be loud knocks on the door—some rude, some polite. The soldiers would check my parents' papers as I stood by watching. They'd open closets and look behind furniture, searching for weapons and the "terrorists" who were our freedom fighters. One, I remember, addressed my father as "sir" when he saw his British passport. Another walked off with some cash left on a table.

"What's that?" a soldier asked once, gingerly holding the dun-colored, oval metal ball he found in a bedroom closet, just a shade smaller than an American football.

"A bomb," Dad said, eyes twinkling.

The soldier jumped.

"Insecticide," Dad explained, pointing to the words "Bug Bomb" embossed on the metal. He was enjoying the young man's embarrassment, a light reprieve and minor revenge at a time when there wasn't much to joke about.

Without quite understanding what was at stake, I registered my parents' horror when the Irgun bombed the British headquarters at Jerusalem's King David Hotel in 1946. Ninety-one people died in this bombing and many more were wounded, Arabs and Jews as well as British. I also heard dark whispers about the Irgun's attack on the Acre Prison citadel and Irgun men being executed there. Later on, in 1948, there was a powerful bombing on Jerusalem's Ben Yehuda Street—revenge for the King David attack. Three British Army trucks, driven by Arab irregulars but assisted by the British, were detonated, killing fifty Jews and wounding 100. These and other deadly acts kept piling up beyond the immediate radius of my life, though I could feel them lurking.

At some point I started overhearing the mysterious words "*ha'umot hame'ukhadot*" and "*leyksukses*" mentioned in news bulletins. They concerned, I learned later, the United Nations' impending Lake Success vote to establish a Jewish state in a partitioned Palestine, still British-administered at the time. With our house standing by itself, far from others, I did not wake up before dawn on November 29, 1947, as Amos Oz describes it in his luminous memoir, *A Tale of Love and Darkness*. There weren't nearby neighbors with whom to gather and hold our breath as the vote was being tallied and broadcast into the streets. I only heard the count later that morning, re-broadcasted just before I was allowed to join the crowds that flooded Tel Aviv's streets.

The whole city, it seemed, had erupted into euphoric dancing. Like other children, I joined the adults who, holding sweaty hands and stomping on the asphalt, danced the hora in dense circles—circles within circles, and circles spinning out to form new circles as far as the eye could see.

4. Home Front

*T*he dancing went on and on that day, letting the euphoria sweep aside the knowledge that war was ahead. In fact, we'd been at war all along, even if it was undeclared. The Jewish self-defense organizations that grew into militias and included clandestine training and caching of weapons said as much. Many of those dancing and chanting would soon be in uniform. The *yishuv* had already heard the Arabs cry *itbakh el-yahood*. Though I hardly understood what it meant, let alone implied, "*itbakh*," close to the Hebrew "*tevakh*," was a scary word, too. It means "butcher," not just "kill."

Everything changed after May 14, 1948. Israel announced its independence and the Arab countries declared war, even as the gates opened to a flood of traumatized and destitute Jewish survivors. Many would sign on to fight within hours; many had already done so. Able-bodied refugees would be taken off the boat, given guns, and sent to fight with almost no training. I knew hardly any of that at the time, let alone that our struggle for statehood was not just about us but about the Palestinians too. A ten-year old, I'd hear unfamiliar Arab names among the endless newscasters' jabber but had no way of understanding that the coming war, whatever that meant, was part of the momentous struggles for ethnic, tribal, religious, and national self-determination that had been rocking the entire region.

Of our war, the war of '48, the air raids are what I remember most intimately: the distant boom of explosions, the tile floor shaking under me, and the clammy touch of bodies crowded into the corridor that served as my family's shelter. I can still hear the sirens wailing under a sky that suddenly seemed low and dense, as if pressing down on us. One or two small airplanes might be heard circling above, about to drop their bombs. Sometimes there was no sound, though you could feel the earth shake. Sometimes an explosion could be heard, a boom that seemed suspended for a while before its echo trailed off. Often these planes seemed right above our tiny one-story house, its whitewashed roof so vulnerable in the fields that surrounded it. At the sound of the sirens we'd retreat to the corridor. Nobody rushed or cried out, not even my sister, barely four. Mom might turn off the flame under a pot or gather her knitting. I'd bring along homework, my sister a toy or picture book, Dad, when at home, the newspaper.

Mostly we'd sit quietly, waiting for the "all clear" signal. Sometimes my parents would try to locate the explosions by their sound:

"This one seems a bit north from here, near the sea," Dad might say as another "bou-um" sounded.

"Isn't that near Camp Yonah and the military hospital?" I'd ask.

"Err… yes, in that direction," Dad would nod, looking at Mom. By then even I knew that she was volunteering as a nurse's aide and had avoided a recent bombing only because she was off duty that day.

My sister continued playing as bombs fell, humming snippets of a song she'd learned at playgroup. Mom would sit still, hugging her knees and listening intently. When a bomb exploded close to our house, the walls would shake. I'd raise my eyes to the transom window at the top of the bathroom door, checking to see that the strips of brown tape glued to the milky glass were still holding.

"Do you think they're bombing Sarona?" Mom might ask, her voice rising in concern.

"They" went unnamed. Were they Egyptians? Jordanians? Syrians? Who, in 1948, had the propeller planes needed for such bombing?

Sarona, like the improvised hospital at Camp Yonah, had been a British camp, sitting on German "Templar" lands, one of several nineteenth-century colonies established in Palestine by this German Christian sect. The British expelled the Templars and requisitioned Sarona which became, with the British gone, Hakirya ("The City")—a jumble of Quonset huts and farm buildings that served as the fledgling state's government center. The Ministry of Defense, the military's general staff, and our one radio station were all housed there, prime targets for bombing and dangerously close to our house.

Mom's question about Sarona implied another question: Will they hit us this time? There might have been tension in the rising pitch of her voice but no fear. Our fate, her voice implied, is bound with the state's. For me, at ten, this quiet courage defined our reality. "War" seemed abstract, carnage invisible. I knew it mainly through distant booms and tremors and through the grainy monochrome photographs that would sometimes appear in the daily *Ha'aretz*.

My parents' estimates of the location and distance reassured me. Of course I sensed their tension with each explosion, but the danger felt abstract. There was never any talk of ravaged bodies, and my mother never talked about what she saw in the military hospital. Only as an adult did I let myself imagine what it may have been like for her to wash a lacerated body or change the dressing of an amputee. "Think of the survivors," she said years later. "It's worse to be wounded than to die in a bombing."

One morning Mom came running into the house, her face white. A piece of shrapnel had almost hit her as she watered the garden. Somehow the air-raid siren failed to sound and the shrapnel lodged in the wall, barely a foot from where she'd been standing. We never plastered over that dent.

Mostly we were silent during those air raids. The feeling of stoic calm broke only on the days when our maid, Mazal, was with us. Mazal—her name means "luck," implicitly "*good* luck"—was in her twenties, slim, graceful, and assured, with fine bones, cinnamon-colored skin, and curly dark hair. I knew her as the "grown-up" who helped my mother in the kitchen or swept our rooms.

It was only gradually, as I came to understand how Israeli racism separates one Jew from another, that I registered that Mazal was a Yemenite, a Mizrachi Jew from an Arab country and therefore low on our ladder of social privilege. What I saw at the time was her panic during those air raids—a panic that marked her difference. At the sound of the air-raid alarm, Mazal would rush into the corridor. Trembling and crying, her lips moving in barely audible prayers, she'd crouch with us on the floor, clutching at any available arm or leg.

I was embarrassed by this panic, so utterly forbidden within our family's code of behavior. Exposed and vulnerable though our tiny house truly was, we all sat through each air raid patiently, shut in with our thoughts, all except Mazal. "Oh God, please God ..." she'd moan, at which point my mother would pull away, folding her legs under her skirt so that Mazal wouldn't be able to grasp at them. When Mazal would next turn to my sister or me—never to Dad—we'd pull away too, imitating Mom's example.

I couldn't understand Mazal's panic. For me, the calm of that corridor meant safety. Even those estimates of where the bombs were falling comforted me. My parents' self-containment affirmed their British past—Mom's in Liverpool, Dad's in colonial Cape Town. I remember them mentioning more than once the Londoners' equanimity during the Blitz as they sheltered in the Underground tunnels. I could hear in these stories a lesson for how a "good, brave child" is to behave.

I now see how Mazal's panic threatened to crack the walls of equilibrium my parents erected with such determination. She gave voice to the fears we silenced. She was right in thinking that we could have died any minute under a flimsy roof that could easily cave in on us. Her frantic body argued that self-control does not always work and revealed, moreover, a lie: in this newly patched-together nation we're not "brothers," no matter how often we might sing "Hinei Ma Tov"—"How good and pleasant it is to dwell as brothers together."

Now, sorting through memories as I write, I feel again the child's numb incomprehension but also my adult's search to retrieve. I see me as I was in '48 tracing and retracing her steps to school, the grocery, the library, a friend's house—and feel again the chill of war's somber emptiness: fewer cars, fewer pedestrians, a lone army jeep speeding by, a lorry full of dusty soldiers. I can describe the lorries, point to landmarks, recount an anecdote, but what connects them is hard to reach.

I imagine Tel Aviv's deserted wartime streets as an old film, a scratchy black-and-white strip of celluloid that jumps when the teeth don't catch properly in the sprockets. A woman emerges from an apartment house, shopping bag in hand. She shades her eye for a moment as she lifts her head to look up toward the pale sky, and disappears back into the dark entrance of her three-story apartment building. A stray dog crosses the street. Somebody shakes a rug over a balcony's railing but quickly yanks it back again. A car engine is heard revving out of sight. Outside an empty coffee shop the chairs are stacked; nobody is expected. A shutter has been half-lowered over a pharmacy's plate glass window and door. A child is walking by, wearing a raincoat darker than the background shades of gray. The street, normally alive with sounds and movement, is at a standstill. The camera pans across sandbag walls blocking the entrance to some apartment houses. The city's breath is barely audible, just a faint din.

As I imagine it, this archival footage is looped to replay its scene sequence indefinitely: A woman emerges from an apartment house, shopping bag in hand…

I yearned to tell Deborah about how this sense of menace felt to the child that used to be me, but the words felt listless. Memories would surface at odd times, as we walked in Tel Aviv, hiked on a trail, or traveled by car, spurred by a place, or a song, or a scent drifting toward us. But how was I to convey my child's sense of near-paralysis, facing terrors I couldn't quite name?

One incident I did mention. It concerned the dogs that began roaming in Tel Aviv during the war. Deborah had just stopped to pet a passing dog, its smiling owner holding the leash, when another memory surfaced—of emaciated dogs, mangy and flea-bitten.

For years I'd forgotten those dogs—Arab, I realized only in 1986, as I read Isaak Diqs's memoir, *A Bedouin Childhood*, to my son. Diqs was barely older than me in '48 when he returned home on a school holiday to find the entire tribe gone, his family decamped. Only the charred ashes of cooking fires marked the tribe's presence, and the dogs still foraging for food. The ownerless dogs that roamed my neighborhood must have come from the nearby villages of Summayel, Sheikh Muwanis, and al-Jammasin al-Gharbi, I realized, and perhaps even farther out.

Now, seeing Deborah pet a happy, healthy dog, I told her this story. With her own dog, Sophie, dead in Boston, I knew she'd feel it deeply.

"Diqs himself was abandoned," she said, looking far off. "Nobody warned him that the tribe might leave."

"Yes, vulnerable," was all I could think to say. Me, my son, Diqs, all the same age. It could have been any of us, but it wasn't.

"One night," I continued, "I awoke to sporadic gunshots. The next morning, on my way to school, I saw dead dogs lying on the pavement. No blood, though one had a neat gunshot wound."

Deborah said nothing. Heartbroken, she kept an improvised shrine of flowers and a photo of Sophie by her bedside throughout her stay in Tel Aviv.

This story of the abandoned dogs became entangled with my memory of the sandbag walls that cropped up around town, shelters whose very sight filled me with anxiety because they meant we *needed* shelter. These padded burlap fortress walls, rising higher than my head, fronted the pillared lobbies of apartment buildings with dark enclosures that, over time, came to smell of stale urine. There was something scary, even illicit, about these dank, narrow places, yet at the sound of an air-raid siren they provided protection.

Plate glass windows were another marker of danger, crisscrossed with bands of tape to prevent shattering and backed with dense blackout curtains to be drawn at night. The blackout was enforced by men drafted to serve in the Civilian Guard. Too old for combat, they patrolled the streets, some of them barely speaking Hebrew. Bent, stiff-jointed, and equipped with a flashlight and whistle, they made sure no telltale light escaped through a badly draped window. "Hey, you!" you might hear a shaky old man's voice shout, flashlight pointing at the offending window. "Yes, you! Close that curtain—now!"

My parents and I, smug behind our well-draped windows, would peek to see the guilty face across the street and a hand hastily drawing the curtains. We'd laugh, though it was not a joke. A sliver of light could kill us. Also not quite funny was the story of our "swimming pool." It concerned my father's decision to provide us with a real shelter, something better than the corridor where we hunkered down during the early bombings. Dad dug a deep trench just outside the kitchen door, near the pepper tree whose pungent red and green berries kept the flies away. It was a fine trench, large enough to hold all of us, its clay steps carved neatly into the hard clay earth and a sheet of corrugated metal serving as a roof.

"Good hard clay!" I still laugh. With the first rains it turned into a reservoir of scum and algae that didn't drain for months. To his credit, my father, the engineer, bore our teasing gracefully.

I loved Dad for his mishaps, even as I felt embarrassed for him and knew that they irked my mother. The "swimming pool" was of a piece with his nominal military career, a stain on his manliness at a time when the words "hero" and "man," *gibor* and *gever*, were almost interchangeable. My father was a bit too old for combat duty, a married father of two and not particularly fit. In a snapshot taken of him on a 1949 trip to the Negev, he is standing by some monument wearing a raincoat and holding a rifle, looking more like a bank clerk than a fighter. He did not fit our idealized image of a strapping member of the Hagana's elite Palmach units—the lean young men you'd see on posters and in magazines, speeding in Jeeps, hair blowing in the wind, with an Arab kaffiyeh scarf rakishly draped around a tanned neck.

Since every able-bodied man was needed, my father was assigned guard duty. He'd put on his uniform after work and spend the night standing behind a sandbag wall on a flat rooftop that faced the Jaffa border and the worrisome Hassan Beq mosque, from which snipers shot into Tel Aviv. There was a joke circulating at the time, in which one such guard couldn't be found when it was time to replace him. He was only found the next morning, standing on the wrong side of the sandbag wall. That wasn't Dad, though he too was something of a dreamer. One night he walked absentmindedly off that roof, broke a leg, and spent several weeks in bed. Later he was assigned to the Engineering Corps, next door in the Kirya, where he no longer needed to wear a uniform.

While we could laugh about the "swimming pool" and Dad walking off that roof, there was no ignoring the fact that these were grim times. Though there was no television to bring the war into our homes, the sirens, radio broadcasts, bombings, sandbag walls, and the military vehicles rushing by never let us forget it. Everybody knew somebody, or of somebody, in uniform. On their way to a quick visit home or in transit to another front, these young men and women wore their disheveled khakis, balaclava "sock" hats, and acquired Arab kaffiyehs as a badge of honor. No helmets or dress uniforms. How they acquired those kaffiyehs was never discussed. They were our glamorous, devil-may-care people's army, invincible.

There were also the wounded you occasionally saw in the street: a bandaged head, an arm in a sling, or a man walking on crutches, perhaps even missing a leg. Their numbers grew over time, though these were the "well" ones, able to be outdoors, not those my mother saw at the hospital ward. "The nurses dumped on me the worst jobs," she told me years later, and not much more. Only now do I dare imagine what it meant. Once in a while she'd bring home a trinket or a glossy black-and-white poster that one of her patients passed on to her, mass-produced items that the Committee for the Soldier distributed to the wounded "in recognition of ..."

I never learned anything about the young men who passed these gifts on to my mother. Most of those she took care of were foreign volunteers, assigned to her because she spoke English. I see her as she was at the time: slim, softly curling light hair, blue eyes, and a ready smile, bending over a hospital bed to remove a bandage, adjust a blanket, and comfort a scared youth.

I hadn't thought about these foreign volunteers for years. It was mainly our own Sabras who peopled the heroic stories we told ourselves. I was therefore surprised to chance on a monument to them in October 2014, when my friend Jacoby joined me in retracing some of my travels with Deborah. Jacoby had already seen the scenic Gilboa road and Beit Shean when, some days later, we were in a forest commemorating the Burma Road that, in '48, provided crucial access to besieged Jerusalem. The tall dark stone rectangle welcoming us to a clearing turned out to be a memorial to the foreign volunteers of the Machal brigade who died in '48.

Name after name was chiseled into the polished rectangle, listing dates and countries of origin, among them veterans of the Spanish Civil War and World War II, not necessarily Jewish. Later I read that of the four thousand Machal volunteers, 123 died in battle, including four women. A website showing the names and photos of "machalniks" who'd served in the Palmach's Desert Beasts unit lists two wounded: Al Twersky of the United States, who lost a leg and is seen in a photograph wearing a floppy hat, and Ronnie Cheskelson of South Africa, whose wound is not specified. Were any of them my mother's patients, I wondered?

"So sad," Jacoby said, and fell silent.

Searching her face, I saw tears in her eyes.

I was taken aback. I did not expect her—a longtime social justice activist working for the Palestinian cause—to be moved. Years later, she wrote to explain her feelings:

> "I cried about the collapse of the hope and the dreams.
> Those fighters, from so many places, including the Spanish
> Civil War, came believing they were building something,
> called to do that, to join the struggle for something new,
> needed, and good."

Of course we adored our soldiers, especially the Palmach Brigades, all of them Sabras in our myth-making wish for a Sabra nation, all native-born. After centuries of abuse and dispossession they'd be the guarantors of our newborn state—"*medina ivrit*," as we called it—secular, Hebrew, not "Jewish." We civilians were mustering our own resilience while still reeling from the traumas of World War II. There was pride in it but also a heritage of pain that leeched into every crack and fissure of our daily life. Like the tattooed numbers visible on many arms, the broken Hebrew that swirled around us—all those accents and grammatical errors—testified to calamities we could not forget.

Inevitably, with our young men and women at a front, some neighborhoods vulnerable to sharpshooters, and people everywhere worrying about air raids—with ears cocked at every siren and eyes noting every sandbag shelter—nerves were frayed. In every home, it seemed, frazzled housewives struggled with food shortages. The newly minted word "*tzena*," meaning austerity and referring to strict food rationing, was on everybody's mind. "Should I or shouldn't I buy eggs on the black market?" a housewife might agonize when a man appeared at her door—as one once did at ours, flashing open a raincoat to reveal a boxy bus-driver's change pouch with four eggs nestled under its leather cover. To counter such black-market temptations, alternatives were extolled: "Seven olives have the same nutritional value as one egg," a radio announcer assured us, while *La-Ishah*, a women's magazine, covered ways to cook the lentil-size *khubeiza* pods growing wild in the fields.

A desperate grasp at survival seemed to permeate Tel Aviv, even if I couldn't have named it at the time. It hung in the city's humid air like an odor, one that I felt especially when standing on the food lines where I was sent several times a week. People would line up in front of a grocery shop the moment a new supply arrived, with passersby joining before they even found out what was on offer. Of course these lines spoke of scarcity, but they had to do with much more than just flour, sugar, or a can of Spam. Phantom memories of losses and starvation in Europe's ghettos haunted those lines—a starvation more obdurate than anything my grandmother experienced during the siege in Jerusalem. For many of the bodies waiting, pushing, and shoving, the food lines still meant a desperate holding on to a life seared by horrors far worse than the current war.

I remember those lines vividly: people jostling, arguments erupting, everybody tense and tired, and all of us aware that Mr. Lachman, the neighborhood's one-armed grocer, may soon run out of whatever became available that day. We all knew our parts: Mrs. Greenbaum would again be reprimanded for trying to edge ahead of whoever was in front of her, Mrs. Shapiro would complain about the peanut butter or Spam that her children wouldn't eat, and old Mrs. Ben Bassat would keep checking the sky, worrying that her swollen legs wouldn't carry her to shelter fast enough if sirens were to sound. "Ya Allah!" she sighs, rolling her R's. "What can one do? *Ein Breira.*" One memory is especially vivid: Mrs. Shapiro lowering her shopping bag to ease an aching shoulder, her sleeve rising to reveal the numbers tattooed on her arm. She was talking with Ruti, mother of twins, whose husband, we all knew, was fighting in a not-to-be-named somewhere, *ey-sham.*

In my memory these lines occurred in the perpetual damp cold of rainy days, with me shifting my weight from foot to foot, my soggy stockings sticking out at the toes where the leather had been sliced to allow for another year of growth. More than a head shorter than any adult on line, I feared the restless bodies that dwarfed me and recoiled from the voices that rose and fell, questioned and argued and consoled, in a rudimentary Hebrew accented every which way. We all knew one another: the Ashkenazi women, a few still in their dressing gowns, the Mizrahi women in faded floral dresses and hastily tied head-kerchiefs, the occasional nightshift worker who clambered out of bed on his wife's behalf, bullying his way toward the front of the line, and Lea the greengrocer, a Holocaust survivor whose husband meandered silently, emaciated, his eyes hollow, mute.

While the food lines showed me war as a turbulent gathering where individual tragedies and needs jostle and sometimes crash against one another, life at home taught me the calm of war readiness. One day, returning home from school, I found myself in a steaming kitchen separated from the dining area by a scrim of floating strips of gauze: bandages drying on an improvised laundry line. My mother and grandmother were seated at the dining table rolling clean bandages while bloodied ones were twisting and winding in a pot of disinfectant bubbling on the stove. Draped on a nearby chair were more white strips—bedsheets cut into ribbons. It would be years before I let myself imagine what use these bloodstained strips might have served. It did not occur to me, either, that bandages were too scarce to discard or that the hospital was too short of hands and space to sterilize them. To this day, the smell the Lysol makes me remember those brown and yellow stains on white strips of gauze twisting around one another in boiling water.

"May I help?" I asked.

Her ear cocked to the radio, my mother gestured to an empty chair at the table. Disentangling a white strip of gauze from the clean pile that Savta slid toward me, I followed their example, rolling the gauze carefully into a neatly packed cylinder. Then another, and another. The feel of the rough white gauze between my fingers was strangely reassuring, as was the growing pile of pristine rolls that gathered in the middle of the table. They spoke of competence and recovery, of war being kept at bay, and of ordinary people like us making recovery possible.

I did not want to imagine any other possibility, though of course there was no escaping them. In this tiny country the front and the home front were not that far apart. The fighting was often fierce. Our soldiers were not always advancing. Some were wounded; some died. The entire *yishuv* seemed to be listening to the hourly broadcasts and special bulletins that blared into the street out of open doors and windows, coming from radios left permanently on. We'd hush to listen to reports of *our* advances and losses, not "theirs":

"Three bombs fell near ..."

"The enemy retreated to ..."

"All returned safely to base ..."

"The wounded were evacuated to ..."

"A son fell in the battle of ... member of kibbutz ..."

The fighters were always "sons," once in a while a "daughter." As the announcer's carefully calibrated voice read the Sabra nicknames of the fallen—Benny or Tzvika or Danny or Shosh—we felt we knew them intimately. There was a smattering of other names too, Mizrahi names like Zecharia and Nissim, or European names like Berle or Lolek, residues of diasporas Israel was leaving behind. It was mainly the Ashkenazi Sabra names that came to typify '48—names that felt rugged, brave, and beloved.

Whenever the names were read, a wave of sadness would wash over us. Heard in the street through an open window, a passerby would pause, likely to know that family or kibbutz or village or hometown that lost its "son." They were all our sons. "Kibbutz N. just lost a son," I overheard a woman say to a total stranger, on my way home from school. "Yes," the other sighed. "My sister-in-law has an old friend in that kibbutz. She must know the parents."

There were also the other broadcasts, those that appeared regularly at the end of the hourly news, in a program called *Mi Makir, Mi Yodea* ("Who Recognizes, Who Knows"), where an announcer would read names of people looking for loved ones, relatives and friends who vanished during the Holocaust and its aftermath. Each name a life, each syllable a tiny grasp at hope.

"Clara B. from the village of ..., Beserabia, looking for her sister Esther B., last seen in ..."

"Yizhak W. from the ... neighborhood of Warsaw, looking for anyone who knows the whereabouts of ..."

"Shula and Rivka S. looking for any news of their parents, Leib and Rocheleh S., last seen in ..."

And so it went, a never-ending litany that replenished itself every hour. Nobody could remain untouched, not even those who had no relatives in Europe, like my family. The very list spoke of so much anguish. Many of these names still had the sounds of the shtetl clinging to them: Pesia, Fanya, Leibe, or Shloimeh. It could have been me, I thought, barely allowing myself to imagine what that "it" might have been. It could have been any of us.

The radio knit the *yishuv* into a family, binding us to a war effort that focused solely on our own collective survival. It was only our "sons" and "daughters" that we were thinking of, not those of the Palestinians. Together we willed ourselves into a surreal state of acute seeing mixed with blindness, a selective numbness on high alert. We heard the news. but my parents never discussed the contents in front of us children and I did not ask questions. I learned to be quiet, teaching myself to be numb. War became the new normal, and yet everything about it was a mystery. The Palestinians' expulsion from Summayl, an easy walk from our house, occurred as if elsewhere, out of sight.

It would take years for me to learn that our new homeland came at a cruel and lacerating cost to the Palestinians, whom we exiled from theirs. It would also be decades more before I'd find myself visiting Israel with Deborah and allow that visit to show me the Nakba.

But at least to some extent my move to the United States helped me to see my own history somewhat differently. In 1961, newly married to an American student and living in a rent-controlled tenement at the edge of New York City's Harlem, I discovered a poverty for which I had not been prepared. The American Blacks and immigrant Puerto Ricans crowding into the walk-up tenements of my neighborhood were nothing like the smiling, fresh-scrubbed white Americans who had beamed at me back home from the glossy covers of American magazines and even glossier advertisements. Listening to Pacifica's listener-supported radio WBAI, I learned about civil rights marches and clashes: fire hoses, police dogs, activists at lunch counters and some murdered by the Klan. Working in the periodical section of New York City's Public Library, I discovered publications ranging from Ku Klux Klan newsletters to I.F. Stone's *Weekly* and the *Southern Patriot,* the latter considered "seditious" for its reports on race and labor struggles. At City College, where I enrolled, students were volunteering to join Freedom Rides.

By 1961, my fellow students at City College were writing essays about the treatment of Native Americans and questioning our professor's praise for the progress made since the Civil War. As the civil rights movement grew and "Ban the Bomb" marches turned into calls to "Bring Our Boys Back Home," I began to wonder about my Israeli wars, too. Maybe it was hearing about the My Lai massacre in Vietnam that made me recall Kufr Qasim where, in 1956, forty-eight Palestinian farmers were massacred in central Israel, twenty-three of them children, as they returned home from their fields during a curfew they hadn't been informed of. Maybe it was the founding of SDS (Students for Democratic Society) in 1960 that made memories of the Israeli anti-Zionist socialist organization Matzpen (1962) return with new clarity.

Imperceptibly, both Israel and the United States were tugging at me, teaching me to open my eyes.

5. Brothers Dwelling Together

*I*t's a mysterious process, this opening of eyes, often imperceptible and hard to define, a matter of will as well as opportunity. Ever since I'd first told Deborah about the cactuses, in 1993, and especially after our time in Beit Shean, I felt dogged by a silent history shadowing the one I knew. By 2005, during Deborah's first visit to Israel, I was seeing my country in new ways that I was still reluctant to name. Avoiding the Nakba, I talked instead about the seismic upheavals of "absorbing" masses of refugees and destitute immigrants—a truthful account she'd care about but also, for me, a self-justification that let me bypass the Nakba. It is a triumphalist story of regeneration tarnished by what it does not say about the very immigration we extol. Our "ingathering of exiles" was our Manifest Destiny, driven by a desperate wish to be a "free people in our own country," as our national anthem has it. Inevitably, it was also a settler-colonial project, imbued with racism both external, toward the Palestinians, and internal, Jew against Jew.

I'll never forget the crowding and chaos of this "ingathering," including my long hours waiting on the food lines. Anybody who had a spare room had to take in strangers during those early years of upheaval, my great uncle and aunt among them. The small apartments of the Kiryat Meir estate housed two families to a two-room unit, with fights erupting over the shared kitchen and bathroom and husbands coming to blows in the street. Harder yet was the fate of Jaffa's Jewish refugees, most of them Mizrachim, who spilled into any available space after the '48 fighting began, turning Tel Aviv into a shantytown. There were families living in shipping containers and in corrugated iron and cardboard shacks, lone individuals curled behind sandbag walls, and families crowding into entrance hallways, half-hidden by threadbare blankets hanging from fraying ropes. On rainy days steam would rise from the flooded pavements, releasing the musty smell of damp bedrolls and unfamiliar foods cooked on rickety primus burners. None of the children I sometimes glimpsed behind those partitions went to my neighborhood school.

Like the world at large, we too recoiled from the Holocaust's survivors. Unsettling though it was to see their tattooed arms, the tattoos also whispered to us that we, Ashkenazi old timers, were better than them, a truly "free people" untainted by the diaspora's wretched legacy of victimization. To our arrogant Ashkenazi eyes, all Mizrachi Jews seemed "backward," "problematic," and "primitive": Yemenites, Iraqis, North Africans, and other Mizrahim and Sephardim. Arab-seeming in custom and skin color, their language, food, clothes, music, and even liturgy challenged the Europeans' relative wealth, their control of the country, and their smug sense of superiority.

The Israel I grew up in was not the proverbial melting pot but a pressure cooker with its valve loose. There were too many traumatized people among us, with too many histories, languages, cultures, and kinds of pain. For all the embrace of the often sung "Hinei Ma Tov," taken from Psalm 133, we were hardly brothers, let alone together. "*Hinei ma tov u-ma na-im …*" I sang to Deborah. "Behold how good and how pleasant it is for brethren to dwell in unity." But are these really Jews, the old *yishuv* wondered?

I sensed these tensions even as a child. At four, I already knew enough about skin color to call my ruddy newborn sister "Yemenite" when I first glimpsed her in my mother's arms. It was a family joke: my sister grew to be a blond and blue-eyed child. I was clearly aware that "they," in this case Yemenite Jews, are not like "us," the European Ashkenazim we took to be the Jewish norm.

A bittersweet reminder of what "Yemenite" meant to me around that time is on record in two framed collages I made as a child. I chanced on them after my mother died, stashed in her closet for years. Deborah happened to catch sight of these treasures spread on a table in front of me. The colorful cutouts are as bright as ever, clear against the fraying, discolored background.

"You did that?" she asked. "I'll frame them. And this one too," she added, picking up a collage with several monochrome cutouts of a gun-toting Dick Tracy that would now claim a "hip" pop-art edge.

"Look, somebody dated them in pencil: 'Linda 1942'," I said, touched by the hand that thought to sign and date them, feeling affection for the child—me—who accepted with such trust the world she was assembling with scissors and glue.

Now on my wall, two of these collages tell the story of my universe at age four: an archetypal pioneer in shorts and sandals firmly holding a spade, his badly glued rake having migrated into its twin collage; a representative set of farm animals (cow, sheep, donkey, camel, with a nuclear chicken family of three); orange, cypress, and palm trees, one each; and a washerwoman in a headscarf sitting on the ground, knees akimbo, scrubbing laundry in a zinc pail. A child is hanging laundry near her, wearing a red dress and a frilly white apron much too pretty for the task.

That dainty child was the imaginary me, awash in storybook notions of domestic femininity, making herself useful without staining her apron or crushing her dress. Even at age four I already knew that the washerwoman was Yemenite. She looked, dressed, and was seated on the ground just like Rumia, who spoke Hebrew with rolling R's and guttural A's and did our laundry in Herzelia. Naive though these images were, they spoke to current realities and tensions yet to come, including Yemenite babies stolen for adoption into Ashkenazi families, North African Jews rioting in Haifa's Wadi Salib in 1959, and the emergence of Israel's Black Panthers protest movement and political party in 1971.

These are just some among countless other economic, legal, residential, cultural, and religious conflicts that continue to separate Mizrachi, Sepharadi, and Ashkenazi Jews from one another, including communities within and among them: Arab Jews, European Jews, Jews with Spanish ancestry; Jews from Eastern Europe and those from the West; "Arabs" from the Near East and those from the Mughreb; Jews from Iran and others from India. With millennia of displacements across porous boundaries, ancestral identity becomes a measure of self-worth, and ethnic grievances can be sharp.

My earliest direct insight into these enmities happened in high school when my freckled and blue-eyed Ashkenazi friend Miri, an orphaned Holocaust survivor, was not allowed by her guardians to date our friend Micha because he was a "frenk." Sixteen years old, Miri and Micha had been inseparable. I was puzzled: Micha, a proverbially "tall, dark, and handsome" youth, was one of us, a Sabra who eventually became an air force pilot. Our tight-knit Ashkenazi group of friends was dismayed but unquestioning. The injunction seemed reasonable, even if nobody could explain why. The word "frenk" was enough.

Deborah was moved by this story. As a teenager, in her evangelical family, she was to stay away from Jews and Catholics.

"Jews I understand, but Catholics?"

"Even worse," she laughed. "Popish! Even if they call themselves Christians."

"Jew" and "Catholic," "Ashkenazi" and "Mizrachi"—one knows, or imagines, or invents meanings. Among us, Ashkenazim, any olive- or brown-skinned Jew, Sephardi or Mizrachi, was a "frenk." The word had currency even as Israeli socialists, almost all Ashkenazim, marched in large May Day parades singing "The International" in its Hebrew translation.

The radio was always turned on in our busy kitchen when I was growing up. It was the beating heart of our home and, to judge by sounds wafting into the street, the heart of many homes. For years there was no television in Israel, only the radio and its two channels. Later, as my mother aged, a small transistor radio would keep her company, affirming the mythical wonder of the life we Israeli Jews were building in our young homeland. The familiar songs we all heard, and could at least hum if not sing, confirmed that we were "brothers together." Even newly arrived immigrants who did not yet know Hebrew could remember at least some of the words.

I'd hear these old songs during my visits home, the new ones never really replacing the old. It was something to share with my mother during the many hours she rested in bed. One evening—by then Israel had several TV stations—we watched a compilation of short interviews where immigrants reminisced about their early days in the shabby transit camps that housed thousands of immigrants during the early years of statehood. One woman, though, an Egyptian immigrant, smiles on film as she recalls their Friday night dances.

"We used to dance to 'Kakarula,'" she tells her interviewer, nostalgia creeping into her voice.

"Kakarula?" he asks, mystified.

"Yes," she confirms, humming the refrain to the 1948 love song "Shkharkhoret."

There is no "kakarula" in this song, though that's how this woman heard and remembered it, not the Hebrew lyrics she couldn't understand. What she heard was actually the phrase "*Kach kar'ou la*" ("that's how she was called"), about a soldier's love for a pretty, dark young woman.

Mom and I exchanged an insider's smile, loving this immigrant for her endearing mistake, which was so reassuring: just a woman remembering Friday evening dances and a pretty song, not the difficulties of transit camp life, the resentments, or the *yishuv*'s ungenerous reception of people like her.

Another evening, listening to Mom's favorite "golden oldies," Shoshana Damari's deep voice came on the radio, singing her best-known song, "Kalaniyot," about a girl picking red anemones for her mother. A song about the passing of time, it spoke to my mother's lost youth and, in a different way, mine. But what struck me most, hearing it anew, was Damari's thick Yemenite accent.

"Nobody speaks like that anymore, not even Damari's children," I said, thinking about the thousands of Moroccan, Libyan, Iraqi, Kurdish, Yemenite, Tunisian, Syrian, Egyptian, Iranian, Turkish, Indian, and Ethiopian Jews who are now Israeli, alongside the Ashkenazim.

"In practice," I added, thinking of our many lingering accents, "the ideal of 'the ingathering of exiles' didn't work. We weren't 'ingathered,' just made to cohabit."

Mom nodded faintly, leaving me to ruminate about our ethnicities. While Damari's accent may have been marked from birth, I thought, its harsh sounds defy the Ashkenazi *yishuv*'s decree of what is to be normal Hebrew. Hers is the voice of some of Israel's poorest and least respected Jewish communities, including Rumia and Mazal, a voice that retrieved and amplified this music as a badge of honor.

Perhaps my mother was just tired when she closed her eyes and stopped talking, but I think she wanted to escape both the nostalgia and disenchantment that haunted this conversation. When I tried to shift the conversation to the immigrant village of Petachia where, in the mid-1950s, she'd travel by bus three and four times a week to do community work, she didn't respond either. For her, daughter of the early dreamers of the budding *yishuv*, Israel's recent history involved painful misgivings, including the ongoing militarization of the country and the increasingly brutal occupation of Palestinian territories. By the 1990s I heard her describe Zionism as a colonial project that went wrong, already an anachronism by the time her grandparents landed in Palestine in the 1880s, just as European colonialism was falling apart.

"We could've stayed in England," she said more than once, thinking about meeting my father in London, where he was studying engineering.

"Living through the Blitz?"

"Yes, even that."

Two years later, when Deborah and I were touring what remains of Abu Kabir and Salameh, south of Tel Aviv's modern sprawl, I remembered that conversation.

"This is where the Nakba and our own racism meet," I said. "Among ourselves and in relation to the Palestinians."

The only Palestinian relic we could identify in Abu Kabir was a vandalized Muslim cemetery in a depressing state of dereliction, with Jewish apartment houses clearly encroaching on it. How long would it remain, I wondered, surveying its vandalized tombstones and neglected dome-roofed sepulcher, a *makaam* overgrown with weeds. But in nearby Salameh, now Kfar Shalem, we were greeted by a more telling marker of Palestinian life: an imposing mosque standing in the midst of a Jewish community occupying what used to be a Palestinian town of five thousand inhabitants. For years I had heard of this neighborhood only as an impoverished and turbulent annex to Tel Aviv. I knew that many of its Mizrachi immigrants were Yemenites flown over in "Operation Magic Carpet" in 1949–1950. But by the time Deborah and I got there, some of Kfar Shalem had already been cleared for new construction, rimmed by apartment blocks.

Poor though this Jewish community was, the small, mostly one-story houses we saw were well maintained. They'd been whitewashed, their tiled or earthen small patios swept clean. Here and there someone planted a grape arbor, someone had herbs or geraniums blooming in an old oilcan. Pride of home was visible everywhere, but also graffiti and posters calling on people to resist eviction. I have since read that this struggle dates back at least to 1965, when developers first began to eye Kfar Shalem's real estate, so close to the center of Tel Aviv. Legal battles, rallies, and demonstrations followed, including the 1982 police killing of one protester as he tried to defend his home.

"Just like Jaffa, where people are also being evicted," she said. "Do you think they have a chance?"

Looking at the new apartment houses, I had my doubts. "The land is too valuable to let them stay," I said.

"So why don't they make common cause with the Palestinians who are also losing their homes in nearby Jaffa?"

"Duh?" my raised eyebrows said. "Because they are Jews," I said, slamming the car door shut, as if this was a definitive answer.

That evening, with Kfar Shalem still on our minds, Deborah and I strolled along Tel Aviv's seafront. The cafés and restaurants lining the paved walkway were humming with people, and the tall hotels and apartment houses that rise above them shed soft light over the crowded scene below. It was not a moonlit night, and yet you could see the people swimming in the tepid water, a dark head or a raised arm outlined for a few seconds when light bounced off the crest of a wave. Old Jaffa was faintly visible to the south, a dark mass rising above the water's edge, outlined against the slightly less dark sky.

The nearness of airy, concrete-and-stucco Tel Aviv facing the old, stone-built Jaffa recalled what we had just seen: abandoned Palestinian village ringed by modern apartment blocks creeping forward as if to swallow the remaining village houses.

"The lucky immigrants," I said, "got public housing near cities, but many were dumped in abandoned Arab villages like Salameh or in so called development towns."

"Like what we saw in Beit Shean," Deborah said.

"And Yeruham and Dimmona and other desolate places where immigrants are settled with next to no employment. And it wasn't all luck. Some ethnicities were considered less 'civilized,' than others."

"You know," she said, as we continued to walk. "It's not only me who's seeing things for the first time. You are too."

I nodded. She was right, though I still didn't welcome this new seeing. Walking back home, I was silent, happy for the darkness enveloping us. The traffic was slowing down along Ben Yehuda Street, and the souvenir shops that crowd it were dark behind their metal shutters. Every so often a half-empty bus rumbled past us. The street was growing quiet.

Enjoying the ease of the moment, I let my memories drift to the relief of Tel Aviv's return to ordinary life once the 1949 ceasefire was signed. We children could once again roam the fields that stretched between my neighborhood of Kiryat Meir and the now deserted village of Summayl, collecting bullet casings. Some casings still had bullets inside them, and some had gunpowder at the point of contact. Nobody seemed to worry about accidents, even when some boys found a way to empty the gunpowder and set it on fire, sparks crackling in all directions. One large casing, a prized mortar shell I found near our house, sat for years on the floor of my room, holding a bouquet of dry thistles, a bohemian cliché of those post-war years.

It was strange to suddenly remember, now in Boston, that mortar shell. I hadn't thought about my old room for years, the room where I'd stopped being a child: the narrow bed, the fold-up desk, the framed reproduction of Franz Marc's *Gazelle*, with its soft wash of greens and mustard-browns, the boxy record player on the floor, and near it, the mortar shell casing. That casing, I now think, marked my growth out of adolescence, a marker of questions I was yet to ask. Its tarnished metal spoke of deadly power while its silky smoothness whispered of pleasure. It was my first insight into the twisting paths of killing.

6. Jerusalem

Jerusalem was the one place Deborah *had* to see before returning to the United States, yet the prospect made me uneasy. Millennia of histories entwine, clash, crash, fade, and reawaken in these crowded hills, where everybody jousts for territorial and spiritual ownership. How was I to lead this outsider into Jerusalem's bloodstained palimpsest of occupations, written and rewritten into its very stones, touched daily, year after year, by the same sun?

And there was more to my reluctance—a sense of the city's betrayal of its promise, even if that promise has always been a delusion. "If I forget thee, O Jerusalem, may my right hand forget its skill," Psalm 137 affirms. But which Jerusalem does it speak of? The heavenly city of the imagination, the city I knew as a child before '48, or the one it is becoming today?

There was some nostalgia in my wish to connect Deborah to "my" Jerusalem, where my grandmother's apartment at the edge of Beit Hakerem, facing the city's western rim across from the Valley of the Cross, had always been more than home to me. But that beloved apartment, I had since come to realize, was within walking distance of Deir Yassin, which saw the most notorious massacre of Palestinians during the '48 war. Whatever twinges of nostalgia I still feel choke on this history. The Jerusalem I was about to show Deborah is a city mauled by passions, greed, and righteous self-interest.

What do the millennia of prayer and yearning that Jerusalem had inspired amount to, I wondered, as I mulled over what to show Deborah. How was I to convey the sublime claims lodged in this city by its three Abrahamic religions when it has long been a battleground for ownership spurred by those same claims? And where do sublime feelings end and land-grabs start amid all that rhetoric? Involuntarily, the same memory haunted me every time I pondered these questions: the rousing climax of *The Birth of a Nation,* D.W. Griffith's notoriously racist film of 1915. Threaded into the plot's concluding celebration of Ku Klux Klansmen galloping to rescue its white protagonists is a diaphanous rendition of Jesus entering the "heavenly city," sanctifying the Klan's arrival in a soft-focus halo.

Much of present-day Jerusalem, I reminded myself as Deborah and I were preparing to go there, is as foreign to me, an Israeli, as it is to her: the Christian sites, the Muslim ones, even the ultra-orthodox Haredi neighborhoods where secular Jews are not welcome.

We found a tiny ground-level apartment carved out of the back of a Palestinian mansion on a dead-end street named Dor Dor Vedorshav (literally, "each generation and its interpreters"). A quaint name, so "Jerusalemite," even Talmudic, in its requiring each generation to research and debate its era anew. It was a leafy, short, dead-end street, flanked by other elegant Palestinian mansions. Lavish in fine masonry and architectural detail, with the deep green of their gardens relieved by bursts of red and pink bougainvillea blossoms climbing up walls and spilling over fences, the street seemed a refuge from the city's hurly-burly. Not for long, though, as a chalky-white gravel road extension had already been laid down, opening to a bulldozed area flattened for new construction.

Come evening, the heady scent of jasmine would waft toward us as we walked past garden walls. Daytime, sounds of hammering and sawing at the mansion across the street signaled renovation under way. Except for our house, all the others had already been renovated: you could glimpse fashionable drapery behind restored windows and gleaming new locks on garden gates. "A Private Luxury Mansion rental," www.hotel.com advertised on Dor Dor Vedorshav Street. "An old oriental house … spacious garden" advertised another.

The couple that rented us our lodgings did not seem to belong in the neighborhood. The wife was doing laundry outdoors when we first arrived, dressed in a faded flowered dress and headscarf reminiscent of our Yemenite laundress, Rumia, in Herzelia. The husband, in stained work pants, was repairing something in a courtyard that was more a service area than a patio.

By looks and accent they seemed North African, probably non-owners whose family, still large when they first arrived in Israel, had been assigned an abandoned Palestinian house by the Caretaker of Absentee Property. The building, a faded beauty, was primed for renovation.

The story of this neighborhood became clearer to me a year or two later when I chanced on Amos Gitai's film trilogy, *House*, where the Palestinian Dajani family's home on Dor Dor Vedorshav Street is a stand in for others. Shot between 1980 and 2005, these three interconnected documentaries trace the biography of this house. While much of the footage centers on bodies and machines rennovating this house for its new (presumably Israeli) owner, the film's close observation of the labor involved and its attention to the Palestinian laborers doing it, exposes the politics that churn beneath the seemingly neutral surface: who does this labor, why, and for whom?

In the film, we meet the Palestinian owners who had fled Jerusalem in early '48, after the Deir Yassin massacre, and learn about the impoverished Romanian and Algerian Jews who were given this and similar houses early on. We learn about a professor who lived in the Dajani house for a while and the affluent French and Anglo-Saxon Jewish owners who cherish the romance of "oriental" architecture. But we also learn about the Palestinians whose labor makes possible this Jewish acquisition. This, too, is a Nakba story: a biography of a house that was cherished at its height, known in its decline, and was then reclaimed into new glory.

Gitai's Dajani family home must have been one of those Deborah and I passed daily on Dor Dor Vedorshav Street. Like many Israelis, I registered the lovely Palestinian architecture in a haze of seeing and not seeing, including, I must confess, some coveting. How lovely it would be to live in such a house, with its hand-hewn masonry and the ornamental wrought iron detail still gracing the garden's water cistern. On my way home from a dusty day of sightseeing, I let these vestiges of Palestinian wellbeing seduce me with their promise of gracious living.

Like many tourists, Deborah and I visited museums, gawked at the massive grandeur of the Old City viewed from the terrace of the King David Hotel, enjoyed a drink at the American Colony Hotel that had been a Turkish pasha's palace, and browsed in gift shops. But mostly we meandered through the Old City's maze of markets, fragrant with spices, coffee, and sweet pastries, but also selling souvenirs, brooms, and laundry soap, and echoing with the cries of men rattling pushcarts through the narrow, cobbled alleys.

Like others, we walked along Via Dolorosa, where pilgrims retrace Jesus' footsteps on the way to his crucifixion. We climbed up to the *Haram al-Sharif* (the Dome of the Rock) and walked down to the *Kotel*, the Wailing Wall, just below the Muslim compound, crowded with Jews praying by the stone remnants of their destroyed temple. We circled the city's ancient fortifications, breached and patched by a succession of conquests, walked through the newly excavated Roman Cardo street, and continued to the now-restored Jewish Quarter.

So many histories are fused into the masonry and soul of this Jerusalem: where the stones are washed with the gold and pink glow of the afternoon sun, the striations of human occupation bleed into one another. The strife never stops, not even at the Holy Sepulcher, where crowds were milling about the dank cavernous space. Franciscans, Anglicans, Greeks, Armenians, Dominicans flitted by in their black, brown, and white robes. A lay group led by a Franciscan monk was tracing the Stations of the Cross. A lone Ethiopian priest, a delicate-boned youth in dark robes, was fast asleep in the few square feet assigned to the Ethiopian church, his head resting on a bent elbow. Others, unaffiliated like us, were also there, some praying, some just gawking. Cameras clicked, the flames of candles quivered. Commerce was lively just outside: rosaries, prayer cards, and candles, but also *kaffiyehs*, soft drinks, postcards, and snacks.

"Big deal! The 'Holy' Sepulcher!" Deborah scoffed as we emerged from the echoing interior of this crepuscular shrine. "Byzantium's Queen Helen arrives here some three hundred years after Jesus walked this earth and identifies 'holy' locations as she traipses around the countryside, including this place of his supposed burial."

Deborah's radar for incongruities delighted me. Hidden under her quiet façade was a sensor, always alert to dubious truths.

"You obviously did your homework," I laughed. The Holy Land, as we were discovering, is awash in wishful thinking.

Back in the Old City's din-filled alleys, Deborah noticed an inconspicuous side entrance into the Haram al-Sharif compound, governed by the Palestinians' Muslim *Wakf* endowment. "No. Only Muslims," a uniformed

Waqf custodian said in struggling English, fingering his prayer beads, not even bothering to stand up. But compensation was at hand: an old vendor whose offering of assorted Korans and prayer beads included small, flat boxes covered in red velvet. Inside each was a paper-thin brass sheet resting on white satin, with elaborate Arabesque calligraphy cut delicately into it. A prayer? A blessing? We bought three, the third for a friend back home.

"The *Waqf* guard wasn't hostile," Deborah remarked, "and the old man was nice about selling us these boxes even if we are 'infidels' and women no less."

"I never know what to expect," I said." We clearly don't belong here. Until 1967 the Old City was under Jordan, barred to Israelis. I still feel like an intruder."

"And you are," she said, as we continued to weave our way through the market's alleys. "We are. At least I'm a foreigner, not an occupier."

We paused, each seeing in the other her own self as Palestinians might see her: two older women in jeans, somewhat disheveled, at least one of them Jewish, maybe even an enemy, maybe the wife, mother, or sister of the Israeli soldier who had barged into their home, arrested a cousin, killed a relative, or served them an eviction notice.

Would we ever be able to put aside this reflexive sizing up of one another other, I wondered? Would the first thought always be, Is this one enemy or friend? I was silent as we headed for the *Kotel*. Feeling my feet unsteady on the uneven cobblestones, I suddenly remembered being there as a child, taken by her parents down what might well have been the same narrow cobbled alley—the only way to reach the *Kotel* at the time. I remembered my parents swinging me, a gleeful three- or four-year old, down shallow steps and into the narrow space of prayer where old men and women were praying side by side, swaying, weeping, tucking missives of need into the wall's crevices.

"It's so different now," I said, surveying the vast open plaza in front of the *Kotel*. The alleys I described, the steps, the old people at prayer, all gone. "This plaza used to be the old Mughrabi quarter," I said. "The Moroccan Quarter of Jerusalem, razed to clear the space for prayer. In 1967, my parents made one of their rare, expensive trans-Atlantic phone calls to tell me about it. The entire quarter had been bulldozed immediately after the Six-Day War, they said, appalled.

I since learned that 135 houses were razed, including an ancient mosque. In less than three hours, 650 people were rendered refugees, with others found dead in the rubble. The demolition was rushed to clear space for the Jewish holiday crowds expected to visit the newly accessible *Kotel*. The expelled Palestinians, given no time to take any of their possessions, were loaded on trucks. Until it was bulldozed, the Mughrabi quarter had been their home for more than a thousand years. It was a gift from Saladin to his North African followers, endowed in 770.

That day, as Deborah and I stood on a slight rise at the edge of the paved area, the plaza seemed so peaceful, barely touched by the distant din of traffic. The Wall, patched over centuries of conquest, towered above the holiest Jewish place of worship, with the golden cupola and glistening tiled walls of the Muslims' Dome of the Rock higher yet, guarding the rock imprinted with the hoof of Muhammad's horse, Buraq, as he rose to the heavens. Al Aqsa mosque was tucked out of sight from where we stood, but the conical roof of the Benedictine Abbey of the Dormition was visible nearby. Soon it would again be time for prayers. The tolling of bells would mingle with the muezzin's amplified chants in a discord that would hover over this plaza, where Jewish prayers were being murmured and chanted. *Haredi* men in black congregated in tight clusters, with others milling and praying at their own pace—some in their own black cloth or knitted kippahs, others, who had no head covering, in disposable black-cardboard kippahs.

I don't believe Deborah had ever seen such a large gathering of Jews at worship, maybe not even a small one. Surveying the scene through her eyes, I explained that every head covering signals its own variant of origin and belief: the shape of a fur hat, the crown and brim of a fedora, the stuff of a kippah, and those disposable cardboard kippahs, are all coded, even a tourist's baseball cap. The knitted kipphas, I explained, are often worn by settlers who are 'Judaizing' biblical Judea and Samaria, never calling it the Occupied Territories.

As we talked, a commotion seemed to be brewing near the partition erected to separate the women's end of the *Kotel* from the men's. A small group of Women of the Wall had arrived. Wearing kippahs and embroidered prayer shawls, they were demonstrating against this gender barricade. Yet another wall, I thought, another unfinished war.

Later that afternoon, as we sipped Turkish coffee from tiny cups in a small restaurant near the Old City's Jaffa Gate, Deborah asked me if I'd ever seen the Mandelbaum Gate. She already knew that until '67 that heavily guarded gate had been the one official point of transit between the Israeli and the then Jordanian parts of the city.

I never saw the Mandelbaum Gate, I told her, but I remembered seeing a segment of the barrier running through no-man's land. It had to have been in 1959, when I was studying at the Hebrew University. I don't remember how I got there on that blustery winter day. Maybe I just lost my way when I found myself a few yards away from the border, blocked by a large concrete wall. Ten or more feet high, it filled the space between two tall buildings, their windows concrete-sealed, their faces pockmarked by bullets and fringed with curls of rusting barbed wire, the whole separating Israeli and Jordanian-held Arab Jerusalem.

I could see that scene yet again: the earth strewn with filthy rags, smashed bottles, wind-borne paper, and rusting tin cans riddled with bullet holes—a buffer zone that allowed no passage. I remembered raising my eyes and seeing, just a few yards away, the rounded top of a checkered red-and-white kaffiyeh held in place by a black *agal* rope—the standard Jordanian military uniform: a sentry, the barrel of his rifle peeking near his head. A sharpshooter? The barrel was pointing upward, not toward me, but it could have easily been lowered.

Though neither of us said it, Deborah's mentioning the Mandelbaum Gate may have been spurred by our plan to join a tour of the Occupied West Bank, including the new separation wall that Israel was building. We'd already seen photos of that high concrete wall snaking its way through the countryside, separating farmers from their lands, children from their school, families from one another, regardless of the Green Line border agreed on in the '49 armistice. As planned, the next morning found us siting in a minibus with a few other Americans, all of us new to the area but aware of the politics at stake. With only a half-day, the tour kept to the area surrounding Jerusalem, where new settlements, built high on hilltops, asserted their command over the Palestinian villages nestled farther down. The separation wall itself was still being built, but seeing even just sections of this mammoth barricade, winding through built and open Palestinian lands, was crushing.

I remember Deborah saying something about the Occupation and me, looking around us, shushing her. It was not a conversation I wanted to have in front of our Palestinian guide or our silent fellow-tourists. "Later," I mouthed, gesturing toward them. You never know where such conversations might land you, though in truth I didn't need her, an outsider, to underscore the shame I was already feeling. We'd already learned that our guide's family was originally, before '48, from Lifta, near my grandmother's Jewish suburb of Beit Hakerem and Palestinian Deir Yassin. We also knew that the expulsion of Palestinians from their lands and homes did not end with the Nakba, but had been and still is going on steadily in the West Bank and Jerusalem under all kinds of pretexts: military needs, questionable ownership, illegal construction, unauthorized residence, ever-changing legislation, and relentless settlers' assaults that dispensed with pretexts altogether.

"Expulsion" doesn't really say it. There were and still are house demolitions, terrifying late-night arrests, and violent confrontations. Children as well as adults are imprisoned and interrogated brutally. Tensions keep mounting as Palestinian families find themselves homeless while Israeli Jews take over their neighborhoods. A few days before this trip, as Deborah and I strolled along a new promenade overlooking the densely populated Silwan neighborhood, three Palestinians boys, age nine or ten, threw little stones at us, clearly outsiders. The boys were giggling, and the small pebbles—hardly stones—missed us, perhaps on purpose. It was just a gesture, but they had surely seen larger stones hurled in earnest by older boys and men. The message was clear: we want you out of here.

Later that day, no longer in the minibus with strangers, I told her about my having been to the Kalandia terminal a year earlier. I went there with the Israeli organization of Machsom ("Checkpoint") Watch, established to protect Palestinian passage. Abuses at the checkpoints were notorious, with sick people as well as workers delayed or denied passage, often for no clear reason. We, Jewish women, old enough to be the soldiers' mothers or grandmothers, old enough to shame them into decency, had arrived at the Kalandia terminal before dawn to ensure that the soldiers would not obstruct the Palestinians' passage. The men were crowded into steel cages, pressing those ahead to move forward through turnstiles that could be stopped at any minute. Most of them looked away, though when one of them looked me in the eye, my heart sank. What use were we in fact? To him we were still the occupier, still the enemy penning him behind bars.

For a short time after the '67 war, once Jerusalem's '48 barrier had come down, peace seemed possible. Israel would exchange the captured land for peace, some of us supposed, though even then nationalist feelings were aflame: the euphoria of seizing Jerusalem, "liberating" it as many saw it, was hard to resist. People sang Naomi Shemer's "Jerusalem of Gold" in a rapturous ecstasy of collective ownership that proclaimed the city as only ours, not shared. The song came close to replacing our national anthem, "Hatikva," ("The Hope"). By then, the hope voiced in "Hatikva" felt obsolete. We had achieved it. We have become a free people in our own country.

Sometime after calling to tell me about the destruction of the Mughrabi quarter, my father called again. It was still the summer of '67, but this time he sounded cheerier. "We are all streaming into the Arab side, and they are all streaming into ours," he said. "Everybody is shopping and looking to see what's cooking in the neighbors' pots."

He meant "Palestinian," though in '67 we still used the word "Arab," and many still do, ignoring the national identity that the word "Palestinian" asserts. "Arab" was the generic term used in the British census: anyone speaking Arabic was "Arab." Implicitly, the entire Arab world is the Palestinians' home. No wonder Prime Minister Golda Meir of Israel said: "It was not as if there was a Palestinian people in Palestine and we came and threw them out and took their country away from them. They did not exist."

"If only the leaders would stay out of it we'd live quite well together," Dad said, letting reality intrude.

But, as he rightly guessed, it did not take long for our leaders to make it clear that they had no intention of fostering whatever coexistence ordinary people on both sides were tentatively trying out. In the euphoria of acquisition we Israeli Jews did not pause to consider what it might mean to keep the new territories that we came to control with such a dizzying speed. Millennia of long-lost historic Jerusalem were invoked to justify holding on to these territories: the tombs of ancient prophets and patriarchs, the age-old suffering of our people, and the blood spilled by our young warriors to regain them. We couldn't give up our new territories, or wouldn't.

To this day, my father's mix of wistful idealism and realistic irony fills me with loving sadness, as he saw both the possibility of peace and the seeds of its destruction. By the time of these two phone calls I already knew that in the 1930s, before I was born, my parents had been members of Brit Shalom (covenant of peace), an organization that argued for Arab-Jewish coexistence even as Zionism swept the land. Founded by philosophers Martin Buber and Ernst Simon and by Rabbi Judah Magnes, Chancellor and President of the Hebrew University, all of them German-Jewish intellectuals, Brit Shalom's position was controversial. Labor Zionism dismissed it as delusional. Right-wing students, including young Ben-Zion Netanyahu, Benjamin Netanyahu's father, petitioned to dismiss Rabbi Magnes from his position at the head of the Hebrew University. Though Brit Shalom never drew many supporters, I'm still moved by my parents' sharing its aspirations.

In 2015 I came across a slim paperback, yellowed with age, propped up among my books. I wouldn't have noticed it were it not for a sliver of brittle spine that fell into my hand. Titled *Towards Union in Palestine: Essays on Zionism and Jewish-Arab Cooperation* and published in 1947, on the eve of Israel's birth as a state, it belonged to my parents. In it, Magnes, Buber, and Simon warn against Zionism's standing apart from the Arab world into which it had inserted itself, arguing instead for a binational state. They published this manifesto—a heart's cry—even as the tides of history were pulling Arab and Jew apart. The British were still nominally in control of Palestine, yet fighting had already erupted.

What made my parents hold onto this renegade booklet? So much of their library got discarded over time, and yet they kept *Towards Union in Palestine*. With tensions between Palestinians and Jews already rising by the 1920s and made worse as growing numbers of displaced Jews kept arriving, did the dreamers of Brit Shalom really expect this notion of a binational state to find followers? Did my parents?

"It was hard to find any Arabs willing to join Brit Shalom," my mother told me shortly before she died, sounding bitter as she lay in her darkened room, the oxygen machine gurgling softly by her bed. It is sad, even tragic, certainly fateful that there were no takers. By the 1930s, when my newly married parents joined this tiny group, the lines were already sharply drawn. Few Jews would've considered joining Brit Shalom, let alone Palestinians.

No wonder, I realize in hindsight. Zionism is an ideology of siege and self-preservation. It rests on the belief that the whole world is set to destroy us, in every generation, as Passover's Haggadah reminds us annually: *Bekol dor vedor* ... And as for the wealthy Palestinian elites who wouldn't take the hand extended by Brit Shalom, what did they have in common with a handful of utopian German-Jews, "cultural Zionists" who failed to enlist even their own kind? Surely little, and the Palestinian peasants and urban workers even less. In those pre-state years the Jewish slogan was not only "Free Immigration—Hebrew State," but also "Hebrew Labor." Singing the "Internationale" under billowing red flags, our labor unions and cooperatives nonetheless did all they could to exclude the "Arabs" from the labor market.

Deborah never got to see my parents' Brit Shalom pamphlet or Amos Gitai's *House* trilogy. By the time I'd seen the films and then, some years later, chanced on this booklet, she was living in New York and I in Boston. But even so, our four short days in Jerusalem had already shown us that nothing is ordained. "There are choices," either one of us might have said as we surveyed the plaza that used to be Jerusalem's Mughrabi quarter.

It was in this spirit of choice, in the early seventies, that my friend Peter and I had revised the Passover Haggadah for our families' use. The Haggadah is not a scripture; it can be questioned and revised. Among other additions and adjustments, we excised the sentence that calls on God to pour His wrath on the "nations" (*goyim*) that do not know Him, and the pessimistic reminder that in each and every generation—*bekol dor vedor*—"they," faceless and nameless, rise to destroy us. Now, as I write about Deborah and my time in Jerusalem, my thoughts turn to Dor Dor Vedorshav Street. Its name calls on each generation to inquire anew, just as Peter and I were doing and as the Haggadah, too, instructs its celebrants to do so.

Once again I see that lovely dead-end street as it was in 2005: the gracious houses, the shaded gardens, the bougainvillea spilling over a wall. How many, I wonder, bother to inquire into its strange name, *Dor Dor Vedorshav*? Who cares, or even knows, that this dead-end street was originally called Dajani Alley?

7. Cactuses

"You know, this history—the childhood stories, your parents, the country—they matter to me too," Deborah said one evening as we sat at a beach café, our feet dipping in the cool sand. It was toward the end of her first visit, with only a few days to go. "And let's face it," she added. "It matters to you, too, in new ways."

She was right, even if I didn't welcome that insight. Her visit made me confront histories I preferred to forget and consequences too painful to face. With this in mind, I suggested a day trip to Tzippori, our final one one in 2005, recreational, not political. But when Deobrah asked "Why Tzippori?" I couldn't quite answer. The name had some long-forgotten meaning, something to do with Jewish history. Or maybe a wonderful panorama, since "*tzippor*" is "bird" in Hebrew?

Tzippori was a several hours' drive up north, leaving no time to dawdle. "Anther time," I said, gesturing toward Nazareth as we sped onward on a new by-pass road, only to join the heavy traffic chugging through the center of Kafr Cana.

"Hard to imagine Jesus attending a village wedding here," I said, driving past a busy bus depot, a Starbucks, a noisy scooter repair shop. Hard also to believe that this is the small village I remember from before '48, where I saw "a biblical scene," as my father called it: a threshing floor where a camel and a mule circled and circled, right by the roadside.

Built-up Tzippori wasn't yet visible as we paused at the village turn-off to take in the low-slung, densely forested hill rising above newly plowed fields. Velvety at a distance, the deep green that covered the hill was interrupted only by a massive square tower rising against the pale horizon, indomitable in its command of the lands below. The usual JNF pine forest, I thought, noting a few patches of a lighter silvery green visible among the uniform plantings. Something odd, I sensed, pushing the thought aside.

The modern village of Jewish Tzippori finally came into view. Tucked into the hillside, its white stucco houses beckoned through a screen of lush gardens, their pitched red-tiled roofs rising above the foliage. On this mild summer day the village seemed asleep: no cars revving their engines, no people going about their business, no children bouncing a ball. A few crows rose out of a leafy tree, circled, and settled down again. The slight breeze still carried a trace of spring, a brief delay of the fullness of summer's heat.

The nearby archaeological park was bare of tourists on this midweek workday. An old, well-tended olive tree, tastefully replanted by the visitors' center, welcomed us. We paused for a cold drink, paid admission, checked a pictorial "In the Footsteps of Jesus" map that had inch-sized people in supposedly biblical attire journeying along a dotted line, and picked up the glossy brochure the government's Office of Tourism prepares for visitors.

The brochure informed us that Zippori had a rich Hellenistic, Jewish, Roman, Byzantine, and Crusader history, as well as earlier populations known only to the erudite. The site includes the remains of both a fifth-century synagogue and a small basilica honoring Tzippori as Mary's birth-place, but the highlights are Roman, including an amphitheater and a lavish fourth-century mosaic floor whose beautiful portrait of "Mona Lisa (or "Venus") of the Galilee" now adorns a line of Israeli cosmetics and assorted souvenirs.

Much of this history was new to me, traceable through the string of names the place acquired over time: the Greek Sepphoris and Diocaesarea, the Crusader Sephory, the French Sephorie, and so on—all but Arab Saffuriya. More familiar was my murky sense of a Jewish past retrieved from my school days fifty years earlier, now clarified by the brochure: Tzippori became a thriving center of Jewish learning early in the third century, after the destruction of the Second Temple. I had forgotten about that episode, buried in the epic march of Jewish catastrophes and achievements we studied. And yet, after the sack of Jerusalem and the Bar Kokhva rebellion, Tzippori was home to major Jewish academies (*yeshivas*), the seat of the Jewish High Court, the

Sanhedrin, and the place where Rabbi Yehuda Ha-Nasi compiled the Torah's oral commentaries into the Mishnah codicil, precursor of the Talmud.

As we emerged from the visitors' center and headed for the site itself, Deborah paused to scrutinize the brochure. "Romans, Sanhedrin, Mishnah, and Crusaders," she said, looking at a photo of the big tower we had seen at a distance and now realized it was Crusader, "but nothing about the Islamic centuries or the Ottomans?"

She was right, though the thought hadn't occurred to me. What happened on this hill after the Crusaders abandoned it, leaving only their watchtower? Here was Benvenisti's question needling me again, the one I remembered concerning Kawkab el-Hawa: How come we Israelis, so interested in the Crusaders, ignore centuries of Muslim presence in this land? The question was no longer new to me, though I did not expect Tzippori to bring it up again.

As in Beit Shean's archaeological park, here too we were guided by well-marked paths, explanatory signs, and roped off areas laid out to lead visitors toward the highlights. When is a place simply old, to be ignored or disposed of, and when does it become valued as "ancient"? I wondered. The fragments of vanished civilizations preserved here are honored as memorials to long-gone power, aspiration, strife, and loss. "The Mona Lisa of the Galilee" still smiles faintly amid mosaic fragments that register a glory long gone. Her creamy complexion and curly hair are, at once, a reminder of the flesh's beauty and a memento of its passing, but the glossy brochure is utterly silent about the Muslims who lived here long after the artisans finished piecing this mosaic, stone by stone, to delight the Roman owner of a sumptuous villa.

I was still thinking about the ironies of what is or isn't "ancient" when I absentmindedly stubbed a sandaled foot against one of the whitewashed stones edging the path. Straightening up, I froze, noticing for the first time the huge clumps of prickly pear cactuses that lined our way—a dense, spiky mass towering above my head. Were these meant to be an ornamental touch? A path marker?

These cactuses were regal: silvery gray-green sentinels growing on parched, stony ground. There was no escaping what they meant. Both Deborah and I knew that in Israel, prickly pear cactuses often mark the presence of Palestinian life.

Yet I had never seen such tall cactuses up close. Of course this particular variety was common in Palestinian villages when I was growing up, and remnants of cactus hedges continue to be visible throughout the country. But until this day in Tzippori I saw those pale green clumps only at a distance, never close enough to measure my height against theirs or feel the spines of their long hard thorns within easy reach. Now, as our feet crunched on the gravel path, the very vigor of these giant succulents shocked me.

There was something primordial about them, so adapted to harsh conditions. "Hard to eradicate" would be the neutral way of describing their stubborn clinging to life. As Deborah and I'd acknowledged twelve years earlier during our few days in Washington, DC, they are also a metaphor. Mute, they witness and guard a history that is itself hard to eradicate.

"I need to take these in," I said, stopping to study them more closely while Deborah stood by quietly, shading her eyes. She, too, was staring at them, frozen, never reaching for her camera.

Rising above my head, the cactuses' fleshy presence seemed to assert an unstoppable will, existing as if by force of an atavistic compulsion to self-reproduce. No complex botany here, no trunks, branches, leaves. Leaf-like oval pads simply emerged out of their predecessors, reaching sideways and upward, piling on top of one another. Some bottom pads had already dried up and hardened into a brittle gray mass that could be mistaken for a trunk, and some masses of pads had buckled under the weight of top-heavy newer ones, leaving them to decompose in the merciless sun. Bending down, I saw that some of the collapsed pads, still oozing their viscous discharge, were already sending roots into the baking earth. New shoots were already beginning to form, peeking out from the decaying matter. They felt eerily feral, these bloated silvery pads, so hungry to propagate, their life renewing itself out of rot with shocking tenacity. It is like a horror film, I thought, this ravenous, waterlogged insistence on staying alive.

I am not sure how long I stood there, staring at the rampant plant life that bordered our path and then bending to look more closely. Once I stopped to notice these giant bushes, they seemed to be everywhere, lining the park's marked paths.

"So these are the village cactuses you told me about years ago?" I heard Deborah's voice, seemingly from far away. "The ones you said you can't let me photograph?"

I just nodded, bending to tighten a sandal, silent. What was there for me to say? After all, she was a free agent, I told myself, looking at her standing with her camera bag slung on her shoulder. Who am I to dictate what she can or can't photograph?

Deborah's reminder of our Washington, DC, "cactus" conversation in 1993 had the ring of, "You see, I can have my way after all." But I also sensed a tinge of empathy in her teasing voice, her gentle touch on my arm, meaning, "I'm sorry you can't get away from the Nakba."

We stood there a while longer, overwhelmed by this profusion. The park was too well maintained for us to suppose that the park rangers simply couldn't keep up with the growth. The cactuses edged the paths neatly. Somebody's been clearing the paths from fallen pads.

Do the politics of this landscaping not occur to anybody else, I wondered? For the Palestinians the cactuses are a symbol of *sumud*, "steadfastness" in Arabic, akin to our Hebrew *tzamud*, "adhering." For us, are they just a decorative hedge?

"There has to be more to this place," Deborah said, adjusting the strap of her camera bag.

Turning to look back at Tzippori as its wooded slopes receded behind the rear window of our car, a grainy black-and-white image insinuated itself into my memory: an archival panoramic photograph of that same hillside as it had been in 1932, reduced to shades of gray. I'd first seen this photograph in Ra'anan Alexandrowicz' film *The Inner Tour*, years earlier. Remembering it now, as we were leaving Tzippori, the shock of the image returned. Here was the same hill extending generously to the left and right of flat fields, just as Deborah and I had seen it from the access road, except that the old photograph showed a crowded Palestinian village covering the entire hillside—eight hundred houses by the British census of 1931. Other than a lone house still standing in the foreground, the only other building the two views have in common is the massive Crusader tower, the *Quala'* in Arabic. The Palestinian village is entirely gone, replaced by a cloak of green.

It would be some years before I'd allow myself to imagine the life that existed in Saffuriya, before the Nakba, before it became Tzippori: stone houses crowding the hill, grain drying on rooftops, women carrying water jugs from the well, chickens and children underfoot, a donkey swishing flies away, distant voices from the olive grove during harvest time. Men would be visible in the fields below, plowing, sowing, or reaping, depending on the time of year. That Saffuriya only came alive for me when I read Adina Hoffman's book *My Happiness Bears No Relation to Happiness,* where the life of the Saffuri poet Muhammad Taha Ali offers deeper insights into the Israeli-Palestinian conflict.

When Deborah and I drove away from Saffuriya-Tzippori, in 2005, Hoffman's book had not yet been published. Eventually I learned that Muhammad Taha Ali and thousands of other Saffuris ended up in Nazareth, naming their new neighborhood Saffafre after Saffuriya. But that came later. In 2005 it was mainly the forest and the park's giant cactuses that left me restless, that and the archival photograph. We knew that we had to return—to Saffuriya, not Tzippori.

There was no masking of truth in the photograph. The sight of the densely populated village had me wondering what drove us Israelis to such extremes of destruction. The very thoroughness of the erasure felt vindictive, and maybe it was. After all, we were not clearing land for large-scale urban renewal here, as happened in Beit Shean. It took extensive logistical planning to blast this huge village so thoroughly and then plant it over, tree by tree, with thousands of imported pines. How much dynamite was needed? How many people worked on this project, and for how long?

The standard account says little, as I discovered later. Saffuriya, we're told, put up a tough resistance to the Jewish forces. There was no major massacre here, as happened in some other cases. But unlike many villages that surrendered to the IDF, Saffuriya met the Israeli forces with fire. Both the destruction and the forestation were standard practice, designed to prevent Palestinians from reclaiming their lands.

Adina Hoffman provides a richer context. She describes Saffuriya's years of suffering before '48. The situation became especially desperate toward and during the First World War: forced conscription and labor under the Turks, a cholera epidemic, typhus, and starvation. And the situation worsened under the British, who responded to the rising tide of Arab nationalism with curfews and searches, house demolitions, and executions. Younger Saffuris were inspired by the Arab Revolt of 1936–1939 and the charismatic Syrian nationalist leader, Izz-al-Din al-Qassam, who had recruited peasants and urban Muslim laborers to his pan-Arab anti-colonial organization, the Black Hand, which in the 1920s and 1930s fought against the French and then the British and Zionists.

These young Saffuris saw themselves as freedom fighters, I realized, after reading Hoffman's book. The same as our own militias—the Hagana, Irgun, Palmach, and Lehi. To the British we were all "terrorists," while we Israelis dismissed the Palestinian fighters as "gangs." Yet a '48 Hagana report describes Saffuriya's men as "fierce warriors" and the village as "the most dangerous center of Arab nationalism."

We, Palestinians and Jews alike, wanted the British out, but we also wanted each other out. Like us, the Saffuris were militant and determined nationalists. Resistance does not die easily, as Hoffman shows when she traces the connection between the Saffuris' resistance and Izz-al-Din al-Qassam. The Qassam rockets that Hammas' Izz-al-Din al-Qassam brigades have been firing into Israel from Gaza even as I write, affirm that lineage. No wonder Israel wanted to expunge Saffuriya.

Back in Boston that fall, winter, and spring, it was understood that when we returned to Israel the following summer, photographing the Nakba would be our project. Deborah would still join me in Israel for two or three weeks. But what little we had already seen in 2005 forced me to confront my own ambivalence regarding Israel's self-invention. At issue were the truths I—and my entire nation—did not want to acknowledge, tangled as they were in suffering and dispossession on both sides.

I still understood only a little of this when we returned to Saffuriya that second summer. This time we ignored the antiquities and headed straight for the forest, where we found a bewildering network of dirt roads, any one of them seeming as good or as bad as the next. We simply took our chances. Supposedly there were recreation areas in the forest, picnic tables and the like, though we never found them. Instead, we came across forest sections named for large donors inspired by the glamour of the young nation's independence, among them a section donated by Guatemala in honor of its own independence.

All the dirt roads looked alike: loosely packed red-brown earth, barely wide enough to let two cars squeeze past each other. The trees looked alike too, not only of one species but also of a uniform age: same height, same branches, same thickness of trunk. Once in a while, when we came across a thicket of cactuses still growing among the tall pines, we'd park and search the area on foot. Again and again we found nothing. What's there to photograph, we wondered?

We were at it for hours, looking in vain for some sign of the village. Even the cactuses, when we did come across them, were just dense clumps of tall, fleshy pads studded with dagger-like thorns. Whatever they guarded at ground level was invisible, and it was quite possible that they hid nothing.

At some point I gave up, too tired, hot, and dusty to care. Even our bottled water had become too warm to drink. When Deborah parked to explore yet another clump of cactuses I refused to budge.

I had enough!

She shrugged, determined to continue. I watched her walk cautiously down a slope toward a new thicket of cactuses that had caught her eye, her sandaled feet sending pebbles downhill, little puffs of dust rising. I closed my eyes, leaning against the car's headrest, preparing to doze, when I heard her call.

Skeptical, I clambered out of the car and hurried down the short slope toward her. More tired than I had realized, I found myself sliding on loose clods, barely missing the spiky clump where I landed. I could see Deborah's blue denim shirt half-hidden among the towering cactuses, her hand gesturing toward a narrow space that seemed to open among their pads.

"Come here," she called. "There's an opening."

Crouching to enter, I was immediately trapped by thorns snagging my T-shirt, tearing at my hair, scratching my arms. Still, within a few steps—creeping through them seemed to take forever—I could see why she'd called me. Five hand-chiseled stones, neatly squared, were still attached to one another in a curve that had been, at one time, an arch. A few similar stones lay loose near by, all carefully cut, buried under the huge cactuses.

This was all we found that day, back in 2006, our second time in Saffuriya.

Though we did not know it at the time, let alone know where to look, apparently more could have been found. Two abandoned cemeteries are buried there, the remains of a mosque, some stones left from demolished houses, and a Palestinian house converted into an Israeli bed-and-breakfast, presumably inside present-day Tzippori. Those in the know—Saffuri refugees and some Israeli activists—can identify landmarks: a remembered tree, a stone, or a telltale land formation. Outsiders like Deborah and me had to depend on intuition.

It was with a wry sense of familiarity that I later came across the following account of a BBC journalist, Isabelle Humphreys, who visited Saffuriya in 2002, guided by Ziad, a "pure Saffuri" in that all four of his grandparents were born in the village. "I tear the knee of my trousers," she writes, "trying to get over the barbed wire fence into the closed area that was once Saffuriya. I take a picture of some unrecognizable stones on the ground that once belonged to the mosque. Ziad points among the trees to the place where his family used to live …"

In the following three years, as Deborah and I crisscrossed Israel in search of traces of the Nakba, we would relive Humphreys' experience. Tripping over some stones, my jeans would also tear, and I, too, would have to squeeze through barbed wire fences. Like Humphreys I'd stare at forests and wonder how somebody, any "Ziyad," could tell that here, exactly here, stood a house of which nothing remains. Like her, Deborah would wonder what to make of "some unrecognizable stones." Every so often we'd argue about what this or that land formation meant. The enigma of decoding would continue to dog us. How can one tell fieldstones from rubble? The scant remains of a house from those of a mosque? The pine trees that tell you where a home used to stand from other pine trees, exactly alike, that don't? It is a reticent land, as Deborah and I were just beginning to discover, steeped in distrust, prohibitions, and contested claims—a paranoid land, reluctant to disclose its secrets.

PART II: MAPPING

She had suddenly understood, it seemed, that it wasn't just about waiting under the sycamore tree to hear what the Jews wanted and then to go home, but that her home and her world had come to a full stop, and everything had turned dark and was collapsing; suddenly she had grasped something inconceivable, terrible, incredible, standing directly before her, real and cruel, body to body, and there was no going back.
—*S. Yizhar*

And we felt that something incomprehensible is happening around us, hard to grasp and perhaps even hard to feel, sweeping us in its flood into a world that encircles us with hallucinations, a world of sudden signs and wails that descend from the skies, turning the world around us into a gale of silence…
That's how my mother learned that Haifa fell.
—*Mahmoud al-Asaad*

Lower Galilee: a cypress boundary separating vestiges of Palestine from
newly cultivated Israeli lands.

8. Maps to Nowhere

During her first visit to Israel Deborah didn't photograph much. She was to come as an ordinary tourist, stay in a hotel, and see the sights. Walking in Tel Aviv and even in history-choked Jerusalem, her camera mostly remained untouched. It was a time to look, learn, and think, not snap pictures.

"You said the Nakba is out of bounds," she reminded me shortly after she'd arrived the second time, in 2006, leaning over the railing at my mother's balcony in Tel Aviv.

"To both of us," I said, remembering that only on our second visit to Tzippori did I realize that the pale patches I'd noticed among the distant forest pines were cactuses.

Below us was a street lined with walk-up apartment blocks, their flat roofs a wasteland of broken television antennas and solar water tanks, screened by the red brilliance of flame trees in bloom.

"All those touristic clichés!" Deborah said, when I wondered about her not even photographing Jerusalem. And, anyway, she explained, she needed to figure things out. Having one's subject isn't enough. There are always questions of treatment: what camera to use, what lenses, which film stock would be best for the local light, should it be color or black-and-white, and more. She needed to know the place and understand her own relation to it, including the effects of scale and distance as they shape meanings. She needed to take her time.

It was hardly the first of such conversations, but it was our first at my mother's home, a change in plan I did not anticipate.

"Oh, I meant to tell you: Deborah needn't go back to the hotel. She can stay here," Mom said a few days before Deborah's arrival.

"Are you sure?" I asked, surprised. "Didn't you tell me last year that you don't want my friends staying here?"

"Yes, but this is different," Mom said. It was as close as she ever came to accepting Deborah into my life.

Welcome though it was, I remained uneasy. My parents' new apartment still occupied our home's old plot. The same furniture, books, art, and kitchenware were all in it, down to the chipped yellow custard cups. It still felt like my childhood home, a place where a partner didn't belong.

Still, working openly on the Nakba was the bigger transgression, defying as it did a national prohibition. It was easier to pass Deborah off as just another landscape photographer, one in a long line of pilgrims, missionaries, travelers, surveyors, archaeologists, geologists, naturalists, artists, diplomats, military men, and romantic dreamers eager to know this land.

The time when I'd refused to let her photograph Palestine's cactuses was long past. After what little we'd seen of Israel just a year earlier, documenting the Nakba was no longer a choice. For Deborah, recording the history of a people not her own was a matter of dispassionate interest, mediated through the lens of a camera. For me, feeling the earth under my feet and inhaling its familiar scents as my gaze roamed over the land left no room for detachment. After years of being steeped in both Zionist ideals and willed myopia, tracing the Nakba as it registered, literally, on the land, meant seeing the scars etched into the intimately loved landscape of my youth with a double vision, where the conflicting claims of the Palestinians and my own heritage were both exposed at once.

This double vision would never leave me, though the immediate challenge during Deborah's second summer was practical. The main lesson we were to learn was how hard it was to find the demolished villages Walid Khalid lists in his encyclopedic register, *All That Remains; The Palestinian Villages Occupied and Depopulated by Israel in 1948*. Roads to standard tourist sites like Jerusalem, Beit Shean, and Tzippori were well marked, but not any access to those old Palestinian villages. The search for these fast-disappearing villages—bombed and dismantled, covered in forests, buried in cactuses, or absorbed into new Jewish construction—became our major mission.

In this we were rank novices. Back home after our first visit, our work took over: me teaching film and literature at the University of Massachusetts

Boston and Deborah photography and critical studies at the Rhode Island School of Design. The Israeli-Palestinian "conflict," as that ongoing fighting is commonly called, was hardly our specialty. Still, inspired by Benvenisti's *Sacred Landscape*, we had spent the months between our first and second visits reading whatever came to hand, often written by a young generation of researchers, the "new historians" who were re-examining Israel's standard accounts of its becoming.

This rereading of history suited Deborah's interest in history's quirky myths, much as she questioned Queen Helen's ability to identify Jesus' burial place three centuries after his death. For me, however, this new research made for painful education, leaving me all too aware of what the creation of a Jewish state meant and still means for the Palestinians. My love of the Israel I grew up in—our ideals of pioneering and self-sufficiency, our songs, the hikes by which we got to know the land, the camaraderie, the suffering and aspirations, and the revived Hebrew language through which all of this found a voice—were all at odds with this new knowledge.

While this conundrum never let go, it was overshadowed by a sense of practical failure. After all, how does one locate a village that is not on any map and has no tangible signs to confirm that it ever existed?

I no longer remember how Deborah had managed to locate a reasonably priced English language copy of Khalidi's *All That Remains*, but it was as close to a guide as we had that year. With its entries for over four hundred depopulated villages, this massive volume included the most recent British survey information for each village, framing what Khalidi's researchers had found still standing in the 1980s. The British counts of populations, schools, religious affiliations, crops, and home and land ownership provided the back-drop against which Khalidi's updated census of destruction can be measured. In fact, the count is still higher, since Khalidi excludes cities and towns and Bedouin villages in the South. Even so, *All That Remains* is a crushing register of a way of life that was shattered, leaving only fragile traces, as its mournful title reminds us.

"No traces of the houses remain on this site, which is marked by numerous fig trees and a smaller number of olive trees," Khalidi writes of Yajur.

Of Lubya, "Levi pine forest has been planted … The debris of houses is buried under these forests. Scattered wells further mark the site …"

"The Village site has been completely built over by the kibbutz of Urim," he writes of al-Imara.

Jilya's "area is fenced in and inaccessible."

"The village has been obliterated," we learn regarding al-Dalhamiyya.

"Stone rubble provides the only indication of the village's location ..." regarding Hadatha.

And so it goes, six hundred and thirty-six outsize pages filled with small print.

Back in Tel Aviv after one of our failed searches, I found Deborah slumped in her chair, looking depressed, with *All That Remains* open in her lap.

"It's awful to see how little remains," she said, moving the heavy volume off her lap.

Usually she was the silent one, but this time it was me.

It's my own people, I thought. Our own Zvika and Dani and Uzi, who expelled these villagers on our behalf. We are all in it together: those of us who had fought but also our parents, our lovers, our teachers and neighbors and classmates, and now our children and grandchildren.

"Maybe that landmark would help us find the place, Zachariya," said Deborah, pointing to a village mosque Khalidi mentions.

I peered into the book. We already knew that even such landmarks are hard to find. Yes, an abandoned mosque may still stand in Zachariya, but how were we to find it, surrounded as it was by a sprawling new development? In forests or rocky hillsides, in kibbutzim and new and old towns, even in Tel Aviv—where does one begin to look? Again and again, we had had to depend on a mix of luck and perseverance, and often we failed, returning home dusty and dispirited.

One memorable afternoon, following Khalidi's cues, we traveled several hours only to find a dying olive grove, the stony ground under it matted with the stubble of dead weeds and brittle thorns. The scene was familiar to us, except for the broom shrubs that choked the entire grove. These stubborn parasitic creepers, which flourish in dry lands, sent their tentacle-like branches twisting up into the olive trees' canopies. They spread from tree to tree, covering the grove in an impenetrable, blanket. It had taken years of abandon for such an invasion to take hold. Not unlike the cactuses of Tzippori, this rampant profusion.

While this sight was particularly dismaying, failed searches were becoming a daily routine. Our new Israeli maps proved useless, and, while Khalidi's book lists what can be found with impressive thoroughness, it does not help one locate the place or landmarks he mentions. Over and again we had to guess whether to turn this way or that as we meandered through a new Israeli town, walked aimlessly in an empty field, followed a goat path up some hill, or tried to penetrate a cactus thicket.

That Khalidi mentions landmarks without offering a way to find them makes sense. His book is a register, not a guidebook, and the Israeli landscape is changing fast. Settlements spread, new roads are cut, new cultivation takes over. His maps are just outlines demarcating Ottoman administrative units, regional *villayets*, the village in question indicated by a dot in an otherwise blank space. There are no coordinates inside these maps, no roads or nearby place names, though the text does mention the Jewish settlements that now sit on village lands.

Even when we chanced on a landmark it was hard to know what we were looking at. How can one tell that a certain Jewish grocery was once an Arab schoolhouse, that an art gallery was once a mosque, or that the gate to a kibbutz swimming pool was once the entrance to an Arab house, as was the case in one kibbutz near Wadi Ara?

Again and again we searched for villages we'd researched the night before, entering little crosses and names into our Israeli road map to mark our tentative guesses. We'd set out in our increasingly dusty rental car, its roof sticky with pine sap, the back seat cluttered with maps, Deborah's camera bag, Khalidi's tome, bottled water and egg salad sandwiches, only to return home tired and discouraged. Some days we almost gave up. Rural Palestine, such as it had been, seemed altogether gone.

Then one day a breakthrough. Again not knowing where to start looking for that day's landmark—the remains of a well—we took our chances on a dirt road. It was just a guess, as the road cut through yet another stone-strewn field, leading nowhere as far as we could tell. But then I noticed a flat piece of concrete lying in the field some distance from the dirt road, barely noticeable among the dead grasses and fieldstones, but obviously out of place. What was it doing there?

It had been a long day and Deborah wasn't eager to stop for yet another failed exploration. But she pulled over.

Cutting a path through brambles and stones, we progressed slowly, Deborah ahead of me, when I heard, "Look at that!"

She'd reached the concrete slab and was pointing with her toe at a section slightly raised above the ground. Under it gaped a dark void. I threw a small stone into the space. It took a while before we heard the faint sound of it hitting bottom.

"Khalidi's well," she said.

We stared at each other, not quite believing we actually found it.

There was nothing else of interest in that field, just that sheet of concrete covering a well, but over time we developed a sixth sense that helped us interpret meager information. It almost always involved a hunch and a secondary road, sometimes hardly more than a footpath. Sometimes it was just a distant irregularity in the landscape, an unexpected tree or a crumbling agricultural terrace that hinted at a possibility, often with no path at all. Sometimes the paths turned out to be goat-tracks that would part ways and reunite in aimless webs that led nowhere. Sometimes a stone-strewn dip turned out to be a

Khalidi's well.

well. It was a trial-and-error process, except that the errors grew fewer as our instincts sharpened.

"Look," I'd say, pointing at a current Israeli road map that had no mention of the Palestinian village we were looking for. "It is supposed to be more or less here [finger pointing], so we can try this road or perhaps that one [finger tracing one roads]. Maybe there will be a dirt road, or we'd luck out and find something like the schoolhouse Khalidi mentions."

Sometimes place names helped, as they did when we learned that Beit Shean had been Beissan and Tzippori used to be Saffuriya. That's what happened when we were looking for Ayn Ghazal.

Khalidi writes that Ayn Ghzal was near Ijzim and Jaba'," I said to Deoborah, "in the 'Little Triangle' that in '48 controlled the coastal highway between Haifa and Tel Aviv. So it should be somewhere on the spur of Mount Carmel, roughly here," I said, pointing. "And *Ghazal* means 'gazelle,' which is *ayala* in Hebrew, and *ayn* in Arabic is the Hebrew *ein*, a spring, so…"

"Aha!" she interrupted me. "So Jewish Ein Ayala! Right here, look! And it's near Geva, so maybe Palestinian Jaba?"

"Yup!" I laughed, watching Deborah enter a neat X on the map next to Ein Ayala.

Lifting our heads from the map spread on the low coffee table next to Khalidi's open volume, we grinned, enjoying our budding competence. Insights like these might only be guesses, but they offered armchair sleuths something. Putting an X on the map didn't guarantee success, but it was a tiny gift of hope.

Khalidi does clarify that Ein Ayala occupies the lands of Ayn Ghazal, though we noticed it only after this conversation. He also mentions a shrine, a *makaam*, nearby, probably near Ein Ayala, I thought, remembering a newspaper article I had read about it years earlier. Unlike many abandoned shrines, this *makaam* was cared for—by an old Muslim man who regularly watered the garden. The photograph showed a typical small cube of a building topped with a domed roof, the tomb of Sheikh Shahada, a local sage.

The next day, after touring Jewish Ein Ayala in vain, I noticed a narrow road leading to its Jewish cemetery. There was no reason for us to follow it except that the cemetery looked peaceful, its wall of ink-green cypress trees rising into a cloudless blue sky.

We never got to the Jewish cemetery. A stony field stopped us. It was a derelict Muslim cemetery, we saw as we drew near, and there, facing it across the road, was Sheikh Shahada's shrine. Of course the *makaam* would be here, near the burial ground of the Sheikh's companions.

The *makaam*'s location high up in the Carmel range gave it majesty as it overlooked a steep descent into the ravine below. You could see the road snaking up toward us from the coastal plane. In the old days, before cars zoomed around these curves, the ascent itself would have been an act of will. But it was especially moving to see that the *makaam* was revered. Someone, perhaps the devout Muslim described in that article, or his son or grandson, was taking care of the shrine. An ineffable feeling of sacredness enveloped the place, that and *sumud*, the Arabic word for adhering, for holding on.

The shrine had a clean coat of white paint, as did the small stones bordering the garden path and tree trunks, the whitewash being a local protection against burrowing insects. The small garden surrounding the shrine had been swept and watered recently. There was a simple plastic chair in the garden and a watering can. Standing on tiptoe to peek into the building through the small window, we could see another chair near the draped bulge of the Sheikh's simple tomb and, on a small window ledge cut deep into the stone wall, a drinking glass and a well-thumbed Koran.

The invisible man who cared for this *makaam* seemed ineffably close, his hand dipping a brush in a can of whitewash, opening a spigot, moving a chair, or leafing through the Koran. Tiptoeing silently, in reverence, all we could hear were our feet crunching on gravel and birds twittering above us.

Though over time Deborah and I became better at charting our journeys, our guesses continued to wobble and morph. Even when we managed to locate a place Khalidi had mentioned, we still had to read the land's vital signs: a stony field that might or might not be a cemetery, masonry that might or might not be Palestinian, a concrete slab that might or might not cover a well.

Sometimes we made mistakes, as when we chanced on a group of broken concrete floor slabs that were not the remains of Palestinian houses, as we'd supposed, but tent floors for what had been a temporary Jewish immigrants' camp that housed Jewish refugees shortly after the '48 war. Often it was Deborah, more anxious than I to find signs of the Nakba, who'd leap to conclusions. While she craved proof, I clung to doubt. Call it caution, but the truth is that I, for my part, yearned for just a little bit less proof.

"Deb, you are too quick to find the Nakba everywhere!" I'd say, picking up on that old argument that began on the road to Beit Shean and continued for years.

Resolving such disagreements required more research than either of us could manage. It happened once again when Deborah found a charred kewpie doll in the rubble of a nondescript cinder-block house, not necessarily Palestinian, demolished at the outskirts of a Jewish village.

"Deb, this is not a Palestinian kid's doll. There's no way it could have been lying here since '48."

Later, I learned that manufacture of kewpie dolls like this began only in the US in 1949, an unlikely year for shipping dolls to any child in this war-torn land, let alone a Palestinian village child whose family would have most likely been expelled by then. This time I felt vindicated, though I'm no longer sure. Maybe it wasn't a kewpie doll? Maybe it was some earlier model? Surely there was something else at stake for me beyond being right. Though at this point I had committed to helping Deborah with her photography, I was still bedeviled by what we saw and what we were yet to see.

There was no escaping what I knew and still know. I *had* to be her guide. I know the language and, in my way, have lived the history; I recognize the local stones, tiles, tools, toys; I can read Hebrew graffiti and even some Arabic; I could point out to Deborah the Nachlieli bird (wagtail) that presages the first rains and spot the shy, crested Duchifat (hoopoe) that, as one children's legend told it, used to transport King Solomon to his secret palace in mythic Tadmor. I had seen the Milky Way on silvered nights and breathed in the scents of early dawn, when the dew was still on the land.

I knew all this firsthand, yet even as I wanted to know more, I also hoped to know less. Our arguments were about knowledge, fueled by the puzzle solver's craving to tame the unknown, to reach a place where there is only one answer: yes or no. But our arguments were also about my wishing that our guesses would prove wrong. There was already plenty of unambiguous evidence of the Nakba. Must we look for more?

For Deborah the doll was an archaeological clue, like the dented metal jug she would find two years later in a dark corner of an abandoned house in Akir, or the fragments of ornamental floor tiles she collected and lugged back to the US—some forty feet of them when laid end to end, no two alike. Finding evidence of the Nakba suited the forensic probing that shaped all her photography and writing, exposing truths that defy the complacent stories we tell ourselves.

I, too, know the pleasure of finding clues, though my pleasure was haunted by thoughts of demolition and looting. Somewhere, in every village trace, lurked the shadowy presence of the people to whom the floor tiles or jug or doll used to belong, and near them, almost corporeal, I saw our own dusty and sweaty sons, brothers, fathers, and husbands, emptying villages on my behalf. My joining Deborah in her search to record the Nakba was not, finally, forensic. Like a tongue searching out an aching tooth, I was searching for a relief that would not come. And yet I could not bear to keep the Nakba relics I'd found, not even the corroded faucet I'd spotted in Beit Shean. The only relic that felt remotely innocent was a white porcelain teacup shard that had the British NAAFI insignia (Navy, Army, and Air Force Institute) stamped near its smooth white rim. I took it to be proof of "their" occupation of the country, not "ours."

I did keep a small, crumbling plaster star, four inches across, which I found among rubble not far from the impoverished coastal Arab town of al-Lidda, now the "mixed" Arab-Jewish Lod. I found it on the floor of an abandoned building, vandalized over many years, as the dates of scrawled graffiti showed. The Hassidic revival slogan of "*N-Na-Nach-Nachm-Nachman me-Uman*" (named for Rabbi Nachman of Breslov) mingled with crudely penned Hebrew names and salacious drawings. The word "TRANSFER," spray-painted more than once in large, emphatic, squared Hebrew letters, called for the Palestinians' eviction, not bothering to say from where to where, or how.

9. Zochrot

To look at it, there is nothing special about the small plaster star I rescued from a field house near Lod. With its edges worn, you can hardly tell it's a star. Packed with care, it traveled in my luggage as if it were a locket or a bit of old lace, a memento mori of persons I never met. When I unpacked it in Boston, delicately unfurling the tissues that swaddled it, a puff of grainy plaster settled in my suitcase. Now the star rests among my books, dusting the shelf with the granules it continues to shed. Keeping it is my retort to the call for "TRANSFER," which seemed so ubiquitous the year I found it. Left where it fell, the star would not have survived trampling feet.

It's not surprising that the old "TRANSFER" graffiti were allowed to fade over time. They became redundant, implicit in the dream of a Jewish homeland, voiced by Theodor Herzl, lurking in Lord Balfour's guarantee of a Jewish home in Palestine, supported by the United Nations partition vote, and affirmed by slogans chanted by the *yishuv*. A place of our own, so the argument went, was the only way we Jews would ever survive anti-Semitism. The hardbound books crowding my grandmother's shelves brooked no disagreement: the collected work of Herzl and Ahad Ha'am, Ben Yehuda's Hebrew dictionary, and bound volumes of the pioneering Hebrew language periodicals, *Hatsfira, Hamagid*, and *Hamelitz*.

This was patrimony of my grandfather's, an early Hebrew-language journalist and delegate to the first Zionist Congress (1897), committed to establishing a Jewish "home" in Palestine, already a "state" in Herzl's thinking, already more political and territorial than Balfour's vague "home." I never knew this grandfather, and yet he seemed hugely present, his eyes deep-set under an immensely high forehead, gazing from the black-framed sepia photograph that presided over my grandmother's tiny apartment. His legacy held the young me in awe.

In high school we read Ahad Ha'am's writing, but not his caution about what Jewish statehood might mean to the Palestinians, though the argument had been simmering under the surface of Zionist aspirations all along. To be sure, some did: Arthur Rupin, Henrietta Szold, and a few other "cultural Zionists," and including the Communist party, the Marxist-Zionist Mapam party, and the tiny Brit Shalom group. But they were not the Jewish mainstream in which I grew up. Did my mother ever reconcile her admiration for her illustrious father with her growing sense that we Israeli Jews, mostly European Ashkenazim until statehood, were colonizers who must integrate into the Middle East if it was ever to become our home?

For me, returning to Israel only periodically, the widespread "TRANSFER" graffiti came as a shock. I was used to evasive silence around the fate of Israel's non-Jewish citizens, not this graffiti-born eruption of explicit territorial cleansing. Instead of vagueness regarding the "Palestinian question" I found an Israel where being Jewish, as fuzzy and debatable though it is, had become a political platform that excluded all non-Jews from equal citizenship.

Looking at the large sweep of these graffiti I could almost feel the energy coursing through the veins of those who drew them: the arm extended, the torso straining, the breath held and released, the leg muscles flexing to balance this body as it dipped and stretched. I felt a hunger lodged in these graffiti, a corroding sense of the power that came to possess us after our easily won victory of the Six-Day War. It was about territory, certainly, but also about our desperate claim to be fully present as a people, beyond erasure.

During Deborah's second time in Israel I couldn't stop noticing these spray-painted calls for "TRANSFER." They seemed to materialize everywhere, writ large on exterior walls, "billboards" for passing cars. "Look!" I'd say to Deborah, and she would nod as if to say, "Yes, I hear you," though perhaps what she really meant was, "yes, but do I really need to hear that again?"

There were more practical matters to worry about. Most immediately, we were still hampered by inadequate maps, even if we got better at aligning Khalidi's information with current road maps. Though the much-thumbed pages in our spiral road atlas acquired X marks and newly penned names of Arab villages that no longer existed, many of our forays continued to be fruitless, more tiring and time consuming than the results seemed to merit. So much of our search meant long drives only to walk up a hill toward trees that might or might not have been an orchard, cactuses that revealed nothing, or a rock formation that did not prove to be the terracing we'd imagined.

Here and there we found the remains of a village, but even these successes were accidental. What little we did find in places like Beissan, Saffuriyya, Zachariya, or Ayn Ghazal only made me wonder about what else we might be missing. The X's and Arab place names entered in our road atlas were more about intentions than about accomplishments.

Halfway into Deborah's second visit we finally decided to contact Zochrot, the Israeli NGO that was to host our trip to Tarshiha. Dedicated to commemorating the Nakba, Zochrot was still young in 2006, barely known in the US or Israel, though somehow I'd heard it mentioned. Given how silenced the word "Nakba" was, I didn't expect much help from them, and when Deborah first suggested we contact them, I refused.

In truth, the feeling that our work might be considered a betrayal of Israel weighed heavily on me. This is what my friend Itzik gently suggested one afternoon, reducing me to tears. Though I had entered this work reluctantly and without a clear sense of purpose, the more village traces we found—and failed to find—the more committed I became. The sheer scale of the Nakba, including its consequences across generations, is an existential threat to all of us, Arab and Jew, intertwined as we inescapably are in each other. Making the Nakba known, I had gradually come to believe, is *good* for this country, not a betrayal. When Deborah mentioned Zochrot again, I gave in.

Zochrot's office turned out to be barely four blocks from my parents' house and one city block from Mr. Lachman's grocery, where I'd spent hours standing on line, back in '48. I had passed the apartment building where it was housed countless times. Two flights up from the entrance a woman was beating a carpet draped over a balcony railing; inside, the smell of cooking filled the stairwell. Climbing the dusty stairs, we paused by a door where a small metal plate was engraved with "Zochrot," as if announcing a doctor's or lawyer's office.

Since nobody answered, we simply tried the door and walked in, finding ourselves in a bare white room—the gallery and lecture hall, we learned later.

A few voices could be heard coming from another room, its door shut, but there was nobody in sight.

Finally a door opened and closed behind someone who walked briskly past us, carrying some papers. Somebody else came out, walked by, pivoted to look at us over his shoulder, and retraced his steps toward us.

"Excuse me, are you looking for somebody?"

Brown hair, nice eyes, sturdy and taller than most, maybe early forties, he towered above us. I felt strangely tongue-tied. How to explain what Deborah and I were doing in Israel? I already knew that exploring the Nakba was still unwelcome even in broadly liberal circles. Zochrot was obviously not hiding out, but I still didn't know what to anticipate.

"Well, you see …"I stammered, l speaking in Hebrew. The facts came out in bits and pieces: touring Israel, searching for remains of villages destroyed during the Nakba, the difficulty … It was all true except that I was ducking the question of "Why?"

"Ah, I see," he said, still reserved. "I am Eitan," he added, offering his hand, his grasp qualified. "But why are you doing this?"

I am not sure if or when Eitan and I moved from Hebrew to English. We must have done so for Deborah's sake, even if I was the main speaker.

Words were tumbling out of me in a rush. I told Eitan about the places we'd seen and the difficulty we'd had finding them. I said something about the current Israeli maps not including the original Arab place names and he nodded. I mentioned Khalidi and he looked surprised and pleased. (Later I learned that Eitan himself started with Khalidi's book as his guide.) I described the fields and stones and thorns, the false starts and dead ends, the dirt roads and the hours of travel, but also the occasional finding. I mentioned chancing on Meron Benvenisti's *Sacred Landscape* early on and other books we had read since. Eitan was attentive. He could see we had done our homework.

"But *why* are you doing this?" he asked again.

Surely the need for what we were doing was self-evident, or wasn't it? Saying anything more felt risky. The "why" and "to what end" of our search would need more than a passing comment.

"I think that, well, that one must acknowledge the Nakba if we are ever to have, you know, peace. We need something like the Arab *sulkha*, a communal recognition, an acknowledgement, maybe like South Africa's Truth and Reconciliation hearings."

(The word "*sulkha*," I later explained to Deborah, is like the Hebrew *slikha*. It has to do with apology and forgiveness.)

My brief, halting response felt so inept, and yet it seemed to satisfy Eitan. His body relaxed, his eyes grew warmer, his smile broader. However awkwardly put, my words got to the heart of the matter.

"Did you ever hear of a place called Neveh Shalom—the Arab Wahat al Salam?" I asked, feeling encouraged. I was referring to the village in the Judean foothills where Israeli Palestinians and Jews had been living in a binational, bicultural, and bilingual community for some years, running a peace school and hosting symposia and other events. "The name means 'oasis of peace,'" I added.

"Yes, of course I know it," he said, grinning.

For me this "oasis of peace" was still somewhat mythical, a supposed proof of a wobbly trust that Palestinians and Jews could live together. Apparently for Eitan this unusual place was an ordinary fact, but why was he grinning?

"I haven't actually been there," I said. "The one time we tried to go we found ourselves among giant tanks in the courtyard of Israel's Armor Museum instead."

"Yes, it's near one of those old British police stations. You can see it from the Jerusalem highway," Eitan laughed. "Anyway," he added, "since you ask how I know, I lectured at their Peace School. Others in Zochrot also have a connection to it."

Of course they would, I thought. I should have known better than to even ask.

Connecting with Zochrot was a relief. They had a library brimming with information, held lectures and exhibitions, and organized tours to demolished villages. They also developed curricula, published *Sedek* magazine and booklets, and now have a rich website. We met other staff members: Raneem, who one memorable day guided Deborah and me through Haifa's Arab neighborhood; Amaya, who was developing materials for educators; and Norma, who was researching the nearby village of Summayl, now an enclave of Mizrahi immigrants.

When Deborah and I first showed up at Zochrot, our work was at a low point. It was well into her second summer in Israel, and time was running out. There were too many failures, too many X's entered wrongly on our map. There was nobody to share our frustration, either. Zochrot's gift to us was validation, and it arrived, in part, in the form of two remarkable maps.

One was the standard, large-scale, British Mandate-era map of Palestine, by then available only from antiquarians. Zochrot had it copied and laminated in segments, each about the size of a large dinner table placemat. Arranged in the correct order, they covered all of Mandatory Palestine, noting each settlement, Jewish and Palestinian. For years I'd forgotten about it, though a copy hung in every classroom I attended growing up, with its lowlands and wadi riverbeds in green, higher elevations in a beige that deepened into orange and brown. It was the map that defined our belief that this narrow strip of land is our rightful Jewish patrimony—but also, as I didn't realize back then, the map whose outlines confirm the Palestinians' sense that this territory is inalienably theirs.

Eitan let us take these laminated segments to the local copy shop, where we printed and laminated our own copies. The X's we'd now pen into our road atlas would be accurate. We'd still have trouble finding specific landmarks—a certain well, an olive press, the wall of a house—but at least we could tell where Aqir used to be, or Ijzim, or any other place.

The second map Eitan unfolded for us was too vulnerable to remove from the office. It was the same standard British survey map, but now an inventory of the Nakba. Spread on the library's conference table, the entire country lay before us as it had once been, with all its Arabic place names. Used by the Israeli army to mark Palestinian villages demolished during the Nakba, the map was crowded with the Hebrew word "HARRUS" stamped in large block letters next to many Arab village names.

With its accent on -*rrus*, the Hebrew *harrus* sounds harsh, more so than the English "destroyed" or "demolished," let alone the milder word "depopulated," which is commonly used to describe the Nakba's demolished villages. But beyond the sound of the word, lost on anyone who doesn't speak Hebrew, was the sight of the stamped words: large square letters cut into the rubber stamp in Hebrew's equivalent of uppercase, filling the map with thick dark ink. There was no overlooking the word, stamped over and over. I could almost see the hand rising and then slamming down to press the word into the paper, rushing to make contact before the ink dries.

"This," I heard myself saying, "is a record of disaster."

"It's a palimpsest, a story of 'before' and 'after,'" Deborah said and fell silent.

"Yes, like the glass book we saw in Tarshiha, overwritten layers of script, the old coexisting with the new. A village and then a forest over it," I said, thinking also of Saffuriya and feeling the shocking speed with which seismic changes occurred here.

Eitan was silent as he folded the map. "You should come on one of our tours," he said. "There's one this Saturday, a chartered bus. Come to the Arlozorov train station by ten. Bring a hat and water."

We did. Some of the people waiting seemed to be newcomers like us, standing to the side. Some seemed to be regulars, exchanging a greeting or a few words. A few brought children. I could hear Arabic and even an occasional foreign language, though most people seemed to be local Jews. Scanning the crowd I realized that, other than the women who wore a hijab or people saying something in Arabic, I couldn't tell Arab from Jew. We share the same gene pool, my mother had told me a while back, though once this information emerged, she added, everybody rushed to suppress it.

The tour was to al-Shajarah, a Palestinian village near the old Jewish agricultural training farm of Sejera, where several Zionist luminaries had lived and trained, including Israel's first prime minister, David Ben-Gurion. Who are these people climbing into the bus? Which of them were Palestinian, and how do they feel about us, the enemy, with Palestine's "Shajarah" and Jewish "Sejera" so near and yet apart?

We gathered on a windswept hilltop to hear testimonials from a woman and two men, all three native to al-Shajarah and survivors of the Nakba. Speaking in Arabic and then being translated into Hebrew, they described life in the village before the war, the fighting, and the expulsion, each account heart-withering. Unlike other tours, included was also a Jewish speaker, a descendant of Jewish Sejera, whose memories of the two neighboring villages were transcribed in Zochrot's al-Shajarah booklet:

> On the hill to the left, where there are now new houses,
> [pointing] there used to be an olive grove...the village

mosque stood there. Nothing is left except a few stones, maybe its ruins. And if this is the mosque, the spring can't be far, in that direction [pointing]. I look but can't find the spring…Oh, there it is. The steps are hidden by that giant fig tree.

Inevitably, all four speakers were elderly. That's the only way firsthand memories of '48 can still be told. But what struck me about this Jewish man's testimony was how similar his effort to reconstruct the place was to Deborah's and my struggles: the guesses, the barely visible landmarks, and the frustrating awareness of how new realities conspire to obscure the truth.

I didn't keep a log of these tours; their effect was cumulative, not sequential. They all produced this vertiginous sense of a double image, where what you see and what you are told don't fit together. I felt it on every one of our Zochrot tours, on several Saturdays between 2006 and 2007, as we toured Tarshiha, Khirbet el-Luz, and al-Ramleh, and the villages that used to surround Tel Aviv: Abu Kabir, Salameh, Sheikh Muwannis, Summayl, and more. Whatever their separate histories, in each place I experienced the clashing of "then" and "now," acute and hard to grasp.

On the bare mountaintop that had been Khirbet el-Luz, our local guide picked a pungent sprig of zaatar (wild thyme), passing it on to us before bending to clear away some low-lying scrub. "The old oil press," he said, exposing a cavity partly filled with rubble. Even seemingly intact Tarshiha, where a Palestinian shopkeeper had given me a pen, is marked by this ill fit between "then" and "now," strangely bittersweet because we visited it during its celebration of endurance.

The almost surgical transformation from "then" to "now" was especially visible in the villages that used to surround greater Tel Aviv, where real estate has become high-stakes finance. Sheikh Muwannis was particularly memorable for me. I already knew that Tel Aviv University sits on its lands, including the graceful mansion that is now the faculty club, where I was once treated to an elegant lunch. What surprised me was hearing our Zochrot guide mention the Beidas family as residents of Sheikh Muwannis. It was a name I remembered from childhood: a genial man in a dark suit who would visit my uncle for Saturday lunches and stay to talk business, the man who gave my uncle a forlorn lamb that lived in the basement for a few days before vanishing out of our lives. The elegant Beidas' grand family home had been pulled down, I learned during the tour, to make room for the Jewish Ramat Aviv hotel that was in turn pulled down to make room for a still more profitable use of the land.

Walking through an Israeli neighborhood that was no longer recognizable as Sheikh Muwanis, I wondered what had become of Mr. Beidas. There were so many ways our lives overlapped, I thought, looking at the people gathered around the speaker, and yet we were strangers to each other. Some of the overlap is still an open wound. Did I dare reveal my personal connection to Mr. Beidas and ask about his role in those land deals or Jaffa orange shipments I suppose he discussed with my uncle before the '48 war put an end to them? There was no knowing what such a question might touch off in my Palestinian tour companions, or in anybody else.

It was entirely different when we toured the large town of al-Ramleh, near Tel Aviv, still "mixed" Arab and Jewish, though increasingly Jewish. Here, for the first time, I experienced the stench of open sewers running in the now-impoverished Arab "ghetto" part of the town, while the elegant homes of former Palestinian notables were being refurbished for civic and private Jewish use. Streets had been renamed after Zionist leaders: Herzl, Begin, Ben-Gurion, Jabotinsky.

As on all Zochrot tours, Eitan brought large yellow street signs to install at key locations as reminders of the town's Palestinian identity before the Nakba. The signs included the name of famed author and politician Emile Habibi, and the Yaffa-al-Kuds Road, for centuries conveying travelers between Jaffa and Jerusalem. We were installing signs in busy city streets, not in some remote mountaintop like Khirbet el-Luz, where no one would likely see them. But the police were prepared for us. Some thirty of us were gathered, listening to a speaker when they arrived.

A predictably noisy altercation followed: a shouting match about city ordinances and free speech, a small traffic jam, curious passersby, all filmed by Deborah, ending when the police confiscated the signs. Though it was getting chilly and dark, we voted to march to the police station, dispersing only some two hours later, when we were threatened with arrest. The message was clear: free speech for some, not all. The "TRANSFER" graffiti may stand, but not "Emile Habibi Street."

10. Making Do

I was buoyant as we carried the laminated copies of the British maps to my mother's apartment. Now we could manage on our own, I hoped, even if we lost some of Zochrot's insiders' stories.

A friend's loan of a place in the ancient Galilee town of Safed was also a promising break. Unlike the coastal plane, where Palestinian villages had gotten absorbed into fast-growing Jewish urban and suburban spread, the sparsely populated Galilee mountains surely would have preserved at least some traces, we thought, and Safed's position near a major crossroads would make our work easy. That, and whatever we might see of Safed's centuries-old history as a mixed Jewish-Arab town until '48, made staying there particularly appealing.

My friend, Esther, didn't exaggerate when she called her place a *khirbe* ("ruin" in Arabic, like the Hebrew *khurva*). It was a semi-derelict two-room space, windowless, dug into the hillside, with a tiny bathroom and tinier kitchen reachable through a small courtyard where the red petals of pomegranate buds were just beginning to unfurl. The arched ceiling and supporting walls had cracked, whether from an earthquake or a bombing was unclear. It was also unclear whether this *khirbe* was in what used to be the Arab or Jewish part of town. Lovingly furnished with faded cushions and frayed oriental rugs, it occupied a blurry no-man's land of national belonging.

It wasn't easy to trace the Nakba in a town where its old Arab and Jewish homes looked so much alike. In 2006, old-timers could still point to a house or a neighborhood as Jewish or Arab, but we could not. As one of Judaism's four holy cities (together with Jerusalem, Hebron, and Tiberius) and the seat of Jewish mysticism, Safed's ancient synagogues, its sixteenth-century

Hebrew language press, and its now bustling Judaica art market have made it a tourist attraction. Did visitors register that the tower in the roundabout at the entrance to the old town is a minaret?

The fighting for Safed in '48, before the British left the country, was long and bitter but hardly unprecedented. Like Beissan and Saffuriya and many other places, Safed had been ruled by Romans, Crusaders, Mameluks, Ottomans, and the British. Along the way, Safed's Jews had endured earthquakes, plagues, and fighting that spurred further fighting, including a devastating Druze attack in 1662, a massacre of the city's Jews during the Palestinian uprising of 1929, and the fighting in '48, which included the massacre of Palestinians in nearby Ein el-Zeitun and the systematic cleansing of the surrounding region.

The land, we discovered, was still hard to interpret. Ein el-Zeitun, for example, was marked on the Mandatory map but we still couldn't find a trace of it. As in Saffuriya, we were yet to learn where to look. We were grateful, then, when Esther's friend Zvi, a retired career army man and a longtime resident of Safed, invited us for breakfast and advice. Zvi, Esther said, knew the area inside out. His house, just a few blocks away from our *khirbe*, will be easy to find, Esther assured us.

The morning was blustery and the alleys, we soon discovered, had no posted street names. Other than a shivering cat hiding under a dumpster we were entirely alone, dripping with rain and lost. A man protected by a large umbrella, ultra-orthodox Haredi as his beard, hat, and black clothes announced, strode right past us, ignoring my "*Slikha*, excuse me, sir"— females to him *treif,* not kosher.

"What's that about?" Deborah exclaimed, though she already knew: "The most appalling aspect of Safed is its ultra-orthodox colonization … orthodox men who flinch when addressed by a woman," she'd written in her journal the previous evening. "We'll talk about it later," I said, as my wet jeans sent cold rivulets into my soaked shoes.

Finally two women emerged from a doorway, orthodox like most of Safed's Jewish population, and showed us the way. It was just a brief lull in the downpour but long enough for us to make it to Zvi's house. He, however, stiffened when I explained to him what we were doing and showed him Deborah's annotated map. This was not what Esther had led me to expect, nor what Zvi had expected. He couldn't avoid answering our questions over a strained breakfast of coffee and toast, but his answers were terse and unhelpful. Mentioning the Nakba even to a liberal Israeli was a mistake.

Our new maps did make the search easier, though not by much. They indicated an area, not its details. The stony, eroded Galilee made it hard to distinguish nature from rubble, with the rubble buried under newly planted pine forests, and where, at this elevation, even the telltale cactuses were gone. Every so often, when we'd see something promising, we'd park and set out toward an outcropping or a tiny old grove that might or might not reward the effort. Our inconclusive debates continued to dog us, though now they'd become a shared search, no longer a quarrel. As we'd come to see, the rubble Khalidi keeps noting with dismaying frequency in his reports, often coupled with the word "scattered," confirmed our experience of how hard it is to "read" the land.

Driving, stopping, searching, finding nothing, and turning back: it happened again and again. Each time there would be a rock formation, a village name, a suggestive clump of native trees, or a swath of man-made afforestation to get us going—a repeating experience of climbing and tripping over rocks, turning back from barbed wire fences, skirting deep crevices, getting stung by nettles after the rain or scratched by thorns before it. Having to decide whether to bear slightly to the right or to the left, uphill or downward, or whether to give up altogether. There was always something to hint at an answer, though too often nothing was revealed.

Yet some things were clear. We found old terracing and wind-lashed olive trees on the bare hilltop of Safsaf, where the exposed elevation may have deterred Jewish settlement. In Sa'sa' we saw old Palestinian houses or parts of houses incorporated into the newer cinderblock settlement. Dallata, now Jewish Dalton, has extensive vineyards and a winery abutting the shrine of Rabbi Ben Yosei ha-G'lilee, with neglected olive trees and the remains of Palestinian walls in sight. And so it went. Qadita was the only place where we saw an apparently unauthorized Jewish settlement, home to hippie-religious squatters, its makeshift houses and a ramshackle children's playground built of scavenged materials.

And there were more villages: Ein al-Zaytun, Nabi Yusha, Jauna, Iqrit, al-Ras al-Ahmar, Taytaba, and many others, each its own homeland where people had farmed, winnowed, drawn water, and harvested olives, each a village where young people had married, children were born, and the old aged and died. Each wall fragment had a builder, each grove a planter, somebody who had a name. And yet the absence ricocheted from wall to wall, from one olive tree to the next.

This book, I'm thinking, is held together by lists, an endless litany of loss. At times, the village names seemed joined in an indistinguishable mass, the rubble too, unbearable yet almost banal.

Among these places, Akbara, just outside Safed, was easy to find, clearly marked on the official map. Like Tarshiha and several other villages, it is now home to "present absentees," as internal Palestinian refugees are called. Driving there on a chilly, overcast day we found a new village: wide streets, well-tended gardens, a new mosque, solid new homes fronted with richly carved doorways, and elaborate garden ornaments. Was this all there was to Akbara? What about the Nakba?

Deborah's camera seemed useless that wintry day. Expecting to leave soon, we decided to explore the village on foot. It didn't take us long to reach the edge of the built-up area, where a steep descent began. We could see the glittering ribbon of a stream weaving through the valley down below us, crossed by a rickety wooden footbridge, just two planks wide. A flock of sheep and a few black goats were crossing, bells tinkling. A man, tiny at that distance and assisted by an even tinier dog, was overseeing this crossing.

We were enjoying this pastoral throwback to earlier times when I heard Deborah let out a soft whistle. As I raised my eyes, old Akbara appeared, uninhabited, facing us on the opposite hill. There weren't many houses left, though those still standing seemed intact. The empty space between them—so unusual in a Palestinian village where houses traditionally crowd together—suggested that many had been demolished. Spread along the incline, this vestige of a village, with its few boarded houses usable yet empty, felt ghostly as it stared back at us at eye level.

"I must photograph this," Deborah said, adjusting her camera bag so that it would sit more firmly across her chest. Half-sliding down the winding path the sheep and goats had made, we reached the bridge, our shoes caked with mud. Walking was easier on the other side, where weeds and stones held the soggy earth in place. The stone houses stood silent, closed in, as if waiting for someone to unlock their doors and throw open their shutters.

"How can they live with that?" I said, short of breath as we trudged up the muddy path on our way back toward the new Akbara. "How can they get up every morning, pray at the new mosque, and send the kids to school with remnants of the abandoned village in full view? What do they tell their children?"

Deborah, steadying her camera on the way uphill, was silent, perhaps thinking, What's there to say? Half an hour later, as we circled Safed's minaret roundabout on our way home, I heard her say, "People make do. One moves on."

Akbara, I later learned, had been a seat of Jewish learning in Roman times, like Tzipori and other Galilee communities formed after the Temple's destruction. An Arab village for centuries, after '48 it became an "unrecognized" dumping ground for the Nakba's displaced Palestinians, mostly those expelled from Qadita. It was officially incorporated into the Greater Safed District only in 1981, after a long bureaucratic battle, when it was finally included in the regional water, electricity, medical, and school services. A condition for new building permits was that for every house built an old one would be destroyed. This was Akbara's "making do," where the abandoned stone houses we saw standing were themselves "present absentees."

And Safed had its punishing history too. There was bitter fighting before the Hagana captured this mixed city, leaving much of it in shambles. I had seen the destruction right after the war, when my parents visited a friend who had been there through the fighting. Of that visit I mainly remember the destruction, where bits of wall were still standing, sentinels punctuating huge rubble-strewn areas. Our host guided us through the devastation, pointing here and there to explain the town's reconstruction plans, including the "Rimonim" hotel that is now a landscaped compound of derelict Arab stone houses restored as guest cottages.

"People make do," Deborah repeated as we approached our *khirbe*.

I was not so sure. Trauma lingers. Its memory enters one's DNA, not metaphorically, but literally.

In retrospect I think of our earlier stopovers in Tiberius and then Nabi Shu'ayb, on the way to Safed, as a prelude to what we saw in Akbara. All three were living places where the past could not be forgotten, each raising questions about "making do."

I first saw Tiberius at age four, when my grandmother went there for the "cure" at the mineral hot springs and took me along to recover from a recent tonsillectomy. The Tiberius I remembered was a prosperous mixed city—a commercial center and a winter resort. Downhill from our pension were restaurants, a fisherman's pier, and the remains of Crusader fortifications. Fashionably dressed Palestinian women were shopping on the main street, wearing short, diaphanous black veils over their faces. At the old Galei Kinneret hotel, my cousins' favorite afternoon sport was getting Ben-Gurion's wife, Paula, to shout at them to be quiet.

The Tiberius Deborah and I found was nothing like that. The black basalt fortifications, fishing pier, and old Scottish hospital (now a five-star hotel and spa) were still there, as was a new small park where a lonesome minaret stood as a piece of "public art." But the stylish center of the mixed town had become a run-down Jewish-Israeli jumble of cheap shops and pushcarts. Stunned by the din of congested traffic, hawkers, and blaring pop music, we were about to return to our car when I noticed a large white dome curving above a high wall, barely visible at ground level—a mosque, we saw once we climbed some nearby steps, cut off from the life churning around it.

And yet the mosque was not cut off, not quite. Someone had left a small black-bound book on top of the wall. Lying open on its back, its cover warped, its weather-stiffened pages rustling in the wind—a Koran. Was it a Muslim marking the mosque's closeness to Allah, I wondered, or a Jew who found it on the ground and did the best he could to return it to its owner?

The very tenderness of this act moved me. It was a moment when the bitter division of "we" and "they" gave way to reverence, whether Muslim or Jewish didn't matter.

The scene at Nabi Shu'ayb was very different, as we discovered later that day.

Since *nabi* means "prophet" in Arabic (*navi* in Hebrew), we expected to find a Muslim shrine that had been abandoned during the Nakba. We should have known better: Nakba sites are not named on current maps and have no roads leading to them. Instead, we discovered that we'd arrived at a thriving Druze pilgrimage site honoring Nabi Shu'ayb—the spiritual founder and prophet of the Druze religion, traditionally identified with Jethro, the Midyanite father-in-law of Moses, as I later learned. The wide oleander-lined road leading steeply up to an impressive newly built shrine, the ample parking, souvenir stands, and snack shops all told us, too late, that this couldn't possibly be a Muslim relic of the Nakba.

About to leave, leaning over the guardrail to take in the view just below the cliff-top parking lot, we could see plowed fields further down, stretching some distance away, and nearer to us, straight down, a small grove hugging Nabi Shu'ayb's steeply rising hill.

"Look!" Deborah called out. There, peeking through the foliage, was the tip of a minaret, its white cupola rising above the dense green.

I don't know how long we stood there, staring. When I finally raised my eyes, I noticed the two steep cliffs that flanked the entrance to the valley below us and remembered "the horns of Hittin"! This was the pass through which Saladin entered the valley in 1187 and won the Muslims' decisive victory over the Crusaders. Of course there had to be a Muslim village somewhere nearby, I realized, including this mosque. I first saw the "horns" on a hike, back in 1953, when Nabi Shu'ayb was still a small Druze shrine carved into the mountain. By then the ancient Muslim village of Hittin, honoring Saladin's victory, was completely gone. All that remained was a stony hill, though a photograph dated 1934 showed a large Muslim village crowding that hill.

It was not easy to make our way to the minaret. It took several tries on dirt roads before we reached the grove surrounding it. All was silent at this remote place. A distant tractor was moving soundlessly at the far end of the tilled fields. Only the twitter of an occasional bird could be heard, invisible among the foliage. Near us, just beyond the grove, stood the crumbling walls of the ruined mosque, brightly lit by the midday sun, its gray masonry looking bleached next to the mottled black-green of the clustered trees.

The building, I learned later, is attributed to Saladin. Even in its ruined state, we could see that its walls had been massive. Despite the obvious damage done by dynamite and the passing seasons, these walls felt adamant. The roof was gone, but a courtyard and even traces of chambers, walls, and arches had escaped the dynamite. Strangely, it seemed a gentle scene, almost as if the mosque was still in use. Walking through and around the ruins, we found ourselves talking softly.

At the time, I didn't know much about Druze history except that the relationship between the Druze and Muslims was strained by religious differences. Only later did I learn that Druze history is one of persecution but also turmoil. It's a history of regional alliances and misalliances, rebellions, wars, and massacres, as the whole area—from Lebanon and Syria to northern Iraq and into Palestine—came under different empires and local rulers. At one time the Druze ruled Safed and Tiberius within the Ottomans' Greater Syria. As a minority among the local Palestinians, in 1948 they at first fought with the Arab Liberation Army against the IDF but ultimately threw their lot in with the newly created Jewish state, fighting with the IDF against other Palestinians. Only in Lebanon and Israel are they recognized as an ethnic-national group in their own right.

There could not have been much love lost between the Druze pilgrims to Nabi Shu'ayb and Hittin's Muslim farmers. The newly renovated Druze shrine that now overlooks what used to be Muslim Hittin's lands is huge, costly, and well-maintained, in stark contrast with Israel's crumbling, vandalized, or repossessed Palestinian shrines. While service in the IDF made the Druze a privileged minority, it also earned them the resentment of other Palestinians. The worst of it is that since the Druze speak Arabic, they are often assigned to the IDF's border units where harsh encounters with Palestinians are frequent. What they may really think about Saladin's mosque just below Nabi Shu'ayb or about their relation to other Palestinians is not likely to be told to me, an Israeli Jew, let alone a woman.

I did not expect to find myself in conversation with a Druze man a day later, when Deborah and I stayed at Shlomi's Youth Hostel, in the Western Galilee. Our spotless white room was furnished with two narrow beds, two gleaming white lockers, and two white plastic chairs. Our third floor balcony, however, offered a hazy vista of eroded mountaintops to the north, increasingly blue in the diminishing evening light, and to the west, a glimpse of the sun dipping behind backlit hilltops.

I was sitting on our little balcony, enjoying a spell of twilight solitude after hours of searching for remnants of Palestinian al-Bassa inside Israeli Shlomi, when I heard a man clear his throat—right next to me. Our tiny balconies, I realized, almost touched one another.

"Shalom," he said tentatively.

"Sh'lm," I mumbled, in no mood for conversation.

"Ayyy, difficult … difficult," he sighed, not taking the hint. "What's to do?" he added after a long pause. He said it softly, almost as if speaking to himself.

The sadness in his voice tugged at me. I couldn't keep ignoring him.

"What's the matter?" I asked, finally turning toward him: a handsome man, I could see, mid-forties, dark eyes, thick mustache, military bearing, guttural Arabic accent, halting Hebrew. Druze, I realized.

It came, pouring out. He'd signed up for career military service, twenty years at the border patrol, manning checkpoints: dusty workers rushing to work, old women with swollen feet carrying bundles, sick people needing to get to the hospital, women with squealing babies. Everybody had to be checked, every package a potential bomb, everybody tired and fed up, sometimes hysterical, almost always hostile. And now what? The twenty years he'd signed up for were up, he said, and he was back home, jobless. He wasn't trained for civilian work and couldn't afford to buy land. He should get married, settle down—but how?

Why was he telling me all this, a gray-haired Israeli stranger old enough to be his mother?

I remembered the flourishing Druze village on the way to Shlomi, just a few hours earlier, where we'd stopped to eat shwarma and got tangled in narrow, steep streets until someone showed us the way. The large, well-tended olive groves we'd passed belonged to this village. Unlike Israel's Muslims, some Druze are doing pretty well under the Israeli government, I thought, remembering Nabi Shu'ayeb. But this support has always been qualified, and now, as I write, the new Jewish Nation-State Law (2018) exposes its fragility. This man, for all his IDF service, is still at a dead end. Of course he'd like to buy land, build a house, and start a family, but jobs and housing are easiest to get in the Jewish hubs, where he is not wanted and where he doesn't want to be.

He was right to assume that I'd be a sympathetic listener, but sympathy was all I could offer. I could just nod and say, "Don't worry. It'll be *beseder*. It'll sort itself out."

He fell silent. We both did. At some point he got up, his chair scraping the concrete floor, wished me good night, and returned to his room. I could hear him speaking Arabic with someone next door.

Though it had gotten completely dark, I stayed on, glad that Deborah hadn't joined me. I did not want to hear her say that he needed to "make do" or "get a life," as she sometimes put it. "Getting a life" is not always easy, certainly not if you're a non-Jewish minority in Israel, like the Druze—a privileged Palestinian minority that is not, finally, privileged. Above my balcony the stars were coming out in a velvety black sky: Cassiopeia, the Big Dipper, Orion's belt. Looking for the North Star, I was no longer sure I could identify it.

This conversation reminded me of my Palestinian friend Yamila, telling me about the disdainful treatment her aging Muslim parents had received from Druze officials as they were negotiating their residency rights. Israel's bureaucratic labyrinth was made deliberately complicated to prevent Palestinians from getting resident status in the country of their birth, Yamila said, with mounting anger.

"Yes, the Occupation, I know," she said, indignant. "But the Occupation is a system put in motion by people who are willing to make it work, not just the Israelis but the Druze too. After all, they are Palestinian like us. They *chose* to serve in the army and keep the oppression going. They could have allied with us."

That was the crux of it, voiced by Deborah as we stood by Hittin's mosque, just under Nabi Shu'ayb: "Aren't they all Palestinians?"

Yes and no, I thought. There had to be a tallying of choices in the early years of statehood—questions of loyalties, survival, and honor. As Jewish victory became increasingly likely, choices had to include costs and benefits. After several strategically planned massacres and sweeping mass expulsions, where every assault became an example to neighboring villages and towns until no neighbors remained, what choices could there have been? Given entrenched local enmities, including those between competing village heads, between Fallahin farmers and Bedouin herders, city dwellers and peasants, elites and masses, Sunnis and Shias, and Muslims and Christians and Druze, very different roads were taken.

So many bifurcations, I thought, remembering our early Independence Day parades, when the "minorities" marched proudly, decorated and in formation, each in its own distinct unit. I remember especially the Bedouins, unforgettable in their glorious robes and decorated camels, swaying slowly past us as we Jews cheered them on. There were also tanks and artillery, planes flying in formation, women soldiers in neat khaki skirts and white socks marching as one, and of course unit upon unit of men, including units of Druze and Circassian minorities, each with its own insignia and dress uniform, though no other Palestinians.

The "Arabs," as we used to call the Palestinians—in this instance Muslim and Christian—were not in the parade. They stayed away, uprooted and mourning even as we, the victors, celebrated our newly founded state. They couldn't possibly hoist on their dwellings the Jewish blue and white flags that festooned the country that day. After difficult debates, painful, acrimonious, and to this day unresolved, they chose not to join the celebration. History shows that, had they chosen differently, they would not have been welcome anyway.

From time to time I still see documentary film clips of those smart woman soldiers marching in their spotless military dress uniform, though the "minorities" seem to have vanished, including the Bedouins, who had been indispensable to the IDF as trackers but are now being forced out of their traditional lands. The Druze, too, are invisible, as their uniforms no longer include the distinctive white kaffiyehs they wore in the past. Even as I write, the Bedouins, my Druze neighbor in Shlomi, Yamila's parents from Bir Zeit, and countless other Palestinians of all backgrounds are losing what few rights and privileges they may have had under law. They are all expected to "make do," as Deborah would put it after seeing Akbara.

We didn't say much, finally, the Druze man and I that evening in Shlomi, nor Yamila and I in Boston. What one thinks and feels about the history that divides us is usually shared only with one's own kind, if that: the pain and the hostility, the shame, the hurt pride, the jealousy, the anger, the guilt, the yearnings, the regrets, the compassion, the distrust, and the sheer fatigue of it all.

11. "In A Land Beloved of Our Fathers"

*I*n 2007 I took Deborah to the outpost of Metula, the small village on the Lebanese border where my great-grandparents were among the original settlers, arriving in the late 1800s. It was a cloudy day, chillier and gloomier than we had expected. The old stone houses that lined the main street, windswept and bereft of greenery, felt exposed, their stones gray, uninviting. Deborah didn't bother to take out her camera.

This place always felt like an outpost, even if it advertised itself as a hub of tourism. Located up north, at the very tip of the finger-shaped piece of Israeli territory that juts into Lebanon, Metula has grown only modestly since my childhood. By the time Deborah and I visited it there were fruit orchards, an ice-skating rink, and a new neighborhood beyond the original main street. The small hotels where my parents and I stayed in my childhood had minor face-lifts, but the short main street, named Founders Street for the first settlers, hadn't changed much. It still came to an abrupt stop near the Lebanese border, where we could see gray concrete fortifications, a lone disabled tank abandoned in an open field, and a wire-girded stone monument facing no-man's land. The steel fence, at one time dubbed "the good fence" because of Israel's then amicable relationship with the Christians and Shiites of southern Lebanon, was no longer "good," certainly not since Israel's invasion of Lebanon in 1982 and its support of the Falangist militia's massacre of Palestinians in Sabra and Shatila refugee camps.

I remember a time when the "good" fence would open to return stray sheep to their owner, and people joked about Israeli tourists who accidentally crossed the border. Sadly, no more. Two parallel steel fences, high, electrified, and equipped with sensors, blocked passage. Between them ran a path just wide enough to allow an armored surveillance vehicle to pass, with landmines quite possibly beyond.

There used to be a story circulating about a Mrs. Greenberg or maybe Goldberg who, out for a stroll one late afternoon, meandered into Lebanon and was taken into custody overnight, till the gate could be reopened. When an officer brought her dinner on a nicely arranged tray—apparently there was even a cloth napkin—she refused the food. "Lady," he's reported to have said, "in Hotel Hermon you pay at least twenty-four [old] shekels for such a dinner, and here I am, bringing you a very fine meal for free, carrying it with my own hands, and you refuse it?" Returning sheep across the border was an ordinary event, but a Lebanese officer knowing the price of a meal at an Israeli hotel truly captures the spirit at the time.

Of our visits to Metula, both before and after the '48 war, I smile to remember a night at Sheleg Levanon ("Snows of Lebanon") hotel, hearing thumps, thuds, and the laugher come from the next room—backpackers on a bed-bug hunt. I recognized that building as Deborah and I walked past it, newly named and a story taller but still shabby. Founders' Street seemed unchanged too. The same low stone houses, including a cavernous restaurant where archival photos celebrating the founders' lives lined its walls. The nearby "Farmers' Museum" was locked, open only by appointment.

There was a time, before '48, when local Palestinians herded Jamoussi water buffaloes, glistening black, among the oleanders blooming along the stream that flowed from the Tanour waterfall toward the Hula swamps. As a child, it never occurred to me that a war would put an end to this pastoral life. Now I know that even the years before '48 were not as peaceful as I supposed, certainly not once the Ottoman Empire began to crumble, but even before that. Now I wonder what became of the shepherds and whether they were among the Bedouins who had settled in Tarshiha.

The Jews who arrived with the First Aliyah and the many who came later had to "make do," as Deborah would have put it. Fleeing the butchery of unspeakable pogroms and virulent anti-Semitism, survival was urgent. But as desperate as many of them were, they were settler-colonists. They believed they were returning to the land of their fathers, even as the Palestinians, with land deeds and house keys at hand, lost theirs. In tragic contrast to the

Palestinians expelled from their homeland, my ancestors believed that they were regaining theirs.

I remember overhearing names—Ben Yehuda, Hankin, Levontine, Aronson, Smilansky—pillars of the *yishuv* and family friends, mentioned with easy familiarity over a Saturday lunch of beet borscht and cholent. At the time I had no sense of who these men were—always men—or what they stood for. At most I'd gather that somebody was a friend from the first graduating class of the ha-Gymnasia ha-Ivrit Herzelia, the first secular Hebrew high school in the country (founded in 1905). We Sabra children had no interest in that early period. To our minds, the land deals, modest farms, and cramped dwellings of those years still had a whiff of the shtetl clinging to them. Our imagination was inspired instead by the young pioneers of the Second and Third Aliyahs (1904–1914 and 1919–1928), the "new Jews" and socialist Zionists who danced the hora, arms hugging each other's shoulders, feet pounding the ground after a long day of tilling the earth and building our cities.

The sketchy family history my cousin Yeheskel compiled tells me that my great-grandparents, Yitzhak and Manya, traveled by boat from Odessa to Jaffa in 1891, lived briefly in the new Jewish suburb of Neve Tzedek (now in Tel Aviv), and moved to a farm in Metula once the Baron de Rothschild purchased that land. Hardships continued: Yitzhak died prematurely, crushed under an overturned cart, leaving Manya with six young children. Though Rothschild's representatives pressed her to give up the farm, she refused, continuing to farm with the help of her two young sons. But even that didn't last. The elder son died from a rabid jackal bite and the younger one left the country to send back money earned abroad, as many did in those impoverished years. But even after her daughters married away from home, Manya continued to farm until her death in Safed's hospital in 1929. Only one of her daughters, my grandmother's sister Leah, remained in Metula.

This genealogy of a tribe in the making, replete with "begats" to the third, fourth, and fifth generation, says little about these immigrants' lives, anxious and disoriented as they must have been when they first arrived in this strange land, finding themselves among people whose language and customs they didn't understand. And it says nothing at all about the tenant farmers they displaced, even if the land was bought legally with official contracts to prove it.

Now, as I look back at this skeletal story, I hunger to know more about the world my ancestors entered—nor only about what they saw and felt but about the gales of history that buffeted the region. What matters to me now is not only the pogroms they fled, but the fact that they did so during the waning and collapse of the Ottoman empire and the turmoil that followed as the West divided its spoils. By the time my great-grandparents arrived in Metula, in the 1880s, the region was already feeling the Ottoman Empire's decline. By 1916, the village found itself at the seam-line of border disputes involving Syria, Lebanon, France, and Britain, as well as enmities among local villages, tribes, and religions. Zionism had reached a point of no return in its encounter with the Arab nationalism that was sweeping the region as Britain and France carved between them a new "Middle East."

My ancestors' decision to immigrate to Ottoman Palestine was, I imagine, a case of desperation colored by passionate faith and tragic innocence. They could have chosen America, as most Jewish immigrants did. Theirs was a blind certainty that the land they called Eretz Yisrael (Land of Israel), still uncharted and under Syrian rule when they landed in Jaffa, was God-given, and that their aliyah had been ordained. Yet I can't help but wonder: What did this immigrant couple expect when they found themselves and their three young children, one still an infant, tossed down from the rickety ship that came from Odessa into the sturdy grip of the men who manned the small fishing boat that was to ferry them to Jaffa's port? Could they even think at that moment, these Ukrainian *shtetle* Jews, carried by Arabs who smelled of unfamiliar spices and spoke in a strange language, as these men, laughing, impatient, deposited them on a narrow bench in their lurching rowboats?

"My first meeting with our cousin Ishmael was not a happy one," wrote Eliezer Ben Yehuda, compiler of the first Hebrew dictionary. "It was not a joyous meeting. A depressing sense of dread, as if facing a fortified wall, suddenly filled my soul." Less restrained was the writer Moshe Smilansky: "The noise and racket, the shrill cries of sailors and Arab porters on the ship's deck and in a filthy rowboat that shook and rattled and almost sank under the weight of people, packages, trunks, and boxes, and finally landing on a swarming, rowdy beach—left me shocked and dizzy as if drunk."

They may have felt just a blank incredulity, these new arrivals, as they stared with dazed eyes at Jaffa's minarets and church spires. Approaching a land that was "promised" and "homeland" only in in their imagination, they may have felt the familiar, centuries-old fears that marked their otherness in Europe rising yet again. "Is this my new world?" my great-grandmother may have wondered, tightening her shawl around the baby. "Is this where I'm to make a living?" my great-grandfather may have asked himself.

They had to be desperate to embark on this journey, but they also had time to question and plan and struggle before deciding to do so. They must have debated and dithered, at least for a while. They had to pack food, bundle essentials, and choose what clothes to take or abandon. There may have been official documents to sign, debts to pay or savings to retrieve from hiding, money to sew into a coat's lining, a prayer book, perhaps a locket or photographs. There may have also been farming manuals, Hebrew language study books, maybe even a book of poems, and of course the wrenching goodbyes.

It was not rapacious colonialism that brought that first trickle of aliyah to this land, and yet it led to the Nakba. My great grandparents and the Palestinians travelled in opposite directions, literally and intangibly. Their aliyah was a chance at a new life, the Palestinians' Nakba was a plunge into an abyss. Yes, it was butchery that drove my ancestors to this new land, long before the Holocaust that befell those left behind. But the ravaged bodies and terrorized Jews that the painter Abel Pann drew in response to the Kishinev pogroms of 1903 and 1905 could have also been of Palestinians, even if the traumas were not the same: more people expelled on their side, more slaughtered on ours. There is no way, finally, to weigh, measure, and compare suffering. Neither of these histories should have happened and both did.

Fleeing the savagery of the pogroms, those early arrivals were desperate to survive, hardly thinking about the Palestinians who paid the price for their survival. There was time enough to consider it, but not the will. Metula's memorial to Rothschild's generosity does not tell us that his men bought the village lands from an absentee landowner, Jabur Bey Riskalas, a Christian Greek who lived in distant Acre, and that this purchase caused six hundred tenant farmers, Druze in this instance, to lose their homes.

We of the *yishuv* took comfort in the fact that such land deals were legal. There are contracts, signatures, stamps, and photographs to prove the sales, though there is little discussion of what became of the tenant farmers whose lands were sold from under them. Here and there somebody did mention the inhabitants of the land—Ahad Ha'am, Arthur Rupin, and a few others. But mostly, I was taught, the newcomers were lit by utopian hopes. They were to "redeem" a land they thought of as promised them since time immemorial, a land they believed was empty and available, a desert they planned to make bloom. "Poh B'eretz Hemdat Avot," they sang:

> Here in a land beloved of our fathers,
> All [our] hopes will come true.
> Here we'll live and create,
> Lives of radiance and freedom.
> Here God's *Shehina* will dwell,
> Here the Torah's language will blossom.

I try to imagine what these shtetl Jews may have felt back in 1891, reeling at the unfamiliar sights and sounds of the alien place where they had landed. And I wonder, too, what the people of Jaffa might have made of these disheveled newcomers, with their bundles and children and babble of strange languages, so unlike the staid Christians who had been passing through Jaffa on their pilgrimages to holy sites. There may have been only a few Jewish newcomers at first, but their numbers were swelling quickly and they were here to stay.

According to my grandmother, Yitzhak and Manya first stayed briefly in Jaffa, in rooms rented above the busy Bostros Street, now Eilat Street, where donkeys and camels and pushcarts must have passed under their windows, and the air would have been dense with the shouts of vendors and the mingled smells of animals, food, and refuse. Moving to airy Neve Tzedek, even if temporarily, must have been a relief. Desperate for work, Yitzhak hired out to distant farmers till he was allocated land in Metula. Arriving there in 1896, he and fellow settlers took shelter in the dilapidated huts abandoned by the expelled Druze until they built their modest homes.

My cousin Yeheskel's genealogy does not say how our great-grandparents, made their way from Jaffa to Metula, but my grandmother, their daughter, did. She'd have been six or seven years old at the time, as I was when I first heard this story.

"It was too dangerous to go overland," she said, proud of the difficulties these First Aliyah farmers had to overcome. "Very dangerous," she repeated, bending toward me, opening her eyes wide to convey the danger. "People could travel to Jerusalem by a covered *diligence* wagon (French accented *-gence*), but going overland to Metula was much worse. There were *listim* lurking along the way."

"*Listim*?" I asked.

"Robbers, bad men with guns," she explained, tucking a loose strand of her hair into her bun. *Chignon,* she called it in French, the *yishuv's* elite language during Baron Rothschild's reign.

I tried in vain to imagine these Jewish settlers, people I never knew, traveling by mules and donkeys across the rugged Galilee terrain. There were no family photos. What did Manya and Yitzhak wear? What did they bring along? Did the baby ride in a basket? Did the other two children have their own donkey?

The diaries and memoir fragments collected in Avraham Ya'ari's bulging two-volume *Memories of Eretz Yisrael* confirm this story of robbers and dangerous journeying, though I never found out who these particular *listim* were. Could some of them have been the same Druze tenant farmers who saw my great-grandparents settle on lands they knew as their own?

According to my grandmother, the safest route between the Galilee and Jaffa was roundabout. "It took several days to travel from Jaffa to Metula," she loved telling me, trying to impress on me the difficulty of the journey. "First we sailed from Jaffa to Beirut and then overland, on donkeys, from Beirut to Metula," one of Ya'ari's writers reports. I don't know how long the sea voyage from Jaffa to Beirut took, but it was four days from Beirut to Safed and the better part of another day to Metula. "When I left Metula to train as a teacher," my grandmother said, "I took the journey in reverse, first to Beirut, then to Jaffa, and then two more days to Jerusalem by the *diligence* stage coach."

While the journey was hard, farming was much harder. To this day, you can see how barren the eroded, windswept hills are around Metula, on both the Lebanese and the Israeli sides. This discouraging sight is what the early settlers must have found, even if there are now orchards and modest gardens greening the village. Clearing the rocks must have been an ordeal, as was access to potable water. They lugged water uphill from the Tanour waterfall, and then had to boil and strain it to remove tiny leeches, my grandmother told me. "Is it possible to explain to today's students," writes Aviezer Chelouche in his family memoir, "how our great-grandparents held on by their fingernails to wastelands in which they would envision their future as a family and a people?"

When I first met my great-aunt Lea, my grandmother's sister—it must have been in 1945 or 1946—I was taken aback. To my child's eyes, Lea, by then a widow in a faded housedress, seemed ancient. Wrinkled and wearing her thin hair in a bun, she looked like a worn version of my grandmother. Was this what Manya would have looked like? The family house felt distressingly cramped, lined up with others much like it along Metula's Founders Street: one low story with a cowshed in the back, its thick stone walls barely lit by its small, deep-set windows. My mother, grandmother, and I sat in the dim front room drinking tea, our elbows resting on patterned oilcloth. Lea served it Russian style, in tall glasses. The conversation was not unlike Yehezkel's "begats": What became of this one? Whom did that one marry? Is she still living in Metula? I knew none of them.

But I did know a story about my great-grandmother Manya, a story that went beyond family lore.

"Look, Ma," I called out one afternoon soon after we'd visited Lea, rushing to my mother with an open volume of my children's encyclopedia, *Ma'ayan*, clutched in my hands. "It's about 'The Savta from Metula,' in a chapter about 'Brave Women.'" Thrilled as I was, it would be years before I'd register that these few stories about brave Jewish women were relegated to an addendum at the very end of this four-volume encyclopedia. At that moment all that mattered was that the story's heroine, "The Savta [grandmother] from Metula," was my very own great grandmother.

The story concerned a time when the three northernmost Jewish settlements of Metula, Kfar Giladi, and Tel Hai came under repeated "Arab" attacks. My grandmother had already told me about these attacks and how the Jewish farmers hid in caves. In the early *yishuv* days, such attacks were committed throughout the country by both by Palestinian peasants and Bedouins, including the Palestinian tenant farmers who had lost their lands. To us Jews, they were simply unspecified "Arab" attacks, the latest iteration of our historic saga of perpetual non-welcome.

The unrest became increasingly turbulent during the Ottomans' gradual collapse. Displaced Druze attacks on Metula stopped once compensation was arranged. But fighting continued as the region became caught up in a Syrian anti-colonial rebellion against France, its new ruler after the Anglo-French Sykes-Picot agreement of 1916. At one point, most of Metula's farmers abandoned the village altogether, traveling by mule and donkey to Sidon, then to Beirut, and finally by boat to Haifa. However—and this is what mattered to me as a child—when the escaping farmers reached the Litani river, the "Savta from Metula," our very own Manya, remembered that she'd left her cows and chickens locked up without food or water. She rode her mule back to the village under cover of darkness, freed her animals, and, after many unnamed hardships, managed to rejoin the others.

This story is long gone from the national registry of remarkable events. Ordinary day-to-day grit did not seem to deserve a story, especially not that of a woman. Among them, another Manya, Manya Shochat, is a remarkable exception: a radical revolutionary, gunrunner, "mother" of the kibbutz movement, and founder of the Hashomer self-defense militia. Closer to my great-grandmother's domestic anecdote is Sophie Pascal's story, great-grandmother of my friend Thelma, told by her descendant, Eliezer Chelouche.

One night, as Sophie was bringing textiles from Damascus for sale at the Jewish settlement of Zichron Yaakov, her cart was robbed by Bedouins. The rain was heavy and Sophie had dozed off in the swaying cart. Awakened by a horse's neigh and stretching, she found herself touching a hand nearby. Realizing that much of her merchandise was gone, Sophie, speaking fluent Arabic, turned her cart toward the nearby Bedouin encampment. Entering the sheikh's tent, she greeted him and the assembled men with customary ceremonial deference, thanking them lavishly for their generosity in "protecting" her goods from the rain. Charmed, the men served coffee and sweetmeats in her honor and sent her home with her textiles intact. Not a word was said about theft. "*Wallahi 'sit Pascal jabara*" they said. By God, Madam Pascal is a brave woman!

Such stories aren't included in Israel's national myth. The people who inspired us throughout my childhood and still inspire many were Tel Hai's heroic defenders, who died fighting off an Arab attack in 1920, close to Metula and the kibbutz of Kfar Giladi. A small agricultural courtyard founded by six Metula farmers just fifteen years earlier, Tel Hai was plunged into regional unrest when, in 1919, Britain ceded territory to France. A few months later, when Arabs fighting to retain an independent "Greater Syria" entered the courtyard in search of French soldiers supposedly hiding there (there were none), an altercation developed and fighting broke out. Eight of Tel Hai's defenders—six men and two women—died, among them the commander, Joseph Trumpeldor.

Though accounts of this incident vary, the ones I grew up on had one thing in common: the battle of Tel Hai was an attack on Jews, fired by anger at our settlement on Arab lands. I first came to question this version a few years ago when reading in Anthony Shadid's memoir, *House of Stone,* that nearby Lebanese villages were also attacked, including his own family's village of Marjayoun, near Metula.

At stake were not three small Jewish settlements and some Lebanese villages attacked by unspecified "Arabs," but a bruising regional instability caused by Britain and France's partition negotiations (notably the Sykes-Picot agreement) and their betrayal of the region's nationalist aspirations. The unrest did unleash clan- and religion- based enmities among Shiites, Bedouins, and Druze, including looters and others settling old scores, as Shadid notes. But looming above that were the newly drawn and redrawn borders that divided Greater Syria into French-controlled Lebanon and Syria and British-controlled Palestine. Trumpeldor's own diary, included in Ya'ari's book, says as much.

For me, growing up during Israel's early years, the story of Tel Hai loomed large. Of the region's knotty history, I saw only the heroic last stand of our few, dying in defense of our homeland. As I learned in school, Tel Hai and Jewish heroism had little to do with the consequences of World War I, the collapse of the Ottoman Empire, the rise of nationalist Arab resistance to French and British imperialism, or the dispossession of tenant farmers whose lands we Zionists bought from under them. As far as we were concerned, Tel Hai was only another example of the Arabs' refusal to accept Jewish presence, emblematic of our millennia-old persecution.

Tel Hai has become a citadel of national passions. The tall, roaring lion stone sculpture that commemorates its defenders is one of Israel's most iconic memorials to its dead heroes, rising on a promontory above Tel Hai's court-yard museum, white against ink-black cypress trees. Etched in the national imagination is the famous sentence attributed to Joseph Trumpeldor: "It is good to die for our country." These are, as our national myth goes, his dying words, repeated in countless poems, songs, stories, plays, and commemoration ceremonies. "In the Galilee, in Tel Hai, Trumpeldor fell," we sang at school, around campfires, and in sing-alongs, the melody weaving sorrow into our collective yearning for national renewal. "Go in my footsteps," the song has Trumpeldor command, "till the last moment."

12. The Silver Platter

*I*t wasn't only Metula that had me thinking about the old *yishuv*. Searching for traces of the Nakba, I began to see my own history in new ways. It was no longer just a question of mapping locations or trying to tell rock from rubble. It meant mulling over causes and effects and reading about this history, including the early *yishuv*'s memoirs and reflections gathered in Mordechai Eliav's *The First Aliyah* and David Ya'ari's *Memories of Eretz Yisrael*—two volumes each. What used to be a jumble of clichés learned at school and hazy memories clamoring for attention began to take shape, leading me to question the national narrative that inspired me for so many years.

One such instance is Tel Hai, whose myth no longer held sway for me—neither in its socialist version where a heroic Trumpeldor, who'd lost an arm while serving in the Russian army, plowed Tel Hai's fields, nor in its nationalist version that pictured the revered one-armed commander wielding a gun. An inspiration for me well into adulthood, the story of Tel Hai's heroic last stand lost its sheen. Its reconstructed Courtyard as a staged "memory site" museum was already a letdown, a banal mummified attempt to vivify a heroic myth. Photos and wall texts, a few curated farm implements tastefully placed on a manicured lawn—it was hard to reconcile this reconstruction with the elevated sense of national sacrifice that the idea of Tel Hai was to inspire.

It is easy to fall back on formulas, I now think, remembering my own attempt, at age ten, to capture the myth's grandeur in the form of a poem. My literary ambitions were high during those pre-pubescent years. My parents, like so many others, had assorted "complete works" on their shelves, both by Hebrew authors and in translation. Clearly having one's own "complete works" was a worthy goal. My literary moment came in the form of a poetry contest sponsored by the children's magazine of the daily *Ha'aretz*, any topic welcome. Of course mine was Tel Hai.

Some weeks later a square envelope arrived in the mail, filled with glossy black-and-white "Views of Eretz Yisrael." Hundreds may have been sent to children like me as a consolation prize. Though I didn't admit it, I knew my poem was terrible. The rhymes were forced, it scanned like a military march, and the passion it proclaimed for "the fallen heroes" was embarrassingly overblown. The opening image of Tel Hai in flames was certainly spectacular, but the spectacle was hollow. Tel Hai did not burn; the fire I ascribed to it migrated from song about the shtetl burning.

"Hey, do I hear the siren's call of nationalism?" Deborah said with a laugh when I told her about this poem. We had just left the museum and were walking up to the roaring lion monument that marks Tel Hai's last stand.

Reading the names of the fallen cut into the stone, my familiar awe at their courage turned to irritation. The lion, upright on its hind haunches, roaring skyward as if in protest, felt crude, not unlike the nationalist bravura of my own poem. The irresistible communal belief was losing its hold on me. Did Trumpeldor really mean it when he said, "It's good to die for our country"?

The roaring stone lion and my passionate poem were signposts along a road I traveled growing up. The message was clear: we Jews must be ready to die for our country.

One afternoon I took Deborah to see my old elementary school. It was after hours and the place was deserted, though nothing much had changed: the same classrooms facing the yard, the same old gym tucked to the side of the small campus, the same asphalt-covered playground, perhaps more cracked than I had remembered. In the gray winter light the place looked shabby and sad. Passing by the gym on our way out, I thought about our annual Chanukah celebrations, when all eight grades would gather in the gym, our teachers and parents and even our dour headmaster in attendance. The tumbling mats, balls, and bars would be pushed against the gym wall, replaced with wooden benches for us children, festive in our holiday clothes, and folding chairs for our adoring parents in the back rows.

I was in second grade when I first clambered up to the gym's stage with eight other girls. We had practiced devoutly for this moment. Wearing headbands with cardboard "candles" attached and yellow crepe paper ribbons pinned to our white dresses, we twirled on tiptoe, arms extended, forming a wobbly circle of "candle lights" to a tune from Grieg's *Peer Gynt Suite*. Other groups followed. Though I never admitted it at the time, these Chanukah pageants were dull, the routine always the same. My mother stopped attending altogether, and I only remember two of the annual installments: the Chanukah play about Hannah and her seven sons and the recitation of Nathan Alterman's poem "Magash Hakesef" ("The Silver Platter").

The Chanukah play was my personal favorite. Based on an ancient Jewish story from the start of the Hasmonaean dynasty, it celebrated resistance to the Greco-Syrian tyrant Antiochus IV Epiphanes (175–164 BCE), who required that Jews bow to an idol he had installed at the Temple.

Sitting transfixed on our hard, backless benches, we'd watch Hannah's sons, starting with the oldest of the seven and moving down to the youngest, choose death rather than bow to Antiochus's idol, with their anguished mother standing by. The crisis would come when the one remaining child, the youngest, melts Antiochus's heart. Moved by his tender years, the cruel tyrant—acted by a tall boy in shiny clothes—proposes a compromise: all the child need do is retrieve a ring that Antiochus would drop on the ground near the idol. Understanding the ruse, the child refuses this reprieve and is killed. We children, the play reiterated year after year, must never deny our God or our people. The Hasmonaean priests and Jewish farmers knew that when they rose in the revolt that reinstated an independent Jewish state.

Stirred by the Chanukah play and the story of Tel Hai, I felt total loyalty to my people, sure that I'd be willing to die for my country. Self-sacrifice was what we were all taught; dying a martyr's death, *al kiddush hashem*, was a virtue. The Chanukah play was just another version of the archetypal story of our resisting persecution: Moses leading us out of Egypt; a shepherd boy fighting Goliath; rebels holding Masada against the Romans; Jewish partisans and ghetto fighters resisting the Nazis; Tel Hai's few defenders facing a large army; and the *yishuv* as a whole, dislodging the British and fighting off vast Arab armies. "In every generation ..." as the saying goes. *Bekol dor vedor.*

In the years that followed my early education, researchers would revise both the Tel Hai and the Hasmonaean stories, in keeping with changing perspectives of their own time. The Hasmonaeans, I later learned, were not ordinary peasants but experienced warriors facing a weak occupier and competing for power among themselves. Trumpeldor's last words may not have been the legendary ones we recited; he spoke Russian, and those present at his death were not sure what they heard. The attack on Tel Hai was not specifically anti-Zionist but part of a sweeping regional unrest. Even Trumpeldor's legacy was up for debate. For some, he embodied the agrarian ideals of Labor Zionism, while others venerated the commitment to self-defense at all costs, even unto death.

The other part of the pageant I remember was its rousing conclusion, when the graduating class would recite "The Silver Platter." I'm not sure whether this custom began at the height of the 1948 war or shortly afterward. Timing would have been tricky. Published just three weeks after the 1947 UN vote to partition British Palestine and printed as an op-ed in the Labor daily *Davar*, not as a "poem," "The Silver Platter" took its inspiration from the words of Chaim Weitzmann, Israel's first president: "A state is not given to a nation on a silver platter." The meaning was clear. By 1947, even as Brit Shalom published its pamphlet calling for a binational state, the *yishuv* had already known decades of attacks and massacres, including major ones in Safed and Hebron and the Arab uprising just a few years later. Sacrifice would be needed, we knew.

Alterman's poem perches at the edge of this abyss. Its Delphic prophecy sees the nation rising in fire and smoke, broken-hearted but breathing, to receive its miracle of creation in terror and joy. Two battle-weary youths, a boy and a girl, stand erect in the moonlight, facing the nation, giving no sign of life or death. "We are the silver platter on which you were given the Jewish state," they say and fall at the nation's feet, wrapped in shadow. Are they the miracle given to the nation, its *only* miracle, as Alterman writes? Are we, the graduating class declaiming the poem with passionate conviction, this miracle? And what are we to make of these two youths' falling at the nation's feet, enfolded in the deepening darkness of a descending night?

Amos Oz also evokes the enormity of the moments before and after the UN vote in his memoir, *A Tale of Love and Darkness*:

... a first terrifying shout tore through the darkness and the buildings and trees, piercing itself, not a shout of joy, perhaps more like a scream of horror and bewilderment, a cataclysmic shout, a shout that could shift rocks, that could freeze your blood, ... and the next moment the scream of horror was replaced by roars of joy.

Though I too saw the *yishuv* erupt in joy, filling the streets with people dancing the hora for hours on end, war loomed ahead. Many had already joined the Palmach, the Hagana, or the Irgun, in anticipation. By the time my graduating class recited "The Silver Platter," in 1952, dressed alike and standing shoulder to shoulder, we already knew that in three or four years we would be the youths ensuring Israel's survival.

The recitation required weeks of preparation. We had to memorize the poem and learn to enunciate and declaim it in perfect unison. We practiced pacing our climb onto the stage and shuffling quickly to line up in straight rows. We practiced standing erect and at attention, staring smartly ahead, military style. The meaning of all this was clear: we all belonged to the nation. In reciting "The Silver Platter" we were announcing our devotion to a "call" that commanded us beyond thought or understanding. It was an oath, a promise to those who would come after us and to the parents and teachers who delivered us to this stage. We were ready to be that silver platter.

Four short years later would find me, now a graduating twelfth-grader, on a four-day hike through the Judean desert. I was one among many seventeen-year-old boys and girls, all of us thirsty, sweaty, sunburnt, and increasingly grimy, with blistered feet and struggling under heavy backpacks, observing a strict water discipline that prescribed three gulps per hour. The plateau on which our boots were pounding was bone-dry and sun-bleached. Every so often I could hear a bird calling, barely visible as it streaked across a searing ash-white sky. The only other living creature we saw was a two-foot-long lizard encrusted in ridged gray armor. Immobile on its hot flat rock, it never glanced at us as we marched by.

Other groups were also marching in this desert, all headed for a swearing-in ceremony at Masada. On the fourth afternoon, as the sun was lowering and the Dead Sea became a flat plate of metallic gray, we converged with the other hikers at an ancient Roman camp still visible at the foot of the forbidding Masada cliff. That night we hardly slept; ahead was probably the most difficult climb of our lives. It may have been two or three A.M. when we headed, single file, for the impossibly steep and dangerous "snake path" that zigzags its way to the top of this ancient fortress. We sung all the way up. Once at the summit, we lined up for the pre-dawn torchlight ceremony where we'd swear our loyalty to Israel and the army in which, in a year, we would all serve.

In *My Promised Land: The Triumph and Tragedy of Israel*, the writer Ari Shavit reviews the origin of such hikes, beginning in 1942, when Shmaryahu Gutman taught a seminar on Masada's heroic place in Jewish history and took the first group of forty-six determined youths—the elite of the Jewish pioneer youth movement—on the dangerous climb up that mountain. Not much was known about Masada before then. A few intrepid souls had braved the steep cliff in previous years, but Gutman's group and the ones that followed made Masada a supreme symbol of national commitment, even unto death.

As Yigael Yadin's and subsequent archaeological excavations confirmed, the sheer cliff that had once been a Hasmonaean fort was turned by King Herod into a fortified palace compound and the unbreachable desert redoubt where, some 150 years later, Jewish rebels, the Zealots, resisted Rome for three heroic years. When the Romans finally finished building the ramp that would let them take Masada, they found the entire Zealot community dead. About to lose their freedom, the defenders committed mass suicide, family by family, 960 men, women, and children.

"How good and how great it will be when we carry our freedom to our grave," Masada's leader, Elazar Ben Yair, is reported to have said. "Only the young Hebrews willing to die will be able to ensure for themselves a secure and sovereign life," writes Shavit, paraphrasing Gutman. "Only their willingness to fight to the end will prevent their end."

Shavit doesn't mention Tel Hai, but I see a straight line leading from Hannah mourning her martyred sons to the legend of Tel Hai, and from that to my eighth grade declaiming "The Silver Platter" and the youths with whom I stood at attention on the flat, stone-strewn top of Masada.

The memory is vivid of so many of us holding our torches aloft, with our bodies barely visible in the pre-dawn darkness. I still remember the feel of the cold wind on my legs and the wind makng the flames of our torches dance as we swore our allegiance to the state and sang "Hatikva," some of us choking on tears. Here and there a face would flicker into view in the light of a dancing flame, or an arm would appear as it adjusted its grip on the torch. I could feel strength coursing through my shins, legs tensing as they supported my body firmly on the ground. I was no longer the seventeen-year old girl, proud that she managed to climb the Snake Path's steep switchbacks. At that moment I was a body that served an idea and a will much greater than any "me" I had believed myself to be.

Never mind that one boy—I never learned his name—collapsed and died during this assembly. The incident was hushed up, though the word passed from mouth to mouth as we stood at attention. It was sunstroke, someone whispered. That water discipline, someone else murmured. The ceremony went on, with that boy dying not on "the altar of the nation" but close to it. His was an almost a heroic death, we felt, awed and secretly shaken. Shivering in the early morning air, tired but proud that our strong legs didn't fail us, we affirmed our ties to the heroic fighters who withstood mighty Rome for three years and chose suicide over surrender.

Out of this awesome history was born the slogan "Masada will never fall again," anchoring the destiny of the present Jewish state in Masada's heroic past. A few years after I climbed up to this precipice, these words entered the IDF's swearing-in ceremony. A related slogan, this one not specifying its subject, was "Never again," invoking (but not naming) the Holocaust and anti-Semitism but open to any unwelcome assault on Jews. It became the slogan of the Jewish Defense League (JDL), a far-right group deemed a terrorist organization by the FBI. Both slogans rest on a view of Jewish history that expects calamity to strike *yet again*, as the traditional Passover Haggadah reminds us annually: "In every generation they rise to annihilate us."

I do not recall hearing these slogans when I was growing up, between 1939 and 1961, though the ground for them was fertile. They emerged and evolved alongside Israeli and diaspora Jews' evolving nationalism,

The Israel I grew up in, at the time still echoing the ideals of Labor Zionism, did feel small and vulnerable, beset by enemies on all sides. The need for self-defense was irrefutable, as my great-grandmother Manya knew all too well and as the fate of Tel Hai showed so dramatically. By 1907 the first local self-defense organization, Bar Giora, was formed, followed by the Hagana in 1920, Betar in 1923, and the IZL in 1937. The name Betar, chosen by Zeev Jabotinsky for the militia he had founded, anticipated the aura that Masada eventually acquired. Betar was the last Jewish fortress to withstand a Roman siege during the Bar Kokhba revolt. It fell some two hundred years after Masada, also after a three-year siege, another symbol of determined Jewish heroism where the few faced the many. Legend has it that the massacred defenders' blood flowed so copiously that it reached the Roman horses' nostrils.

Betar's slogan is an explicit battle cry, one that I heard in the Palestine that was becoming Israel:

> In blood and fire Judea fell
> In blood and fire Judea will rise!

This slogan quotes Yaakov Cohen's poem "The Song of the Biryonim" ("Hooligans"), written in response to the horrific Kishinev pogrom of 1903:

> We have arisen and returned mighty youths,
> We have arisen and returned, We are Biryonim!
> To redeem our land in war's storm,
> We demand our heritage with upraised hand.
>
> In blood and fire Judea fell!
> In blood and fire Judea will rise.
>
> War for freedom, war for the land,
> And if freedom dies, long live revenge!
> If there is no justice in the land, the sword will judge
> Even if we fall like sand, we'll not give up our rights.
>
> In blood and fire Judea fell!
> In blood and fire Judea will arise!
>   (From "Shiron Betar")

Until the Holocaust, the Kishinev pogrom loomed as the most ghastly symbol of Jewish victimhood in modern times. Like Cohen's "Shir Habiryonim," Haim Nahman Bialik's poem "On the Slaughter" was a passionate response to that pogrom, based on direct testimony. We elementary school children learned to recite Bialik's poem by heart. In our young imagination, the pogroms and Arab attacks melded. For some, notably Jabotinsky, the lesson was clear: we Jews must surround our (as we saw it) new land with an "iron wall"; it's only with blood and fire that we can force our will on the resisting populace. As Ben-Gurion wrote too, "Our spilled blood cries out not for pity and succor, but rather to increase our strength and our work in the land."

These words, each a road map to a political future, are steeped in blood. Yet Bialik's poem, as expressive as it was of the horrors of the pogrom's atrocities, includes the following lines:

> And cursed be he who cries out: Revenge!
> Vengeance like this, for the blood of a child,
> Satan has yet to devise.

The history I saw unfold since my school years, as Israel grew strong and flourished, told a story that began before my birth and extends toward a horizon not yet in sight. It extends, I gradually came to see, from the early days of aliyah settlement to a war of becoming—*komemiyut*, as we initially called the '48 war—and on to a war of occupation, from colonization to violent expansion. It's a history that resonated with the words that another popular song, "In the Galilee, at Tel Hai," ascribes to Yoseph Trumpeldor, "Walk in my footsteps … Up to the last moment."

That Trumpeldor never actually said these words didn't matter. Aba Chushai composed these lyrics years later, but they found their way to our hearts.

13. Deir Yassin

One evening in Zochrot's gallery, I heard a lecture on the massacre that occurred in the Palestinian village of Deir Yassin—the most notorious of the '48 war's massacres, committed by people who were weaned on the legend of Tel Hai. I already knew that this massacre was committed by members of the Jewish Irgun and Lehi militias, though how many men, women, and children were actually slaughtered that day, April 9, 1948, is still unclear. Was it 254 killed, as some claim? One hundred, as others estimate? One hundred sixteen, as Zochrot's booklet on Deir Yassin reports? Did the Hagana inflate the numbers in order to disgrace the Irgun and Lehi, as some allege? And what happened to the survivors?

The facts are not trivial. Reports of mass killing, torture and humiliation abound and new ones keep emerging: atrocities inflicted on peaceful Palestinians who had a cease-fire treaty with the Hagana and pleaded to be allowed to surrender. News of this massacre spread quickly, with prisoners paraded in Jerusalem by their captors. It caused countless other Palestinians to flee without a shot being fired. Though the Irgun and Lehi's responsibility for the massacre is known, there are claims that the Hagana could have intervened, and didn't.

Sitting on the gallery's folding chairs with some thirty Israelis, middle-aged and older, I was stunned to see a stocky man rise to shout at the speaker across the room, his face red, his voice hoarse with age and rage, and the speaker respond in kind. Both were old enough to have fought in '48 and probably had. The facts and numbers of Deir Yassin's victims may be debated, but the furious rage that tilted these two aging men at each other transcended the facts. How long, I wondered and continue to wonder, will we on all sides continue to nurse ancient resentments, guilts, and shame?

I did not expect such rage to erupt on the floor of Zochrot. But the name of Deir Yassin festers as a dark, barely mentionable reminder of events we chose to bury but never quite managed to purge. As a child, I rarely heard Deir Yassin mentioned, though when it was, it was the massacre, not the place that people had in mind. One snippet, overheard shortly after the attack on the village, haunts me. Something murmured, about a woman's breast nailed to a door. To this day I do not know whether that atrocity was actually committed, and, if it was, whether it was perpetrated, by us in Deir Yassin or by Palestinians at nearby Jewish Gush Etzion.

Revenge and counter-revenge, and yet what flickers behind my unwilling eyes is the image of a woman's breast, congealed blood at its rim, nailed to a wooden door.

Until the war of 1967, when Israel came to control extensive new territories, Deir Yassin trembled at the edge of memory as the most painful test of our rules of engagement, those much-touted ethics of combat. It was a test we failed, where *tohar haneshek*, "the purity of the weapon," proved a lie. Whatever the facts—the number of those killed, the survivors paraded and executed, the atrocities, the testimonies of surviving witnesses on both sides—it was unbearable to imagine that our "sons" could be at fault.

Most of us present at Zochrot that evening, perhaps all, had served in the IDF. We knew, or should have known, that there is a vast, murky terrain stretching between "ethical" and "unethical" warfare, and yet it was still hard not to think of the Deir Yassin massacre as an aberration. How comforting to see it as something *they* did, the renegade Irgun and Lehi militias that have since been disbanded, not us decent, reasonable Israeli Jews! The urge to put that massacre aside is enormous, although that episode was known as one of the pivotal events of the Nakba.

I was reluctant to visit the actual site of Deir Yassin, though I knew I had to. Surely Deborah must photograph its remains, I thought. At least finding the place should be easy: the neighboring Jewish towns of Giv'at Shaul and Har Nof, both parts of Greater Jerusalem's urban sprawl, now abut or occupy much of the village lands.

It was a chilly winter morning when Deborah and I arrived at Giv'at

Shaul. It must have rained the previous night as the earth was springy underfoot. In what had become our normal practice, we first headed for the nearby open hillside where we thought remnants of Palestinian buildings might still be found. A few shabby stone houses stood here and there, looking gray under leaden skies. In one yard a dog rose to bark at us, in another a white goat stood tethered to a pole, ignoring the chickens pecking at the muddy ground. Though nobody was in sight, a Hebrew blessing pasted on a window and broken-down furniture piled under a lean-to made it clear that the people living here were Jewish and poor—most likely Mizrahim, to judge by the style of the blessing. Were they, I wondered, immigrants squatting in Palestinian homes, as was so often the case? The buildings divulged nothing. Built of local stone, they could have easily been either Palestinian or Jewish.

Stymied, we headed for Giv'at Shaul itself. All we could see of this drab residential development were cracked sidewalks, water-stained stucco walls, and a grid of walk-up apartment houses, with laundry hanging on balconies and prams and tricycles lying in entrance hallways. The laundry looked gray and soggy under the overcast skies; the prams and tricycles were dented, their paint peeling. A man in standard-issue orthodox black could be seen hurrying on some errand, a worn briefcase under his arm. The few women who were out and about wore long dark skirts and long-sleeved blouses, their heads wrapped in kerchiefs.

Except for the predominant orthodox attire, this neighborhood was not different from many others built for the flood of Jewish immigrants and growing families in need of housing. There seemed to be nothing left here of Deir Yassin, and I wouldn't have dared ask a passerby about it anyway. Chances were that a stranger would stare at me blankly, and if I met someone who did know about the massacre, I would encounter only hostility.

"Leave us alone!" an informed person might say. "That's history," another might chime in. "Over and done with. *Khallas*, do you get it? Now it's ours." And it could get nasty, too: "Traitor! F_ck you, whore. D'you wanna give them the country as a present? Let them throw us into the sea?" I heard versions of this, from settlers and politicians quoted in the media, people on talk shows, loquacious taxi drivers, acquaintances, strangers, and friends. Man or woman, orthodox or secular, Mizrahi or Ashkenazi, it hardly made a difference. "We are also refugees," people said. "Do you think that *we* had it so easy? We had no alternative, and still don't. The whole world stood by when we were piled onto those cattle cars. America wouldn't have us. The British sent us back to the crematoria. We had to save our own. Let the Arabs take care of *theirs* and we'll take care of ours. At least they have their own countries next door. We had nothing."

Dispirited, we gave up that day. Help came two or three weeks later, in the form of a casual comment by my friend Nurith Gertz as we strolled one evening along the Tel Aviv beach. Nurith was telling me about a book she was writing, a biography of her husband, Amos Kenan, including the fact that he was among those present during the Deir Yassin massacre. Though Nurith and I first met as academics—she is a highly accomplished professor of Israeli literature, culture, and film—she knew about Deborah's and my work on the Nakba and was supportive of it. Her own work concerned the "conflict" for years, including work on the writer S. Yizhar and co-authoring the book *Palestinian Cinema: Landscape, Trauma, and Memory* with Palestinian film-maker and scholar George Khleifi.

When I told her about our failure to find Deir Yassin, she laughed. "It's right there, in full view. Just go to Giv'at Shaul's bus depot. Standing in front of it, up on the sidewalk, you'd see the State Mental Hospital across the street, with a big sign. That's what remains of Deir Yassin."

A mental hospital! It sounded like a bad joke. Deborah and I must have seen it. It would have never occurred to us that the fenced-in campus with the big "State Hospital" sign could be the retrofitted village.

Udi Aloni's film *Mechilot*, which I happened to see a few days later, is anchored in this irony. Shot on the hospital's grounds, its title means both "tunnels" and "forgiveness." That Aloni's protagonists are Jewish Holocaust survivors who live in a mental hospital is not, in itself, surprising: the Holocaust casts its shadow on many Israeli films. What is remarkable is Aloni's placing these men in this particular hospital, linking the two catastrophes—the Shoah and the Nakba. This is a daring move, a sore conjunction for many Israelis. But there is an added irony here, this one circumstantial: the remains of Deir Yassin are within view of the world's most famous Holocaust museum, Yad Vashem. As Zochrot's brochure notes, on Yad Vashem's side of the valley separating the two, the world is taught to "never forget"; on Deir Yassin's side it is urged to "never mind."

Mechilot was on my mind when, a few days later, Deborah and I stood on the busy sidewalk that runs in front of Giv'at Shaul's bus depot, with a flimsy newspaper and lottery ticket kiosk behind us and shabby stalls selling soft drinks and snacks nearby. Across the street was a high chain-link fence surrounding a sparse pine grove with some buildings partly visible among them. A large sign was displayed prominently at the barred entrance gate: "State Mental Hospital."

Were it not for Nurith, it would have never occurred to us to give this place a second glance. Except for staff, patients, and their visitors, people rushing in and out of the depot were not likely to pay attention to the fenced compound across the street. Most wouldn't know its history or care to know it. Too many Arab houses had been naturalized into the Israeli landscape to be noticed, especially around Jerusalem where the same quarries supplied the same masonry to Arabs and Jews.

Standing with my back to the depot, I tried to blend into the crowd, though in that neighborhood women in jeans stood out. Peaceniks, leftists, radicals, international protesters—scum, anyone who'd notice us might think. No doubt there was "trouble" here before our visit: banners, shouts, chants, police—perhaps even a scuffle. The high fence, the locked gate, and the uniformed guard went beyond ordinary safety measures.

Deborah approached the gate, camera ready, the cap already taken off its lens. The guard shooed her away before she even got the camera into position.

"*Assur*," ("forbidden") he called in Hebrew, his raised hand telling us to back off.

"Why?" I asked.

"Because it's a hospital. To protect the patients' privacy."

What privacy, I wondered? All one could see were buildings screened by trees, closed doors, and tiny windows—no people, not even staff.

"Are you kidding me?" my open hands signaled.

"Move back," his left hand gestured in return, his right adjusting its hold on his rifle. "More."

We moved a few steps back.

"Back," he gestured, planting himself near the guard booth only after we'd climbed up to the pavement across the street.

Sensibly, Deborah suggested that we follow the fence circling the hospital grounds, looking for a breach. This was not to be. This steel fence, seven feet high, felt impermeable. Behind it, at the back of the main hospital building, we could see village houses resting on fallen pine needles, dappled in the shade of the sparsely planted trees. Small, nondescript one-story houses, they were now apparently service buildings, mostly for storage, padlocked.

It was a peaceful scene, seemingly dormant in the mild afternoon light, totally devoid of people. There was not even a broom or a pail or a rag left hanging to make the deserted place come alive. No wonder Aloni set *Mechilot* in this place, I thought. Standing by the chain-link fence, thoughts of this film kept reverberating: them and us, their survival and ours, deadly fear and hate, compassion and forgiveness. Is this history really one of *ein breira*, of there being no alternative, as we Israelis affirm to one another? Do words like "madness" and "sanity," "cause" and "effect," "crime" and "necessity" still mean anything?

Stepping back from the fence, I noticed that our shadows had length-ened, at one with the pattern of the fence's joined links. We were still at the back of the hospital grounds, but the sun had begun its descent behind us. The creamy, golden-yellow sandstone of these simple houses was beginning to take on the gentle pinks and mauves of the afternoon light. The luminous glow is always here, I thought, refracted by the unevenness of the stones.

We turned to leave. Then, as we rounded a bend in the fence, I saw them.

Invisible from the front of the hospital, or from the children's playground that abuts it, or the fence we had just circled, were several yeshivas, built like fortresses. Tall, close to one another, with narrow slit windows that would make excellent sharpshooters' posts, they formed a massive wall that enclosed their own people and barred all others, including phantom Palestinians. Here, I felt, Deir Yassin was, irrevocably, gone.

I am not sure why that erasure felt so final as I stood in front of the yeshivas. Maybe it was the very absence of rubble, the cleansing of traces, that was hard to take. Giv'at Shaul's depressingly run-down spread nearby was also dispiriting. An air of normalizing permanence hung on its ugly walk-up apartment blocks, the women pushing strollers, the men with tattered briefcases, even the boys with ear-locks trembling under skullcaps in the playground nearby.

There was something terribly anticlimactic about this place. It was the site of the worst chapters of the '48 war, as far as I knew at the time, and yet everything looked so ordinary.

A week or two later Nurith took us to see the remains of Qalunya, near Jewish Motza, not far from Deir Yassin. The Motza of my childhood was a sleepy Jewish village dominated by its sprawling Silicate Bricks factory. Passing it on the road to Jerusalem, I always looked forward to the brief appearance of this magical collection of red brick buildings and chimneys hugging the road. But I had never heard of Qalunia, neither that its people had attacked Motza during the Arab uprising of 1929, nor that we captured it twenty years later to secure access to besieged Jerusalem.

By then Deborah and I had found and photographed quite a few villages lying in ruins, but this trip promised to be different. It was a lovely winter day, and Nurith's husband, Amos, came along, making it something like a family outing. For once we also had a guide: Nurith knew the place and wouldn't lead us into another blind scramble. Walking downhill, we breathed air that was cool and fresh after a recent downpour. We needed to be careful not to slip and slide, but now we were on soft wet grass, not dry earth and loose gravel.

At the bottom of the hill we found the remains of Qalunya: a few skeletal buildings and some rusting pieces of agricultural machinery—whether Jewish or Palestinian was hard to say. What was unexpected had to do with Amos, not the place.

Amos was now over eighty, leaning on a cane and walking with difficulty. We had to go slowly so that he could keep up with us. But in 1947 and into 1948, until he joined the Hagana, Amos had been an active member of the radical Lehi (Stern Gang) militia, defined by its actions as "terrorist," although it could equally claim the "anti-colonial freedom fighters" label. Bridges were blown up and British soldiers killed randomly at close range. There was no hesitation about answering the call to "Fire and Blood." On September 17, 1948, Lehi men assassinated the United Nations peace negotiator, Count Folke Bernadotte, changing what could have been a different course of history.

Nurith had already told me that Amos was among those who attacked Deir Yassin in '48. What I did not realize as we started walking toward Qalunia was that he was suffering from dementia.

None of us spoke on our way downhill, but once we reached Qalunia's derelict houses, memories of that horrific assault crowded in on Amos. Nurith accompanied Deborah, who had gone off to photograph the remains of these houses, leaving me with Amos. He paused and, leaning on his cane, was urgently trying to tell me something. Starting and restarting, his speech was slurred and incoherent, though occasional phrases, words, and names tumbled out as we walked: "... the shooting ... Deir Yassin ... at the gate ... the sounds of ... I was left ... Deir Yassin ... They entered ... He carried me ... Deir Yassin ... The sounds ..."

All I could do was listen, nodding to suggest that I was getting it, if only slivers of an elusive story. It's always painful to face the fragility of human speech—the inability to say, to *quite* say, what's on one's mind. But it was harder yet to see Amos, one of the most brilliant men of his generation, fall apart that way. A well-known journalist, author, artist, and public intellectual, he'd been there during the attack on Deir Yassin, wounded during battle. Where, when, and how he was wounded is unclear. Perhaps it was early on at the gate, as he often claimed. Perhaps it was inside the village, as he once or twice conceded to Nurith. Perhaps an hour or so into the battle, but perhaps earlier. Perhaps he really didn't see anything. Perhaps he really couldn't remember.

I later read Nurith's book *Unrepentant: Four Chapters in the Life of Amos Kenan*, which includes lengthy exerpts from her interviews with him. In them Nurith is persistent, Amos intractable, increasingly irritable, even hostile: "I don't remember ... I don't know ... don't remember ... didn't see ... not exactly ... apparently," and again "don't remember." Then, as Nurith's questions close in on whether he killed a Palestinian woman, "No! I don't remember something—that is a weapon—in my hand," he says, "and I'm getting fed up with this interview ... I didn't remember that I shot a woman, I didn't remember. But apparently I shot, apparently it was at a woman."

It's impossible to be clear about what Amos did at the time or said about it later, and that's probably how he wanted it, dementia or not. "With him one can never tell what is or isn't true," Nurith writes in this biography, quoting Amos's old friend, Mika. It's a story wrapped in contradictions and crazed with blind alleys, recorded before he retreated into dementia and made more confused by the time he was trying to tell me about it. The Amos we see in Nurith's book has always been elusive, even as a child. Garbled memory, I now think, is a good way to hide.

On the way back to Tel Aviv I told Deborah about my conversation with Amos, and she explained that she'd stayed away on purpose: she could see that Amos was struggling to tell me something and wanted to give him a chance to do so in Hebrew.

"It's so sad," I said, thinking also about Aloni's film. "Amos carries memories that refuse to vaporize."

We fell silent, letting the Judean hills disappear behind us as we descended into the coastal plane. It was a thick smog-like silence, where my conversation with Amos refused to dissipate. And then another memory insinuated itself, of strolling along Tel Aviv's beachfront with Nurith on that earlier afternoon, when she first told me about the mental hospital. She had just mentioned work on the book that would become Amos's biography, *Unrepentant*. The sky was a sheet of smoggy grayness weighing down on the salty-sweaty beach air and the swirling smells of fast foods. Was it this oppressive air that had prompted her to talk about what became of the '48 generation?

"It's not easy to write about these men once the war was over," she said as we walked south, toward Jaffa's massive cliff rising darkly above the bay. "A whole generation gone."

Surprised, I stopped to stare at her. Until that moment it had never occurred to me to wonder about our demobilized fighters. Tousle-haired, tanned and cocky, with kaffiyeh scarves draped around their necks, they seemed forever rakish, young. By the time I'd reached high school, a cease-fire had been signed, the sandbag walls had come down, immigrants were being settled, and we were singing new songs for the country we were building: a song for the tomato, another for a cucumber, a song for the water sprinkler, and songs encouraging our youth—us—to settle the Negev.

It never occurred to me that, for the '48 generation, a void would have opened once the cease-fire agreement was signed in 1949, as if a trap door suddenly dropped from under their boots. All that energy and willpower, the tensing of the body to attack and to survive, the wounded and dead who had to be carried on stretchers or on backs if not abandoned, the rattle of a jeep speeding over rocks, the rat-tat-tat-tat of a machine gun, the adrenaline rush, the long treks—I never thought about what it might mean to have it all suddenly end, and with it one's sense of belonging to a purpose larger than one's self, to the history that saw us become a nation.

Amos was of that generation. For several years he retreated to Paris. Back in Tel Aviv, he'd pass hours in company with his old comrades, veterans of '48, drinking at their regular table at Café Kassit, the room dense with smoke, noise, and misogyny. With their thickening bodies, raspy cigarette voices, and eyes bleary from alcohol, they were no longer our cocky "sons." Café Kassit was their haven, the home where they would reminisce for hours, imagining themselves the young men they used to be.

I thought of those Kassit days as Deborah and I drove back to Tel Aviv, and then I thought of the Amos I saw when we left Qalunia. The climb uphill was not easy. Our shoes got little traction on the rain-slicked grass, and Amos had to pause every so often to catch his breath. Leaning on his cane, he kept returning to his story of Deir Yassin, expelled in bits and pieces and yet struggling to be heard: "The rush … the shooting … they run … apparently it was a woman."

14. South, to the Negev

Other than a four-day hike toward Masada, the Negev was, to me, just an empty desert to be crossed on the way to the Red Sea resort of Eilat. But in 2008 two small black-and-white photographs, among many displayed at Zochrot's gallery, brought back to me in a flash of memories of another trip into the Negev. Grainy and indistinct, these photographs would not have caught my attention were it not for their caption.

"Falluja!" I gasped, the word echoing in the empty room. Embarrassed, I quickly looked around: nobody there but Deborah and me. We'd been inching our way slowly, bending over the display cases to scrutinize the small photographs and read the typed comments. Curated by Ariella Azoulay and titled *From Palestine to Israel, A Photographic Record of Destruction and State Formation, 1947–1950* (now a book), the exhibit was a collection of seemingly banal black-and-white photographs, often just snapshots taken in haste, tracing Israel's taking possession of the land during the years that came before and continued for a short while after the fighting.

Deborah was unimpressed. "Falluja" didn't mean anything to her, and the photograph had nothing of interest in it, just three Arab men walking in a muddy field. But this photo and another identified as "Falluja, 1949," showing a donkey in an empty courtyard, spoke to me.

The lone donkey shook me—a metaphor for the people who owned and cared for it, now gone, probably expelled toward Gaza, transported on lorries if they were lucky. But it was especially the photo of the men that intrigued me. Its overcast skies and the rain-drenched land stirred tactile memories of the dreary winter morning in 1949 when I, eleven years old, was taken south to see the Negev, shortly after the IDF captured al-Falluja.

All I knew of what was happening in this arid area, originally designated "Arab" by the United Nations' 1947 partition plan (allocating separate territories to Israel and Palestine), was that there was fighting. I'd occasionally hear a place or a commander's name, ours or theirs, but understood nothing. I did know that the "Arabs" rejected the partition plan and attacked us as soon as the state was proclaimed, but I did not know who those "Arabs" were or that the British allowed Egypt, its client state at the time, to invade the "Arab" Negev. Looking ahead to an easy conquest, Egypt's King Farouk issued a large ten-piasters postage stamp dated 1948, showing his army marching toward Gaza and Tel Aviv. Though the supposed two-week-long war turned out to be a terrible trouncing of the over-confident and under-prepared Egyptians, the fight to dislodge them was bitter, its effects in view as we traveled south that rainy morning.

With the Egyptian fighters gone and Israel high on victory, my uncle organized a trip to the battlefields of the Negev—a conquerors' trip.

Early in the morning of our expedition I found myself sitting on a clammy metal bench welded to the floor of a "Tender"—a British World War II army truck. It was still misty when my uncle, my two cousins, my father and me, accompanied by soldiers—all the men armed—climbed into the open back of the Tender in the pre-dawn darkness, still half-asleep,

Somehow we had gotten permission to enter this still-dangerous battle zone, at the time strictly closed to civilians. The sheer bravado of doing so was exhilarating, as was the adrenaline rush of knowing that we—that is, our "heroes"—were the winners. In my imagination I was one of the soldiers, a fighter no longer coddled by the safety of Tel Aviv. Of course we civilians were instructed to do exactly as told: no straying! My father, gripping his rifle awkwardly and dressed in his long city raincoat, was not cut out for the role. He did not have an anorak, let alone a combatant's khaki "battledress" jacket, and, unlike my uncle, he was not one to joke or slap other men on the back in hearty male fellowship. A sweet, gentle man, nothing like those sun-kissed "sons" who were the poster boys of our War of Independence.

The trip must have been more dangerous than I appreciated, maybe even reckless. There could be land mines, the officer in charge warned us. We could be attacked by Bedouins. There were "infiltrators" roaming the country, Palestinians trying to return to their homes. Still, the thought of danger never occurred to me as I sat in the rattling back of our pickup truck. Five years later, in 1954, eleven Israelis would die in a Bedouin ambush at the Negev's "Scorpion Pass," but that was later. On that morning I simply loved the feeling of the wet wind lashing at my face, the lurching under me, the strain in my hands gripping the metal handrail whenever the Tender bounced or swerved.

I had never been so close to a battlefield. The air raids we had sat through in Tel Aviv so recently didn't count, and the bullet casings I collected in the fields near our home were just toys for us children. Now, in the open space of the Negev, I felt older and stronger, almost a fighter already. There was a feeling of swagger about entering a restricted military zone. We were victors surveying our newly conquered lands, barely cleansed of the enemy. I imagined myself ready to face them as our fighters took possession of the land.

It must have rained hard the previous night. The road ahead was slick, the asphalt shining with puddles. Except for al-Falluja, Iraq al-Manshiya, and Iraq Sueidan, known for heavy fighting, the Palestinian villages we passed will remain forever nameless to me, empty and falling apart. Wherever I looked that day, deserted villages were caving in. Built of clay, not stone, their low-lying houses were literally dissolving into the waterlogged earth, with young grass already sprouting on the shapeless brown mud they were becoming.

Here there was no need for dynamite; nature was doing its work. The scene looked faintly encouraging, as the grass on the rain-soaked ruins had the fresh brightness that, for a few weeks before the heat sets in, enlivens this land. Sitting in the speeding Tender, I stared, rapt, at the decaying houses, so different from the sharp-angled, white-plastered concrete of the charted city grid that was my world. To me, the people who were gone from these villages were just shadows, certainly not any Fatma or Ahmed or Yameela I might have met.

The photograph that caught my attention at Zochrot's gallery made these strangers real. Taken by David Eldan for the Government Press Office, it showed three Palestinians: a slightly bent old man leaning on a cane accompanied by two younger men, perhaps sons or family members. Four other men are farther back, all walking toward the photographer. The day is very much like the one I remember from almost sixty years earlier. Visibility is bad. Other than stones and a few houses barely outlined against the distant horizon, there is little to be seen in the flat muddy field where these men are walking. Puddles glisten in the foreground, water gathering in tread marks gouged into the waterlogged earth.

Bending over Zochrot's glass cases, I thought back to that wintry morning when our Tender rushed past fields that seemed an extension of the fields I already knew back home. Plowed ahead of the winter rains, this rich earth would turn into clods of mud with the first rains, but come summer it would crust and crack. The same mud sticking to one's shoes near my Tel Aviv home, the same puddles, and then, in a few months, the same crevices gaping in the hardened surface. It's a land I knew well.

While the memory triggered by al-Falluja's mud was visceral, the main force of this exhibit lay in the note that accompanied it, eloquent in its terse restraint. It reported that Eldan took the picture two days after the Egyptian garrison had evacuated al-Falluja, and that, with the women sent away, the men were being summoned by the IDF for identification:

> One of the elderly men ... greeted the journalist who that
> day accompanied the Israeli forces entering al-Falluja ...
> saying '*Markhaba*' ["welcome" in Arabic]. When the jour-
> nalist asked him why he had stayed, the old man replied
> that this is his home, and though it had been destroyed
> he has many Jewish friends and he's sure that nothing will
> happen to him. After a brief period of military rule, he and
> the rest of the inhabitants will be evacuated.

This man's certainty that his Jewish friends wouldn't let anything happen to him haunts me. By the time I read this, I already knew that old man would be irrevocably betrayed, I already knew how treacherously fragile such friendships proved to be.

The archive Azoulay curated for this exhibition is not melodramatic. Its photos of abandoned homes, Palestinians about to be exiled, the Jewish immigrants who'll replace them, and Israeli sappers posing with dark smoke billowing behind them are all familiar, even banal. The exhibit asks us to note dates, locations, and facts, and yet I find myself worrying about the three men in the photograph, looking dignified in their long white *thobe* shirts and dark abaya cloaks that reach down to their ankles. Did they put on their better clothes for this mini-census taken by the conquering authorities? Should they be walking in such a muddy field?

On that day of 1949, the mists evaporated and the air cleared as we drove farther south. The slick paved roads gave way to unpaved ones where loose bits of dry gravel crunched under our spinning tires. Everything seemed to be covered with dust—the rutted plateau spreading before us, our khaki-colored vehicle, and our own clothes, skin, and hair. We were now in an unfamiliar, parched territory so different from the newly paved roads, irrigated fields, and noisy construction sites near my home. To me the Negev was just an uncharted South where Bedouins roamed with their sheep and camels. It never occurred to me that there would be settled Arab villages in that desert, villages like the ones I saw that morning, melting in the rain.

This sense of the Negev's emptiness changed after the war, once the national call to populate the desert turned it into a mystique. "Go down to the Negev, *ya shabbab*" ("young lions" in Arabic), urged a lively popular song. But in 1949, I could not have anticipated the Negev's soon-to-be future, with its development towns and irrigation and atomic reactor.

There, as our Tender rushed forward, everything we saw was new to me, including places whose names I had only vaguely heard mentioned on news broadcasts. Kis Falluja, Iraq al-Manshiyya, and Iraq Sueidan suddenly were actual villages, their houses already disintegrating, scoured by desert winds. Years later I'd learn that four thousand invading Egyptian troops were besieged by the IDF in this enclave. (*Kis* means "pocket" in Hebrew.) The Egyptian troops were stranded there for four months, released only once the armistice was signed.

For fifty years I barely gave Falluja a thought, not until Azoulay's exhibition brought the disintegrating village back into memory. The rain had obviously stopped by the time Eldan was snapping his photographs. Gazing at his image of the men walking in the muddy field, I remembered the damp chill of a similar day, decades earlier, when I was there, and wondered, what became of a donkey seen in another photograph, standing tethered in an abandoned courtyard. Did it die of thirst or hunger? Did it become a target for shooting practice, like the donkey in S. Yizhar's extraordinary novella, *Khirbet Khizeh*?

Now, as I write, the villages meld into one in my memory, indistinguishable in their ruination. The one place that remains distinct is the former British police station of Iraq Sueidan, "the Monster on the Hill" as the British called it. This massive, dun-colored construction was one in a string of British-built Tegart forts dating back to the Arab Revolt (1936–1939), named for their designer, Sir Charles Tegart. Erected to control major routes along the spine of the country and the Syrian-Lebanese border, they are still recognizable for their distinct architecture and color. I had passed the one near the Jerusalem highway, facing the Latroun monastery, countless times and seen others too. The design was nearly uniform: massive concrete hulks enclosing large courtyards with forbidding towers rising at strategic points. Like other Tegart forts, Iraq Sueidan's is perched on a slight rise, a daunting citadel seen against a bare landscape.

Looming ahead, this impervious fort inspired awe, its massive wings extending to the left and right of a bulky central tower scarred by bullets. Drawing near, I was stunned at the sight of these bullet holes pockmarking the building, clustered by its windows. I sensed that a furious battle must have raged here. I had never seen so many bullet holes, not even in a photograph.

Our guide described the battle of Iraq Sueidan, much as he had done in al-Falluja and Iraq al-Manshiya. He talked about troop positions and movements, weapons and reinforcement, assaults and retreats and renewed assaults, pointing. The men listened intently. We girls stood by patiently, quiet and a bit bored. It would be years before I'd learn that the departing British handed this fort over to the Egyptian forces that invaded the Negev, despite the fact that the United Nations had allocated that territory to the Palestinians, not Egypt. The IDF stormed the fort eight times before the Egyptians surrendered—a crucial victory for Israel. "It took eight failed attempts!" our guide said, emphatically. "And aerial bombardment too!"

To judge by their attentive listening, the men clustered around him found it a riveting story, told so close to the actual fighting. Standing in front of the bullet-ridden fort, they were each called upon to imagine himself a soldier. The story had become theirs, and, though I hadn't realized it at the time, it was becoming mine too, seducing all of us with its myth of heroism.

Perhaps it was the desert itself, with its dry sediments of dusty sandstone, that made for the somber mood that descended on me as I stared at that massive, bullet-riddled Tegart fort. My early-morning bravado was gone. Just a few hours earlier, on the Tender's metal seat, I imagined myself in one of the Negev's famed Samson's Foxes combat units, speeding, carefree in an open jeep, my imaginary checkered kaffiyeh headscarf billowing in the wind. Now, remembering those bullet holes, I think about the violence we call "heroic" and the ideals of selfless sacrifice it entails. We Israeli Jews saw no other choice.

No Choice, (*Ein Breira* in Hebrew), is the title of a propaganda film made in 1949, the year we went to the Negev. This thirty-minute film trailed me for years, its images vivid even now. In it, a young man, lean, strong, blue-eyed and light of hair—the iconic Sabra of our collective imagination—sacrifices his life for the sake of the many. Rushing under fire toward an enemy fort, he lobs the hand grenade that ensures Israeli victory. Lying on the ground, his wavy hair gently blowing in the wind, his last words are, "There's no choice."

Though I remembered the film vividly, even to its final close-up on the dying youth's face tilted toward the camera, a faint smile on his lips, when I reviewed this film years later, I discovered that my memory was wrong. Although the theme of a youth's dying under enemy fire was unchanged, the film's landscape is a rocky hill, not the Negev's dry flatness, and the young protagonist is hardly a Sabra idol. Dark haired and not particularly fit, he is part of a group of newly arrived European immigrants, implicitly Holocaust survivors, still wearing their rumpled European clothes. Attacked on their way to their new settlement, they find shelter behind some rocks. When an airplane drops a package of food and ammunition, this young man ventures to retrieve it and, fatally wounded, manages to drag it back to the shelter. He utters his dying words: "There is no choice," smiling to see the food he has rescued.

Both versions make the same point: there is no choice. A melodious song of the '48 war, "In the Plains of the Negev," often broadcast during and after the '48 war, echoes this theme. In it, a tall youth comforts a bereaved mother. She has many "sons," he tells her, all of them "a steel bulwark against our enemies." Such loss is not in vain. "If you will it, comrades," the song concludes, echoing Herzl's famous Zionist adage, "it is not a fable." It's a message that my generation rehearsed every time we sang about Trumpeldor, recited Alterman's "The Silver Platter," and swore allegiance to the military we'd soon join.

It began at a tender age, this adulation of heroism. There was the song for little "Dane'leh," urging him to eat his "banana'leh" so that he'll grow up to be "a hero in Israel," and about the heroic bee, Zum-Zum, who stung an enemy in defense of her hive and, so, sacrificed her life to save her "people." Gift packets sent to our troops by the civilian Committee for the Soldier included children's hand-drawn pictures and notes. "Dear Soldier, I hope you'll be brave and die for our country," a note might say, decorated with smudgy flowers, guns, tanks, and occasional stick figures.

It is no accident that my own wishful imagination extracted this film from its Holocaust shadows to endow it with the glow of Ashkenzi Sabra heroism. Even the footage is brighter in my imaginary film, luminous, almost blessed. The earth I still misremember in the final close-up on the youth's dying face is the Negev's: flat, bleached, and sandy. Seeing the film at the cusp of adolescence, maybe a mere few weeks or months after I'd stood staring at the bullet-ridden tower of Iraq Sueidan, I shaped it to fit the clichés that inspired my generation. While the actual film trembled with the still-raw scars of the Holocaust, my imagination was responding to the call on my generation to ready ourselves for the fighting ahead.

None of this occurred to me at Zochrot as I scrutinized the archival materials in Azoulay's exhibition. It was the image of dignified Palestinian men walking in the mud that claimed me, and the abandoned donkey. There must have been many donkeys, I now think. They used to be a common farm animal, a taken-for-granted presence in my childhood collage, alongside the chicken and camel and an iconic pioneer.

What a young girl happened to see in the Negev, on a chilly wintry day in 1949, couldn't have been much. We girls were too young to follow a lecture about troop movements and weaponry. Much of the time I must have stared blankly at the scenes we passed by. And yet something obviously remained, a seed that would take decades to germinate. Strangely, it happened not in Israel but at the eastern border of Turkish Armenia, in the summer of 1987, as I sat at the foot of an ancient Urartian castle rising above some fields outside the shabby border town of Van, waiting for my husband and son to return from exploring the castle. It was just a field, where flatness kept giving way to low earthen mounds, with a couple of abandoned mosques incongruously standing amid this desolation.

"Old Van," my guidebook called that utterly uninhabited area. The Armenian genocide, I suddenly gasped. The mounds that gave the field something of a washboard effect had been houses, I realized, when another image superimposed itself on this landscape: Palestinian mud houses melting under torrential rains, grass growing on their roofs. The path leading from Van to the Negev is long and indirect, and yet it took me just an instant to traverse it.

By the time Deborah and I had seen Azoulay's exhibition, much had changed in the Negev, and much is still changing. Fields still turn muddy during the rainy season, but the adobe houses I had seen collapsing in 1949 are long gone. There are new roads, new or expanded cities, towns, and kibbutzim, and newly irrigated fields where even thirsty cotton can now flourish on desalinated water. Iraq Sueidan's Tegart fort is now the Givati Brigade Museum, while the town of Kiryat Gat and several other kibbutzim and settlements sprawl over Falluja's lands. It is all too easy to see this as upholding the Zionist dream: "If you only will it …" as Herzl said. Seen against the Negev's rugged stretches of arid land, its irrigated ribbons of green offer a vivid example of Israel's "making the desert bloom."

But hidden from view is an ongoing, slow Nakba—the violent dispossession of Israel's Bedouin citizens from their ancestral pastoral lands, ongoing as I write these words. The soft Negev earth and the rocky hills nearby swallow this history. What little is still standing of Palestinian life—the rare mosque or shrine for example—is hidden from view. The image of houses collapsing in the rain won't leave my "mental map," as Benvenisti called it—a palimpsest of brittle memories, among them the image of three Palestinian men walking in a muddy field and another of a lone donkey standing patiently in a bare courtyard.

PART III: SOUNDINGS

Longing is an ache that does not long to ache.
It is the aching stirred by pure air coming from a distant mountaintop,
the ache of searching for a past happiness.
Longing ... reminds us that we are afflicted with hope.
—Mahmoud Darwish

And the translators translate pain to another kind of pain,
remembering to forgetting, forgetting to remembering,
curse to blessing and blessing to curse.
—Yehuda Amichai

Bir'im: little more than a front remains.

15. Bab el-Wad

I was there during the war of '48, and in a sense I wasn't. So much of what I knew was oblique: a bullet-pocked wall, distant gunshots, snippets of adult conversations—and Yaffa Yarkoni's disembodied voice, singing "Bab el-Wad." Heard often during that war and for decades later, it commemorates the youths who died keeping the road to Jerusalem open. Broadcast on the military radio station, Galei Tzahal, every Memorial Day, it was a "Taps" for the fallen, mourning the fighters of' '48.

Strong and devil-may-care in their rumpled khakis, these youths, all of them Sabras in our imagination, were our ideal. Turning plowshares into swords, they were our defense and our future. It's a myth that lingers, the image of a vulnerable Israel needing protection. I see it every time my American friend Betye says, "Ah, little Israel," crossing her arms protectively as if drawing a baby close to her breast.

"Oh, so you are a Sabra!" newly met Jews would beam at me in New York when I first arrived there as a young student in 1960. Stories would follow— about fundraising for the young state, about time spent on a kibbutz, about learning and forgetting one's Bar (rarely Bat) Mitzvah Hebrew. Women recall volunteering for Hadassah and Youth Aliyah or sending children to Zionist summer camps, and once in a while, when I first arrived, an octogenarian would still remember gunrunning for the Irgun. These conversations could happen anywhere, from a lunch counter to somebody's living room, including a chance encounter with a Jewish student I met in New York's City College cafeteria.

"What's that?" I asked, wondering about the curiously shaped button she wore in her lapel.

"Two banks to the Jordan, the Irgun insignia," she explained, dark eyes flashing.

I had never seen this insignia before: a strong gun-brandishing arm over a map of a "greater Israel" that includes Hashemite Jordan, with the slogan "*Rak Kach*" ("Only This Way") inscribed at the bottom.

American Jews usually expect me to beam back at them their admiration for the young nation and the Sabras they see as redeeming our tortured Jewish history. Nobody mentioned the Palestinians when I first arrived, and only "leftists" do so now. Rarely does anybody think of the Mizrahi Jews either, although some of them have lived in Palestine for generations. It's the virile, dynamic, Ashkenazi Sabras they think of, youths of European extraction, like me and like themselves.

"Actually no, I'm not literally a Sabra," I confess. My mother was born in Ottoman Palestine, I explain, and my father's family arrived in the early 1920s. I should have been a Sabra but I was born in New York City during my parents' one-year stay there. They returned to Palestine at the start of 1939, with me in a baby basket, soon to become a virtual Sabra. My not being a "real" Sabra used to feel vaguely shameful, as if I were claiming an unearned privilege. "No, I'm not a Sabra, not quite" I still find myself saying, though now ambivalently, seeing the ideal so badly tarnished and wondering what difference could two months make in a newborn's national filiation.

Deborah and I were leaving Tel Aviv's bustling Carmel Market when the subject came up. She had just eaten her first sabra fruit, bought off a pushcart's bed of ice, the thick thorny skin peeled off by a vendor wearing thick rubber gloves. "Not that great," she said. "Grainy, not really sweet."

By then, our third year in Israel, she already knew about the cactuses' significance in Palestinian life, but less about their mystique for Israelis. "For us the fruit is a metaphor," I explained. As the saying went, "Our Sabras are thorny on the outside but sweet on the inside." We Israelis were proud of the cocky toughness of our native-born. Under the Sabra rough, no-nonsense demeanor, we believe, beats a heart of gold, a Jewish heart, sensitive and tender.

Deborah's silent response was unmistakable: Heart of gold? Where did they get all those kaffieyhs?

This Sabra generation was our future, I wanted to explain. As we learned at school, God had the Israelites wandering in the desert for forty years—a whole generation—to prevent the "desert generation," tainted by slavery, from entering the Promised Land. Like them, the native-born Sabras were to cleanse the nation of its diasporic abjection. For years I believed it axiomatically, never pausing to wonder about all those people around me who had foreign accents, many of them parents of Sabras. What about my immigrant schoolteachers, or Leah the greengrocer, or my dentist, Dr. Emmodi? Were they to be shunned as the "desert generation"?

Neither the refugees who streamed into Israel shortly after the war nor some of my friends and classmates were literally Sabras. Many who were drafted with me into the army in 1956 weren't either. The word "Sabra" captured an Ashkenazi ideal, not reality. I think of Mazal sitting out air raids in our corridor, Aryeh from Libya, Yehudit escaping Iraq's Farhud pogrom, Leah surviving the Holocaust in a Romanian village, Miri arriving as a rescued orphan, and even me: none of us were Sabras. There were too many of us who did not fit the image, and many who fit the label but not the image. As for me, a willing student, I accepted the allegory of the abject "desert generation" and its vigorous Sabra counterpart without question. I'd line up with my classmates in our matching holiday clothes, ready for our full-throated singing of "Shirat Hanoar":

> The song of youth, the song of our future,
> A song of renewal, rebuilding and aliyah …
> As long as we have such youth in our homeland,
> The prophecy of Israel is being revived.

Though the message was clear, drawing my generation into the euphoria of utopian nation-building, two films reflect on that song with harsh irony. Each has a children's chorus sing "The Song of Youth" much as we did, dressed in uniforms like ours. Singing with gusto, the children are too young to question what they're singing, though the adult film viewer may. In Gila Almagor's fictionalized autobiography, *The Summer of Aviya*, a harshly conformist Israeli society makes it impossible for the young protagonist, daughter of a traumatized Holocaust survivor, to integrate into Sabra expectations. Elia Suleiman's bitterly ironic film, *The Time That Remains*, also obliquely autobiographical, shows Palestinian school children singing this song with similar gusto, celebrating the very Israeli renewal that brought the Nakba to their own people.

There was no way our Sabra ideal could become available to the non-Jewish native-born of the land, urban or rural: the Muslims and Druze, the Christians and Circassians and Bedouins, including myriad groups within and beyond them, all considered "Arab" by us Israelis. In time, the Palestinians' icon would become the child Handala, often stenciled as graffiti: a tattered ten-year-old refugee, barefoot, with "the hair of a hedgehog," as his creator, Naji Al-Ali, put it. He stands with his hands clasped behind his turned back, symbolizing the plight of the Palestinians. In the early days of statehood, Handala's Israeli counterpart was the Sabra "Uzi" of *Haaretz*, and then "Srulik" in the *Jerusalem Post*: a cheeky kid wearing shorts, sandals, and the cloth *kova tembel* (idiot hat) that was our national symbol, who needles the nation. Unlike Handala, Uzi and Srulik didn't last; Israel was not ready for irreverence.

The Sabras we adored had to be heroes, epitomized by those who fought in '48 to break the siege on Jerusalem. Their dead are kept present in memorials strung along a short segment of Highway 1, the well-traveled road to Jerusalem, with all the over-determined meanings its name carries. Leaving the coastal plain, Highway 1 begins its climb toward Jerusalem, curving here to enter a majestic forested ravine, for centuries known in Arabic as Bab el-Wad ("The Gateway to the Ravine," *Sha'ar Hagai* in Hebrew).

It is an awesome scene, this final climb, at once somber and inspiring, a route I've traversed countless times. What had been a bone-rattling two-day journey in a covered *diligence* wagon in Ottoman times became the arduous collective taxi rides I knew as a child, with sweaty grownup bodies crushing me on both sides as the car swerved around steep curves, stopping every so often to cool the engine or let me throw up by the roadside.

Nowadays it's barely a fifty-minute drive on a smooth four-lane highway—an easy trip that, in our fourth year in Israel, I suggested to Deborah we do by bus. The view is better from high up, I explained, especially on the left. "Try to grab a seat up front," I whispered, standing behind her, my hands on her shoulders, elbows akimbo to protect us from the crush of people surging forward the moment the bus door opened with its pneumatic sigh.

I was looking forward to seeing yet again the forested hills that follow the road, rising steeply on both sides of the Bab el-Wad ravine, and I was not disappointed. Unlike the JNF's thick blankets of uniform pines planted with dogged regularity, the forest felt natural here: spare, unevenly spaced, and varied in age and species. Wispy pines were rising irregularly out of the crumbly red earth, interspersed with slim ink-black cypresses. Though they are not noticeable from a passing car or bus, I already knew that pale cyclamens would be peeking from under rocks after the first rains and that, come February, clouds of white almond blossoms would appear, veiling patches of the rocky hillside. And then, as winter turned to spring, the mimosas would bloom farther downhill, their branches heavy with yellow fuzz balls releasing their dusty perfume into the air.

There's a feeling of time standing still along this stretch of road, since the steeply rising hills that form this ravine discourage building. Other than the paved road being wider than in my childhood, not much seemed to have changed. The Ottoman *khan* ("caravansaray," way station*)* still stood at the entrance to the road, the remains of an old British police station still lingered a bit farther on, and the forest seemed unchanged. Yet I knew this section of road too well not to register the small markings of its history, and it was my chance to tell Deborah more about it.

The old khan, for one thing, had finally been repaired. Built by the Ottoman government in 1869 to serve a growing influx of Europeans, it was run by a Palestinian family and hosted Muslim, Christian, and Jewish travelers: pilgrims, tourists, dignitaries, and ordinary folk, all jostling between Jaffa and Jerusalem on a stony, bruising road, stopping at the khan for tea and sometimes a bed. My grandmother would buttonhole anyone who'd half-listen as she described that two-day trip by *diligence* and the overnight stopover at the khan. Abandoned in '48, it stood derelict for decades, ignored as an "Arab" building, weeds growing out of its crevasses. Its restoration involved a political fight about its naming: should it be named for the right-wing nationalist politician Rehavam Ze'evi, who had nothing to do with the place in '48, or the Palmach Har'el Brigade that actually fought there?

Of all of Israel's battles, the fighting that took place in Bab el-Wad had become a symbol of heroism and sacrifice for which credit must be earned.

What marks that history in particular, visible to all who travel this road, are the burnt and rusting vehicle skeletons that line the roadside.

Deborah had already noticed these abandoned vehicles on a previous trip to Jerusalem. Lying at the roadside just beyond the abandoned khan, to her they were junk, the remains of accidents that ought to have been cleared away. I remember being upset at this casual assumption. Couldn't she see that these weren't ordinary wrecks?

"What's wrong?" she asked, touching my arm.

"Later," I said, too upset to talk, half turning my back to her. "Some other time."

The vehicles she called "junk" were meant to be sacred memorials. Damaged in the '48 fighting, they had been driven by Palmach youths—young women as well as men—to help the Jewish population of besieged Jerusalem, my grandmother among them. Charred, rusting, and riddled with bullet holes, these old armored busses and assorted 1940s trucks couldn't possibly pass for present-day vehicles. I still crane my neck to see them on this stretch of road, mourning the youths who died in or near these rusting hulks.

On this bus trip to Jerusalem—Deborah's and my last, as it turned out—there was a new look in her eyes as she joined me in craning to look at these vehicles and then looked back at me. Insight, I sensed, relieved. What was left of an old battered lorry, its driver's cabinet twisted on its side like a broken neck, was fast disappearing behind us. Deborah understands, I thought, feeling a new kind of closeness, patting her hand by way of a thank-you.

What about others, I wondered, turning to look at our fellow bus passengers: people reading the morning papers, chatting with their neighbors, or catching up on lost sleep. One woman was knitting; another was trying to keep two boisterous children from running up and down the aisle. Three young soldiers sprawled in the back, their semi-automatic rifles resting against the backs of their neighbors' seats. One man was fingering a worn prayer book, his lips moving silently as he read; another had his laptop open, fingers tapping. Most looked like Israeli Jews, but nobody turned to look at those relics of '48 as we barreled past them. Perhaps these rusting vehicles were too familiar by now, certainly not part of the more immediate worries about violence in the Occupied Territories, the economy, or yet another government crisis.

I turned toward Deborah to tell her more about those rusting wrecks from '48 and the heroism of their drivers and escorts. She listened as it all came flooding out in a rush: the siege on Jerusalem; the convoys struggling to deliver food and ammunition to the besieged Jewish population; the improvised roadblocks and ambushes the convoys faced from nearby Palestinian villages; and, down below, the narrow road curving along the Bab el-Wad ravine that had been the convoys' death trap.

Deborah nodded. There was much we could have said, but we didn't: about how the Palestinians who attacked the convoys, coming from the neighboring villages, might have felt about the fight for Jerusalem, and about the death of their revered commander, Abd al-Qadir al-Husayni, at the battle of al-Qastal, just a little farther up the road. And before that, about what they thought of the growing intrusion of Jews into their homeland, including the regional Arab aspirations for national independence, buffeted as they were by the winds of imperialist self-interest. The Ottomans' defeat, and the Arab Revolt of 1916, the Anglo-French partitions and state-creations that followed, the anti-colonial war in Syria and Lebanon in the 1920s, and the local Palestinian uprisings of 1929 and 1936: all ricocheted through the narrow ravine of Bab el-Wad, alongside the pogroms and the Holocaust.

I wonder now about Deborah's and my silence about the Palestinians. In 2008, as our bus accelerated uphill beyond Bab el-Wad, toward al-Qastal and Jerusalem, past Qalunia and Deir Yassin, I still knew little of that history and Deborah probably knew even less. I was mainly steeped in my own Zionist history at the time, myopic and self-interested, even as I was beginning to realize that there was a larger story to be told. The Israeli mystique of Bab el-wad was still too powerful for me to relinquish. It never occurred to me to wonder what the Palestinians—the "other side," the people who attacked us and whom we dismissed as "gangs"—might have known or felt about us. It took years of self-education for me to loosen the hold of this mystique. To this day I still have a catch in my throat when I hear Yaffa Yarkoni sing about these youths.

In archival photographs you can see the Israeli "convoy escorts," as we called them, a young woman sometimes among them, standing casually near vehicles then still intact. Some photos show the Arab positions that overlooked this narrow passage, including a photo of a barricade made of boulders and stones lined across an empty road to prevent the convoys from passing.

There are also photos of our convoys preparing for yet another attempt to break the siege on Jerusalem, their vehicles lined up: lorries, buses, Tenders, and an occasional makeshift ambulance, all supposedly armored, though the "armor" was just two layers of tin sheeting and plywood welded onto ordinary vehicles, with small peepholes cut at eye level.

S. Yizhar's novella *Midnight Convoy*, written ten years after the war, is a painstaking account of a few hours in the life of such a convoy. It describes the glacially slow, meticulous preparation for the upcoming night's journey, increasingly tense as the hours crawl by. Time edges forward with an excruciating mix of inaction and danger, including a young man's chat with a female driver—she seated inside the camouflaged truck's cabin, him standing nearby—as he feels the awakening tremor of what could be, and may never become, love.

Yizhar's convoy ends up having to turn back, its mission aborted. We know that the same journey will be attempted again the following evening, with young men and women setting out yet again as darkness descends.

The skeletal wrecks lying by this now widened and repaved highway are just a few of the ones that couldn't complete the journey in '48. Shelled, scorched, and twisted, they lay by the roadside for years, barely out of the way of passing traffic, their bullet holes and burn marks clearly visible on their dented and rusting metal. But as the rust spread and the road needed widening, they were spray-painted and moved further up the road, each time less recognizable. No wonder that by the time Deborah had seen them she didn't understand what they were. An American friend who had lived in a nearby kibbutz and traveled this road often didn't either.

"So this is your 'Silver Platter,'" I suddenly heard Deborah say.

I nodded silently, letting the view rush by our window, humming to myself the song "Bab el-Wad," letting Haim Gouri's lyrics emerge clearly through the melody I cherished in Yaffa Yarkoni's voice:

Bab el-Wad,
Remember our names for all time.
Where convoys to the city broke through
Our dead lie sprawled by the roadside.
The iron skeleton, like my comrade, is mute.

Guri, himself a Palmachnik, animates these vehicles. They become one with the fighters, mute corpses sprawling by the roadside, like his dead comrades.

"Bab el-Wad" remains the most often heard song of the '48 war, a song that insists on remembering the heroism of sacrifice. I knew it mostly as sung by Yaffa Yarkoni during that war and for years afterward.

"Did you hear what happened to Yaffa Yarkoni?" my mother asked me in 2002. I'd barely arrived from the airport.

Mom's clear blue eyes had a look I knew well, hinting at something faintly improper, her voice already knowing that what she was about to tell would please me, her co-conspirator.

"She finally did it! She criticized the government and the soldiers' behavior in the Occupied Territories."

"And…?" I said, sinking into a nearby chair, not knowing what to say.

"In a program ushering the Day of Remembrance, in an interview on the IDF radio. She compared our treatment of the Palestinians to what was done to us in the Holocaust. It was quoted in all the newspapers: 'How can we, who suffered so much, be capable of doing these things?'"

I was shocked. It took a lot of courage to come out that way. For years Yarkoni was Israel's most popular singer, awarded the prestigious Israel Prize, her singing honored in the IDF archives. Her rendition of "Bab el-Wad" was the definitive one. Heard over and over, her timbre, her cadences, her consonants and syllables and emphases taught the nation to honor its fighters and revere its fallen. More than any other song of the '48 war, and there were many, her "Bab el-Wad" spoke for all of us, voicing the *yishuv*'s love, admiration, and gratitude for the young people who died in that war and, by extension, in all our wars. Sung and broadcast countless times, including annually on Israel's Day of Remembrance, her rendition stood for much more than the fighting that had taken place in a certain ravine. Clad in fatigues, she'd sing for soldiers at the front. Herself a Sabra and a war widow (her husband fought in Italy with the Jewish Brigade in World War II), her iconic "Bab el-Wad" helped shape the emotional contours of Israel's myth of becoming.

Yarkoni was just turning eighty when she spoke out and, predictably, uproar followed. A special gala to celebrate her career was canceled. Tickets were returned. Hate mail streamed in. The decades of adulation were wiped out.

When Mom welcomed me home with that news, in 2002, it was still three years before Deborah's first visit to Israel, four years before we'd start searching for signs of the Nakba, and five years before I'd hum for Deborah a song about mangled vehicles she'd thought were just junk. Ten years later, when Yarkoni died in 2012, I wrote an op-ed about her that was published in the New England weekly *The Jewish Advocate*. It was a love letter and an obit of sorts, where I shared my awe and sadness about the dreams and realities that Yarkoni's singing kept alive, and about her courage in questioning what had become of them. One reader promptly wrote an angry letter to the editor, objecting to my calling her act courageous. Most obituaries about Yarkoni never mentioned that IDF radio interview.

16. Soldier Girl

The clerk sitting at New York's City College Registrar's desk must have thought he wasn't hearing correctly when he heard a woman's voice asking for a veteran's exemption from physical education. Lifting his eyes from the lists in front of him, he saw bobbed hair, a full-skirted dress cinched at the waist, and a heavy three-ring folder clutched to a chest—a typical coed, as female college students used to be called. It was 1961, and everybody else on the veterans' pre-registration line was male. The young woman was me. Half rising, the clerk searched the crowded room for his supervisor while I waited, amused.

With no supervisor in sight, the clerk let me off, but to this day I still see Americans light up with curiosity if I mention my military service. It provokes a newly assessing glance at my body, perhaps some fantasy of the younger me, helmeted, dashing up a hill, rifle in hand. "Ah, a girl soldier!" people think, bemused, looking me over. Questions follow, reasonable though strangely off the mark. "Were you in combat? Did you ever shoot somebody? What did you do there?"

"Oh, nothing much, just office work" I still say, "like many female soldiers." In a sense, it was true. I did spend most of my time at a desk. Sometimes, very rarely, I confess that I used to be in Intelligence, though I never go beyond that. "I danced the dance of seven veils," I joke. "Mata Hari stuff," I sometimes add, ditching the questions that are sure to follow.

My listeners' prurient fantasy of gun-wielding young women in uniform, breasts straining the buttons of their khaki shirts, has little bearing on the gritty reality of my two years in the army and even less on my preceding four years in the Gadna youth brigades that began in the summer of 1952, somewhere between Acre and Lebanon, a rite of passage of sorts. Elementary school seniors, we were about to graduate when I volunteered to attend a summer boot camp for Gadna squad commanders—clamored, in fact, as selection was stringent and I was not initially chosen. Not quite tough enough, our homeroom teacher judged, and she wasn't altogether wrong.

I was determined to prove my Sabra toughness, and two months at a Gadna camp were my opportunity. Words like "arduous" and "stringent" hardly describe the training. Two girls left within a week, using bee stings as their excuse. We, the remaining fourteen-year-old boys and girls, spent eight scorching summer weeks in pup tents pitched on coastal dunes, not a tree in sight. A corrugated tin shed provided shower privacy: boys on one side, girls on the other, with much giggling about seeing and being seen. The only two solid structures near us were a long concrete platform—the *rampa* (rampart) that served as our parade ground, and a fetid, fly-infested "Turkish" latrine. The *rampa* and latrine were all that remained of an old coastal railroad station on the way to Lebanon, one of several defunct Ottoman and British railroad lines crisscrossing the region.

In the course of our training, we trudged for hours through the sand under the weight of heavy backpacks, crawled under barbed wire, and leapt from high up into springy piles of thorns too dense to break skin. The sea was always in sight, always beckoning, and strictly forbidden. The obstacle course was the worst, though everything was worst, including the endless parade practice. And there were punishments, too: for a loose bootlace, for a badly packed backpack, for a body rising too high when crawling, or for just lagging behind.

"Run three times around the camp perimeter! Full gear! Helmet too!"

"Turn back! Start crawling again. No, all the way back!"

"Unpack and repack your gear ten times! Bring it to me for inspection each time. No. Not now! During rest time!"

I accepted it all with clenched-jaw anger. *I'll show them*, I told myself, defiant, but I knew our trainers were right: every slip could risk lives. My feet and nose blistered and my socks shredded to ribbons inside my ill-fitting boots. The air was sticky with salty humidity, so our hair resembled matted straw, and our food was gritty with sand. Running and marching in full gear, winded but singing, proud of our stalwart endurance, none of us gave up. The '48 war was not yet history in 1952. The need to be ready for combat—all of us, girls as well as boys—went unquestioned. In our imagination we were all Palmachniks, singing the Palmach anthem as we marched: "Though the storm rages all around us…We are always ready, we, we the Palmach."

There was a formal cease-fire agreement but no sense that the war was over. We trained with weapons, even if without live ammunition. Crawling meant lifting one's body on elbows and knees just a fraction of an inch while edging forward, scraping knees and elbows and straining to keep one's gun above ground. We learned to advance to a hilltop undetected, hurl dud hand grenades, and find our way back to camp in the thick of night, each of us silent and alone. I remember one afternoon when we practiced a stealthy approach to an imaginary sentry, left arm gripping his chest from behind, right leg wrapped around his legs to immobilize him, right hand holding a knife to his throat.

At the end of August, as I got off the bus in Tel Aviv's central bus station, my legs were more tanned and muscular than ever. Hefting my heavy backpack, I tromped home, proud to hear those ill-fitting boots pound the city pavement. I was still just fourteen but no longer a child.

Changed and changing, I was entering adolescence, even if the Gadna camp suppressed that awareness. Among my friends, breasts began to show. Getting a lift on a boy's bicycle bar with his tanned arms circling you, was charged. We were feeling our way into a terrain that went beyond war. There were also catcalls and dirty jokes, "girlie" magazines on newsstands, and used condoms lying under bushes in public parks—all a prelude to a kind of unsettling knowledge I couldn't yet name. Ignore it, I told myself, forcing the uneasy shock to dissolve into silence when I chanced on a photo of a barely clothed female soldier in *Ha'olam Hazeh* magazine.

Years later I'd remember that feeling when I'd catch an American male smirk about my having been a "soldier girl," but during my Gadna years I was oblivious. As a squad commander, I merely led my classmates on drills and hikes. "Yes, Commander, Sir," some boy might quip, jumping to fake attention. and we'd laugh. Of course I wasn't "sir." I was just assigned certain responsibilities that we saw as non-gendered. The IDF was still a "people's army" in the early 1950s, egalitarian. One wintry week my entire class was sent to help a kibbutz with its potato harvest. For six days, morning to dusk, we'd crouch in the muddy furrows of a place whose name I no longer remember, digging for potatoes. Every so often I'd start a song and the group would join in. Nobody resented this non-military assignment.

I returned home from that potato field with pneumonia, but apparently a letter to my parents followed, citing me for leadership. Years later, when my mother mentioned the letter, I was surprised. Leadership? All I remember is my snot-soaked handkerchief and my bare hands digging for row after row of dirt-encrusted lumps. How come, I wondered, reading the commander's letter? Maybe it was the singing. Nothing special about that. We all felt that we were helping to build the nation's future.

That feeling receded once I was drafted into the army. Basic training was easier than it was in the Gadna camp, but the spirit was different. The fledgling soldiers I met in basic training—women only—were not necessarily eager to be there. Warfare had changed, and the purpose of training women was changing too—no longer about combat readiness but about disciplined obedience.

On the morning I presented myself at the induction center, I didn't know that we were yet again at war. As it happened, I was inducted in October 1956, just as Israel, France, and Britain launched a coordinated campaign to recapture the Suez Canal, recently nationalized by Egypt's charismatic, pro-Soviet President, Gamal Abdel Nasser. It turned out to be a spectacular military victory, but a political disaster for the allies, who were forced to obey the United States' orders to return the captured canal to Egypt. (Twenty-five years later Israel would yield the Sinai Peninsula as well, keeping only the crowded, desperate, and volatile Gaza Strip, often called "the largest open-air prison in the world.")

I arrived at that camp alone, separated from my classmates by a slightly different date of birth, a stranger among two unfamiliar groups of draftees: Mizrahi immigrant women edging uncertainly into Israeli life and a small contingent of Ashkenazi Sabra kibbutz women, tough and dauntless. We made for a sorry lot of eighteen-year- old girl-women in ill-fitting uniforms, lonely and anxious about the new life ahead, many away from home for the first time. In addition to the usual marching and drilling and running and crawling and care of gear, there was also target practice and the disassembling, cleaning, and reassembling of guns. Some women recoiled in tears when ordered to shoot at a target.

We all felt the gender isolation sharply, though in different ways. The kibbutz women had grown up as equal with their male contemporaries, and I, too, had trained with boys and led them in the Gadna without regard to gender. For the Mizrahi women, almost all from observant, patriarchal homes, our all-female world must have felt at once liberating and unfamiliar. Some had not completed high school, and many had never spent an evening sitting around a campfire or hiking, let alone climbed up to Masada. Our commanders, barely a year or two older than us, were all female. Other than maintenance men, cooks, and drivers, there wasn't a man in sight. On the rare occasions when we'd sight male recruits jogging single file some distance away, we'd go into frenzied waving. "Look! Men! There are *men* in the world!"

But it wasn't only our all-female world that became so acutely noticeable in basic training. It was also our ethnicity and social class. Our histories, our jokes, even our inherited traumas as Jews were not the same, and certainly not our social class. The spectral Holocaust still belonged to the Ashkenazim in those days, while poverty and repudiation were the lot of the Mizrahim. To me and to our commanders, the kibbutzniks were the true Sabras, the golden youth who kept the Palmach tradition alive. Most of these young women hoped to be combat soldiers, for which the Gadna prepared me too. But these Sabra recruits also taught me another lesson: act tough and talk back. They never refused an order; if anything, they'd carry it out faster and better than others. But in subtly rebellious ways—a defiant chin lifted, sun-bleached hair tossed back, or a joking retort let drop in harsh, gravelly voice—their behavior spoke of a grit that made our commanders' eyes light up, a grit I quickly learned to make my own.

Sadly, this display of strength was a luxury available only to those who saw it as their birthright and only in the illusory world of an all-women training camp. As we were being discharged, another truth emerged. Assembled in the drab shed that had been dormitory for some twenty of us, each new private was given her new posting. A select few kibbutzniks were picked for specialized courses, but not one of them was given the combat duty she'd expected. Most were assigned to boring secretarial work while a disproportionate number of the Mizrahi women were assigned to the much-disliked military police. By 1956 the claims of gender equality were clearly fraying, let alone the pretense of ethnic equality touted by the song "Hinei Ma Tov."

I was lucky. On that last day of futile arguments, tears, and barely suppressed fury, I already knew that I had a plum assignment because I'd studied Arabic. It was the injustice to the others that shocked me, shredding our already tattered myths of gender equality and the ingathering of exiles. Israel's socialist ethos had always been fragile. Diaries left by kibbutz women, written in the 1920s and 1930s, already describe women being shunted into undervalued gendered labor (kitchen, laundry, and children), even at the height of our socialist idealism. In the cities, this division, including the ethnic hierarchies I'd imbibed at a young age, had always been the norm.

By the time I completed basic training, it was clear that the military, too, diminished people by gender and ethnicity. Disrespect was everywhere, naturalized into jokes about useless female soldiers knitting at their desks. It was a stereotype that left little room for thinking about what we young women actually did or felt or could have done. Our job was to support the "real" soldiers, the men whose manhood and worth were defined by combat and rank. There were thousands of us available to be bossed by the men we assisted, and within Israel's constant state of war-readiness, masculine authority reigned supreme.

I never faced harassment during my two years in the IDF. My own camp was too small, tight-knit, and collaborative to allow for abuse. Here we called officers by their first names and saluted them only in formal situations. Benny, an older career officer, would sometimes give one or another of us "kids" a ride home on his motorbike, and Dov would treat us to a special grilled pita bread he'd bring from his neighborhood bakery. But this companionable ease was exceptional. During basic training, when insult and humiliation are the way the newly drafted are reduced to obedience, bodily fluids and menstrual cramps were used to shame the weak, the dawdlers, and the downcast: "Don't run as if you have a sanitary pad between your legs!" I heard barked at a laggard, male or female, drawing self-congratulatory snickers from those who escaped the insult. "Stand up! You aren't menstruating!" I heard shouted at those who forgot to stand at attention.

I never heard anyone object, and I didn't either. This disgust with women's bodies—with *my* body—was just a manner of speaking, I reasoned, letting the insult ease its way into the twilight of numbed awareness.

The crude power play of gender receded at the camp that became my home, or so it seemed. I remember those two years as almost familial, our group bound by a companionable sharing of work and matched abilities. We shared housekeeping and invented our own slang and jokes. When not at work or assigned guard duty in a stifling, mosquito-infested guard box, we'd play classical music on an old record player, pilfer carrots from a nearby field, and crank up the player-piano that stood in a derelict Palestinian house nearby. On balmy Fridays, as evening descended and the country slowed down for the Sabbath, we'd gather for a sing-along, eager to hear Sami's velvety voice croon the Platters' latest hits, "Only You" and "The Great Pretender."

It was during the Iraqi coup of 1958, when King Faisal II and several others were executed in Bagdad, that a minor incident exposed the lie behind our myth of communal ease. That revolution had our camp on high alert, working around the clock, giddy with fatigue, barely sustained by coffee. Only after several such days and sleepless nights was I finally given permission to go home for a few hours. At 2 AM I managed to hitch a ride, the only passenger in the open back of a pickup truck heading for Tel Aviv. The driver, however, insisted on leaving me on a deserted highway when an easy short detour would have brought me closer to home. He was adamant. No regret, no explanation. Just a curt "no."

In my frustration, I punched his cab's door. There goes my precious furlough, I thought as I started my trek home. My parting word was "schmuck," a fairly ordinary expletive in our Sabra lingo.

The camp was abuzz when I returned. The driver had filed a complaint. "Did you hear what Linda did? Linda, of all people!" The accused: an exemplary soldier. The crime: insubordination to a higher-ranking soldier. The claimant: a young man with a few more months in service than the accused, rewarded with one extra stripe sewn onto his khaki sleeve. The three officers at the court marshal, two men flanking a woman sitting at a trestle table, could barely keep straight faces. My sentence: a "severe reprimand."

For years I was amused to remember this incident, much as the tribunal was at the time, though in reality it wasn't trivial. The issue was not that some young man pulled rank and I was rude in return. The ribbons showing on our sleeves merely counted the number of months we'd had served: three ribbons for him, two for me. But charted across that terrain were privileges that neither of us was ready or perhaps even able to name. This young man was Mizrahi while I was Ashkenazi; he was just a lowly driver, not even a combat fighter, while I was doing the camp's privileged intelligence work; my home was in affluent north Tel Aviv while he was heading home to the then impoverished, un-gentrified Jaffa. And all of it was entangled in the fact that he was male and I female. Except for gender, the cards were stacked against him from the moment he and I were born.

None of this was mentioned during the court-martial. In the eyes of the law, our gender, ethnicity, and social class were beside the point. Israel still had a liberal socialist government in the '50s, and we were all supposedly equal in the army. Yet this young man's animosity towards me, a total stranger who never harmed him, had sources that never got voiced. Who knows what history marked his own family's transition into Israel. Did he even finish high school? How come he was just a driver, rather than a member of one of Israel's hallowed combat units? Once discharged, would he become one of those male drivers who'd lean out of his car window to shout at women drivers, "Lady, back to the kitchen"? Would he even have such a job?

In the years following my military service, women were coming out with stories of rape, groping, and insults. Though neither I nor anyone I knew experienced it, basic training had already taught me that women were devalued. "Weren't you afraid to be dropped off that way, in the dark, all alone, on some empty road?" my American friends would ask. I understand their concern, but see this incident differently. I was not afraid to walk home, just tired. For his part, the driver, too, must have been tired. But consciously or not, he may have also resented my privilege. What matters to me in this story is not the abandonment of a young woman on a dark but safe road but how the driver and others like him might feel about what that young woman represented. The damage to me was trivial; the damage to him was not.

To this day I feel nostalgia for the two years I spent in that small camp where I lived and worked closely with people whom I might have never known otherwise. I still feel fondness for our sing-alongs, the jokes and horseplay we invented, and the geranium cuttings I'd planted in the camp's sandy soil. Remembering Benny and Rika and Dov and Aryeh, I smile to think that we didn't need to sing "Hinei Ma Tov" to feel that we could be brothers together.

It could have been, but it wasn't, not quite. Differences across family origins and wealth on top of gender were challenging Israel's socialist claims and none of us was free of them. These differences were inscribed in skin color, in the shape of a body, and in voices and accents and behaviors even when we all wore the same uniform.

Seen this way, the 1959 riots of North African immigrants in Haifa's Wadi Salib, barely a year after I was discharged, should have been expected. Disrespected and shunted to the margins of Israeli society, theirs was the outrage that erupts when there's nothing to lose. Israel's Black Panther party emerged out of this rioting in 1971, exposing ethnic and economic tensions that still shape Israeli politics. The choice of Black Panthers as the party's name testifies to a clear sense of where its members stood in relation to the country's Ashkenazi elite, and a clear understanding of their affinity with global unrest, way beyond Israel's borders.

17. We, the Palmach

When my old school friend Amira phoned to suggest taking Deborah and me to see the Palmach Museum, I found myself balking. "You absolutely must visit this museum," she said, her voice insistent at the other end of the line. "You'll see. It really gives you a sense of those days. I can keep on going there over and again."

There was no need to explain "those days." She meant the '48 war and the short years leading up to it, when the Palmach shone in our collective imagination in all its glory. Its name an acronym for *Plugot Mahatz* ("Strike Forces"), the Palmach had been the most celebrated militia within the Haganah from 1941 until its much-protested disbanding in 1949. Closely aligned with Labor Zionism and the kibbutz movement, its young men and women represented the soul of the country, the idealistic, tight-knit force needed to dislodge the British and protect the *yishuv*. Once the war of '48 began, they proved to be our bravest and most dedicated fighters. The command I heard in Amira's voice went beyond an ordinary wish for an outing with a friend. Visiting this museum was to be a pilgrimage.

The Palmachniks were etched in my memory: resolute and self-confident young men and women, their swagger buoyant, their stride sure. They were our cherished youths, Sabras in spirit and often by birth, the ones who fought at Bab el-Wad, the ones who made the dream of a state come true. Their insignia was two ears of wheat with a sword placed diagonally across them, so different from the IZL, the right-wing Irgun's arm brandishing a gun across the combined territories of Mandatory Palestine and Transjordan, with "only this way" written below.

Yet by the time Amira called, in 2007, Israel was no longer bravely small. It was occupying the West Bank, Gaza, and the Golan with fierce determination and was known to have one of the world's best-trained armies. By then Deborah and I had seen and read too much to be starry-eyed.

Amira was never one to yield easily. Both her brilliance and her education in the Zionist Far Left put the rest of us Tel Aviv high school youths to shame. I can still see her in class, her blue youth-movement shirt outlined against our classroom's smudged plate glass window as she'd stand up to answer a teacher's question. Holding onto the desk with her left hand, she'd speak with her right palm cupped and circling forward as if to midwife her flooding thoughts, including mysterious words like "dialectica" or "conyunktura."

"We've already seen the awful IZL museum," I told Amira, remembering a boring display of memorabilia, photographs, and documents displayed in what remained of a lovely Palestinian mansion right on the beach, in what used to be Jaffa's Manshiya neighborhood.

"Yes, OK, OK. Manshiya leveled and so on. But that was IZL. The Palmach was different. I'm getting tickets," Amira said and hung up.

"My biggest disappointment," she told me as we stood in line to retrieve our tickets, "is that the Palmach was disbanded before I was old enough to join it.

A photo I found on the internet, taken in 1949, shows the Palmach's third battalion gathered in Safed just before its dissolution, a striking number of women among them. One young man is playing the accordion, head tilted back toward the crowd, leading them in a song. Another holds a crutch. Many are still in uniform.

"They were so much what I wanted to become," Amira sighed.

Me too, I thought. Her words awoke in me yet again the tug of the identification that had engulfed the *yishuv* so powerfully, ingrained in us by stories, photos, posters, and songs. It wasn't only her stubborn insistence on visiting the museum that overpowered me; it was also my own nostalgia.

Just a few years older than we were, the Palmach was our "people's army," leading Israel into its redemptive future as a proud and independent nation, home and refuge to the Jewish New Man. We, the youth of our fledgling country, all wanted to be part of this tightly knit group of comrades who labored on kibbutz lands in daytime, trained for combat at night, but also, when all was quiet, would roast potatoes in the embers of a small campfire, singing wistful songs that still bore traces of Russian melodies. The repertoire was immense, and we knew it all by heart: Yemenite trills, Hassidic melodies, songs about Cossacks galloping along the Dnieper River, Spanish Loyalists fighting the fascists, and newly minted Hebrew songs that occasionally included some Arabic words. *Ya halili, ya 'amali,* we'd sing, loving the sound, not bothering about the meaning.

The mystique was powerful. When I allow myself, I can still imagine that I'm inhaling the billowing dust trailing behind a speeding jeep, powdery in the dry summer air, fragrant after a short spurt of winter rain. As I think of it now, writing on a brilliant but cold winter day in Boston, I can see how, for Amira and even for the more conflicted me, visiting the Palmach Museum was an opportunity to reclaim, however fleetingly, a dream.

The Palmach Museum sits at the heart of secular Israel, near Tel Aviv University, the Yitzhak Rabin Center, the Diaspora Museum, and several other public and educational institutions that define Israel's progress. Facing the street, its towering hunk of gray stone suggests an impermeable fort quite different from the IZL museum's boast of conquest. Visitors are unlikely to register that this museum and its nearby institutions rest on the lands of the former Palestinian village of Sheikh Muwanis, the village of the Palestinian Mr. Beidas who, before '48, used to visit my uncle.

Tourists gather by language groups in a lobby dug below street level, where the very descent into the cavernous dim lobby anticipates the Palmach's "underground" activity during the British Mandate. Young IDF soldiers guide each group through a serpentine, pitch-black tunnel that seems dug into earth and rock. It is an unsteady journey, wrapping you in total darkness. Your feet shuffle on the uneven ground, while your hands feel their way through the narrow passageway. A shoulder brushes against something that feels like a rock; the ground underfoot feels rough, slightly rocky. Enveloped in darkness, you feel as if you, too, are on a mission.

Relief is palpable when the tunnel finally widens to reveal a lit diorama, and then another dark tunnel and another as you are led unsteadily from one diorama to the next. By then you get used to the dark claustrophobia and learn to trust your feet, already anticipating the next diorama. You move in hushed anticipation, knowing that each diorama is a glimpse into the daily life of our Palmachniks.

In each diorama, set in the dim monochrome of forests and tents, the diorama's life-size mannequins come alive as we hear their recorded conversations, now and then softened with familiar songs. "Hokey," Deborah whispers in my ear and I shush her. For all the obvious artifice, the vignettes draw me in. The mannequins are boys and girls conversing in easy friendship in their tents. They could have been Amira, or me. They are still so young, yet unswerving in their commitment, training in some nameless grove, sitting around a campfire, joking about a comrade falling in love, or preparing for a night's assault.

Pausing at one diorama and then the next, we learn their stories. There is news from home, perhaps a letter a youth might share—housing problems, a birthday, food shortages. This sandy-haired guy is a kibbutznik; the tall, gangly one lost his entire family in the Holocaust. There's a yeshiva student, a sixteen-year-old youth who'd lied about his age in order to join the Palmach, and a Yemenite girl who broke with tradition to join. It's the story of sweet, modest, and down-to-earth youths bearing dreams and tragedies beyond their years. The British are still in Palestine in this story, and the outside world surrounding them is dark. "Though a storm rages all around/We are not afraid" is piped in—the opening words of the Palmach's anthem, sung in unison. The people in these dioramas are still training, not yet fighting the Arabs, not anticipating the Nakba. Joining them is the call of the hour. *Ein breira*, the dioramas say. There is no other way.

As we left the dim make-believe of the last diorama, heading for the museum's high-ceilinged lobby, I could feel that old yen to have been part of the Palmach. Even in the twenty-first century, when dioramas are becoming outmoded, it was hard to resist the sentimental claims this crude simulation of our dreams has on our loyalties. But as those who fought in the Palmach, or Hagana, or IZL also know, there is more to this history than sweetness and selfless sacrifice, and this is where Amira and I may part ways.

This museum is a sham, I barely restrained myself from saying as we headed for the door marked "EXIT." "Didn't they ever shoot a gun?" I was angry at the display but even angrier at myself for the nostalgia I allowed myself to feel. There was nothing said about fighting—about forced expulsions, terrorized civilians, or massacres. It was all about courage, comradeship, and service to the nation.

"Linda, what are you talking about," Amira might have said in response. "The Palmach was under strict orders to fight ethically! The principle of *tohar haneshek* ("purity of the weapon") was etched in them."

"But, Amira," I would have answered, "there is no such thing as ethical fighting, ever! And it's known that there were massacres—"

"Those are stories," she might have cut me off. "In the *Hashomer Hatzair* youth movement, we were for a socialist binational state and had the ethics of fighting drilled into us. Anyway," she added, "the museum is about the Palmach's early days, before the fighting actually began."

Had this imaginary conversation actually happened, it would have flared in no time into a blazing argument that would have gone nowhere. Instead, as we exited the museum into the blinding daylight, I fell silent. When Deborah whispered again, "This museum was so hokey," I shrugged, hoping that Amira was out of earshot. I wondered whether Deborah could even begin to imagine the mix of yearning and guilt that swirled in me about the Palmach's ideals, tainted as they were in bloodshed.

Silence is the issue, I thought, remembering Yulie Cohen's documentary film *My Land Zion*, where she interviews her parents, both Palmach veterans, about atrocities. "There was nothing of the sort," her mother says categorically. When Cohen's father tries to demur, his wife silences him in mid-sentence. The prologue to this aborted conversation is a sequence taken at a Palmach reunion, where aging veterans—men and women mostly in their seventies—sing a wistful song of that era. In their singing I hear a yearning for peace, the sweetness of nostalgia, and the silencing of truth, leaving me awash in sadness for my own naïve trust in our goodness. The future did not match up.

There was much I didn't say as the three of us stood outside the museum's back exit. Still entangled in my own feelings, I needed to gather my thoughts, to sort out the said from the unsaid, the myths from the realities as I had come to know them. Yet as I stood there stalling, I noticed another low stucco building nearby, still within the museum grounds, too ordinary to call attention to itself. A small sign identified it as the Palmach Archives. The door was open, welcoming.

Maybe the others felt the need for a buffer zone too. Nobody spoke as we turned toward the open door. A young female soldier in dress uniform, an attendant doing her regular service, was the only other person in sight when we entered the large warehouse-like room. Rows of long tables filled the space, holding large photo albums, each more than three feet wide, open for perusal. The small black-and-white photos mounted on the albums' heavyweight paper were generic snapshots of individuals or groups, snapped when somebody happened to have a camera. Over and again, in one album or another, you'd see young men, hair tousled, khakis worn carelessly, this one wearing the familiar cloth *kova tembel* (fool's) hat, that one a *kova gerev* (a knitted "sock") hat. Every so often there would be a woman among them, perhaps wearing an Arab kaffiyeh. In one photo, Palmach women in shorts line up in a mock chorus line, showing off their legs; in another, men pose with a machine gun. There were large group photos where men stand, tanned, handsome, and cocky, their arms draped on each other's shoulders, crowding to fit into the picture.

It was boring, finally, to leaf through these albums. The photos begin to look alike. The names hand-inked below each photograph mean nothing to strangers. For me the archive was just an impersonal storehouse, a resource for researchers, and a supplier of nostalgia for family members and comrades.

And so, bored, I embarked on a small research project of my own: find the women amid this male camaraderie.

"Oh my god!" I suddenly heard myself say in English, forgetting that Amira was with us. "Here is Arna," I call to Deborah. The Arna seen in this group snapshot was just a female soldier standing among her buddies.

Deborah knew who Arna Mer was. We had both seen the film *Arna's Children* in Boston. But I was not ready to tell Amira about her, not with the archive attendant nearby. Arna was too controversial.

"Yes, it's Arna," the young attendant said, coming toward us. Though she had been standing some distance away, my exclamation must have echoed in the cavernous space.

"We have another photograph of Arna hanging in the museum's lobby," she said, also in English, for the tourist among us. "Enlarged. It shows Arna helping an old Palestinian man. We want people to know that the Palmach cared about the Arabs. That it treated them well."

Don't say anything, my eyes told Deborah. Clearly, the attendant knew nothing about what became of Arna. Maybe those in charge didn't know either, and maybe they did.

I remembered the black-and-white wall-mounted photo only vaguely: a young woman crouching as she offers something (water? biscuits?) to a thin old Arab man sitting on the ground. I seemed to remember legs in shorts and a kaffiyeh. Whoever that woman might have been, her kindness to a frail Palestinian man was shown to confirm the Palmach's ethics of combat.

By the time we visited this museum, I had forgotten about Arna's Palmach days, but once I noticed her in the album it all came back in a rush. I had initially learned about her a year earlier when her son, Juliano Mer-Khamis, brought his documentary *Arna's Children* for a screening at my Boston campus. It was late January of 2006, and the news had just broken that Hamas had won the elections in Gaza. That victory was too sudden for any of us, including Juliano, to know what to make of it. It felt strange to watch this film at that moment of uncertainty, and yet in retrospect, this documentary has much to say about both the history it reflects and the history that was to follow.

Arna's Children tells the story of the Jenin refugee camp's drama workshops and the child actors who participated in them. Founded and directed by her with her son Juliano, the theater offered the children the space to channel the camp's trauma of daily violence. Its second part, however, chronicles the derailing of the children's lives. Filmed as Juliano revisits the camp after the IDF's 2002 assault on it, it shows some of the "children" now holed up as fighters, others already dead. Among the survivors is Zakaria Zubeidi, who made news in 2021 for a daring prison break. In the opening shots of the film, Arna is battling cancer. Her face is gaunt, a checkered kaffiyeh covers her chemo-bald head, yet she is still participating in a demonstration, still visiting the theater, still hugging the children. By the time of the film's release in 2004, Arna was dead.

After the screening, Juliano told us that when Arna died, no Jewish cemetery would accept her for burial. He had to take his mother's body home until they found a remote kibbutz in the Negev willing to offer her a resting place. Recoil at Arna's betrayal, as Israeli Jews saw it, ran deep. She was one of our own, a Sabra born to a Zionist family in Rosh Pina, one of the county's earliest pioneering settlements, and a member of the Palmach. How dare she cross over to the other side! Arna, it turned out, married a Palestinian she'd met in the Communist Party. In the film, when Juliano questions her about her time in the Palmach, she dismisses it much as Yuli Cohen's mother does in Cohen's documentary *My Land Zion*. "Ha! It was nothing," Arna says. "We just ran around in jeeps and made a lot of noise." Some things can't be admitted even by a woman who ended up devoting her life to the Palestinian children and mothers of Jenin's refugee camp.

No wonder I was shocked to find Arna's image included in the Palmach Archive. It was strange to see the tiny black-and-white photograph lined up among so many others. Arna, who seems to be larger than life in Juliano's film—large body, booming raspy voice, wrinkled face filling the screen in close-ups—is reduced in a photo album to a tiny, almost-featureless figure, one among many Palmachniks filling the outsize albums. It was as if Arna insinuated herself into this storehouse of mainstream Israeli history by stealth. It pleased me to think of her memorialized in an enlarged photo in the museum's lobby, even if passersby knew nothing about what became of her.

In 2014, while teaching a course at Tel Aviv University, I returned to the Palmach Museum, this time alone. Nothing much had changed. The mannequins were still engaged in the same conversations, though I couldn't find Arna's large photo in the lobby. Did I walk right by it or had it been removed? The archive, however, was utterly transformed: apparently everything had been digitized. The photo albums were gone, the large tables were gone, and the attendant, invisible, may have been sitting in the new glass booth. To see anything, you'd probably need to show identification, fill out forms, specify what or whom you are looking for, and why. The intimate contact with the heavy album paper that bore the names of these youths, identified by family, comrades, or themselves and painstakingly written under each photo, was no longer possible.

I couldn't see myself submitting an application to see what they had on Arna: "Arna?" the archive attendant would say, looking her up in the computer. She might see a danger-alert code next to Arna's name and peer at me suspiciously.

Back home, searching for Arna on the internet, I found two different narratives, each incomplete—the Zionist story of a Palmachnik from Rosh

Pina and the Palestinian story of the Jewish woman who founded the Jenin Freedom Theatre. Neither accounts for why or how these two lives were actually one. But one day, as I scrolled through Palmach photographs, I found the one missing from the lobby on my second visit to the museum. Yes! It really existed, I exclaimed to myself.

Here she was, her legs bare in her khaki shorts, a kaffiyeh draped around her neck, crouching to give something—even with the magnifying glass I couldn't quite tell what—to an old Palestinian man sitting on the ground. It was exactly as I remembered it. The one detail I did not remember, perhaps chose not to remember, is that Arna has a rifle slung over her shoulder.

Arna was long dead by the time Amira took me to see the Palmach Museum. Juliano was also dead, gunned down outside the Freedom Theatre in 2011. His masked assailant was never identified though suspicions swirled: an Israeli angered by his ties to Jenin's refugee camp? A Muslim abhorring his indifference to social and religious norms? Or a militant Palestinian, as the U.S. media put it? A year later, a Palestinian hip-hop group, DAM, released a single that commemorates his work in the theater and documents the outpouring of love seen at his funeral. Juliano's own film documents Jenin's love for his mother.

Though I return to Israel often, I can't bring myself to visit the Palmach Museum again. Too much remains unsaid in its account of the young men and women who were Israel's "silver platter" of Nathan Alterman's poem. Inspiring in its awed homage to these youths, the poem is also awash in the gloom of a descending night. In it, "the red eye of the sky [is] slowly dimming over smoking frontiers" as its two young heroes, male and female, battle-grimy and bone-weary, "fall at [the nation's] feet wrapped in shadows." "The rest," Alterman concludes, "is to be told in the chronicles of Israel." That "rest" has since come to include the Nakba, the '67 war, and the Occupation that followed. It's a history written across the lives of children who became fighters—in Jenin, in Gaza, in Sabra and Shatila, in Hebron, and more. They were all children, like Arna's.

The Palmachniks who live in my imagination continue to move me deeply. They were the best of us, we thought—the youths who fought the British, accompanied the convoys to Jerusalem, captured Iraq Sueidan, and saw combat throughout the land, "From Metula to the Negev," as the Palmach anthem puts it. Many of them Sabras just a few years older than me, they were the iconic sons and daughters of a nation being born. But they were also the soldiers of S. Yizhar's *Khirbet Khizeh*, whom we see waiting for orders to send an entire Palestinian village into exile.

Khirbet Khizeh's short scenes of the soldiers' idle waiting and the speedy expulsion of the villagers unfolds like a film script, and in 1978 Israeli film-maker Rami Cohen made a film of the book for Israeli television—a film that was summarily suppressed. Any of its shots could have made for a Palmach Museum diorama. One among them could have been of an old Palestinian, no longer able to walk, assisted by a young woman wearing a kaffiyeh, who has a gun slung over her shoulder.

18. Beach Days

Except for Acre, where my family used to eat at Abu Christo's fish restaurant and stroll along the old port, I mainly knew the Israeli coast as a sandy stretch of beaches. Haifa and smaller Jewish settlements did exist along the coastline, but to me, for a few years after '48, "coast" still meant beach balls, umbrellas, and children digging assiduously in the sand. Only after I became aware of the Nakba did another geography emerge from behind the scrim—a slow, lurching emergence that continues even now as I write, and will continue beyond it. One such lurch occurred in 2007, when Deborah and I visited the archaeological site of Caesarea.

"It's a magnificent site," I read aloud from the government's promotional materials. "Wave-lashed location … ancient Herodian port city … restored to create one of Israel's most attractive and fascinating archaeological sites…. Amazing ancient harbor ruins, beautiful beaches … Israeli tourism at its best." For once we'd set out without the usual guidebooks, maps, heavy tripod and camera bag, without even a lunch cooler crowded into the back of our dusty rental car. At least finding this "must-see destination" would be easy, we felt sure. The Ministry of Tourism would see to it.

Visitors were streaming toward the ticket booth by the time we'd parked our car and let ourselves be channeled along a newly paved walkway lined with colorful banners and gift shops nestled under vaulted ceilings. Tastefully selected wares beckoned from behind glass: exotic jewelry, ceramics, imitation antique metal and glassware, textile art for local visitors, menorahs and mezuzahs for American and European Jews. It was hard to resist these shops as we passed by.

When I finally did look up, I froze. "Oh, my!" I said, clutching Deborah's arm. A minaret, brightly lit by the morning sun, rose in front of us, towering above the stone buildings clustered below. I'd forgotten all about it.

For us, steeped in thinking about the Nakba, there was no denying the incongruity of this minaret and its adjacent mosque, stripped of their religious use and seemingly planted there like public art. In our eyes, the minaret loomed as a spectral witness to the Palestinian village that was here before the Nakba. For me it was also a shocking reminder that shortly after that war I had seen this very village and its mosque emptied of people and lying in ruins.

Perhaps it was the sensation of the humid air depositing a thin film of salt on my arms that brought back a rush of memories. Certainly it was the minaret. The vaulted gift shops, I have since realized, had been derelict village buildings when I last saw them, back in the early 1950s. The minaret had been the village's pumping heart—the tower the muezzin would climb five times a day to call believers to prayer. But now both the entry to the minaret and the doorway that opened into the muezzin's balcony had been sealed with concrete. Abandoned, the minaret stood purposeless, ignored by tourists intent on getting to the archaeological site.

"*Then*," I told Deborah, "right after the war, I climbed this minaret. More than once," I said, my voice trailing off as bits of memory tugged at me.

One memory wouldn't let go: a small black-and-white snapshot, now long gone, taken a year or two after the war. At the top is gangly me, in shorts and a white tank top, waving from the balcony.

I see my father now yet again, his hair ruffled by the breeze, standing in his dark bathing trunks way below me, near the mosque, still young, taking the picture. My spindly little sister is standing nearby as he aims the camera up toward me yet again. It was just an ordinary beach day, and a father amused by the feat his daughter had just accomplished. "Look at me, Dad," I may have called out, waving.

Though none of us made much of it at the time, it was unsafe to climb this minaret when my parents took us to that beach, where the abandoned village houses still gaped, empty and forbidding. Like many Ottoman village minarets in Palestine, this one is chunky as it rises above its mosque. An interior spiral staircase, windowless and narrow, opened up under a small cupola into the narrow balcony that still encircles the tower, where the muezzin would have climbed to chant his call to prayer, reminding the believers of Allah's greatness and merciful presence.

The spiral staircase was already crumbling when I ventured in, and the opening into the muezzin's balcony was so low that even as an eleven- or twelve-year-old I had to duck as I stepped over the threshold. I'd grope my way up the stone shaft in total darkness, each foot searching for the wider part of the next triangular step that clung to the central core.

While the climb was creepy, stepping out into a narrow muezzin's balcony took even more courage. I braved those steps more than once and it was scary every time, though emerging into the balcony never failed to exhilarate me. With the sea glistening behind and salty breezes easing the scorching heat, I was enthralled by vistas spreading far below. Clustered nearby was the abandoned village, looking peaceful as it lay empty of people at the rim of the bay, where sandy dunes edged the sea to the north and south as far as you could see. Further inland was a wide ribbon of green farmland sliced by a coastal road that shimmered in sunlight, and finally, demarcating the eastern horizon, the dun carob- and oak-dotted Carmel mountain range, indistinct in the hazy light.

When I look back at that young me, I wonder about her elation. Yes, I loved measuring my young body to the task and the burst of light that dispelled the darkness. But now that I have paused many times since to gaze at panoramas, I wonder whether this bird's-eye view might not also include, hidden in its folds, a sense of dominion—the raw power bestowed by heights—practiced in a child's game of King of the Mountain.

What is there about those vistas that spread below us, beyond beauty, awe, and geographic knowledge? Doesn't their allure lie, at least in part, in a sense of possession similar to what S. Yizhar's Israeli soldiers might have felt in surveying the Arab village they were about to capture, as he describes it in *Khirbat Khizah*? Yizhar's village, seen by these young men from above, seems minuscule, its people doll-like, its fields a distant patchwork carpet. There is, in their gaze, as it rests on the still populated village of 1948, admiration for the cultivated valley and its fertile availability. But there is also a coveting, a drive to possess, and already an inkling of incipient ownership. The land that stretched before us was available to be known, husbanded, and mastered.

I can't imagine that any of this was on my mind as I felt my way up the steps of that derelict minaret. In the 1950s people did not comment on abandoned villages and still rarely do. Many years would trickle by before I'd clutch Deborah's elbow when faced with this phantom mosque from my own distant past, still standing, irrevocably present.

Looking at that minaret, I could once again see my parents and sister settling into a day at the beach: a ground cloth spread out, picnic basket at hand, the tube of skin lotion opened, a beach ball being tossed. Now, welcoming Deborah and me, the same lazy waves were still lapping at the sand, the same salt-laden humidity frizzing my hair, and the same harsh sun burning its way into my skin. All the same and yet so different, as the churning of tourists around us reminded me.

I wonder what became of that photo my dad took, but what would finding an old snapshot accomplish? Would it be anything more than a shadowy effigy of an elusive truth? Isn't the standing minaret proof enough, visible as it is to anyone who cares to notice it, so incongruous amid the hubbub of tourism?

I remember vividly climbing that minaret. What I am less sure about and urgently want to recall is what that half-inch of a child, seen at such great distance, might have understood of those outings to a fishing village so recently vacated by its people. I invoke that image so that I might scrutinize the child who was and still is me, snapped by her father in an ordinary moment of parental bemusement. Scrutinize her? Yes, but also accept her into my being, as even at age eleven or twelve she already knew, or at least sensed, something of the place where she was standing. None of us knew at the time that the people expelled from Arab Qaysaria were actually Bosnians who'd settled in Palestine in 1884 in one of the Ottomans' many "transfers of population." For us they were just generic "Arabs."

It was not proof of the Nakba that rattled me that day in Caesarea as Deborah and I stood staring at the minaret. What struck me was the indifference of passers-by to this relic of a disastrous past—a past that is unseen even when it is in full view.

Neither my father taking that photograph nor the girl that was me could claim that we never noticed the minaret or the derelict buildings nearby. But what did such noticing mean? The word "Nakba" has only lately, and still barely, come into Hebrew use. Passersby hardly register the minarets that still stand in full view: in the park near Jaffa's old port, at the center of

Saffed's roundabout, or at Tiberius's waterfront promenade. Mosques can be disguised—as art galleries, museums, or as restaurants. Minarets are harder to assimilate. The challenge for passersby is whether to see them for what they are, or whether to notice them at all.

If anything, Caesarea's mosque and minaret—assuming they are allowed to remain—are likely to become even less noticeable now that ambitious new excavations are underway. The ancient port Deborah and I only saw submerged is now being excavated; the ancient city walls are being restored. I, however, still remember peering into the fire-blackened, cavernous storage spaces that are now gift shops, piled high after the war with unidentifiable refuse, smelling of smoke and decay.

In the early 1950s, when Israeli archaeology was preoccupied with biblical discoveries that aimed to prove our ancient Jewish presence on the land and thus, our "right" to reclaim it, a turn-around happened. Two imposing, toga-wearing statues, headless and nameless, were found half-buried in Caesarea's sands. Welcomed with great fanfare, they endowed the derelict village with cosmopolitan allure. New excavations unearthed Caesarea's Crusader fortifications, a Roman aqueduct, King Herod's palace, a large amphitheater, and a hippodrome. King Herod, whom we were taught at school to dismiss as a troubled puppet of Rome, an Edomite half-Jew and a "bad man," now became one of us.

The Herodian findings are billed prominently in Caesarea's tourist literature. His sprawling beachfront summer palace now stands as a lighthearted counterpart to his austere cliff-top winter palace in Masada that has become a symbol of Jewish heroism. Caesarea still retains some of that lightheartedness. Its hippodrome now houses equestrian acts in period costume, its cafés and restaurants are full, its beach lively with children at play, its boutiques busy, and crowds stream to the ancient amphitheater to attend musical events of international standing.

I happened to attend two in the early 1970s: one featuring the Preservation Hall Jazz Band, a New Orleans musical institution, the other featuring Mikis Theodorakis, the Greek composer and activist then in political exile from Greece. Thousands of mostly young people crowded the amphitheater's stone benches, holding our breath as the Preservation Hall Jazz Band's aged Black musicians walked onto the stage, the tiny lead singer leaning on a walker. The sound swept us away, and this happened in Theodorakis's concert too, where a large band and a powerful lead singer inspired the audience with rousing political songs of freedom and resistance.

In both concerts I gave myself over to the euphoria I shared with this audience of strangers. We had arrived at sunset, early enough to see the sky redden above the amphitheater's ancient open-air stage. As the star-lit darkness closed in on us we were all transported by the music, drawn closer to one another and to the millennia of history that felt alive in this place.

Now, years later, I wonder about that euphoria. It had something to do with the rhetoric of the occasion, I realize, and nostalgia too. We were all under the spell of Caesarea's ancient grandeur and endurance, and many of us were drawn to the communal aspirations to which this music spoke. The jazz musicians drew us into the vitality of Black America, and Theodorakis's music did likewise with its uncompromising rejection of tyranny, as the program notes made clear.

Mostly Sabra Israelis, mostly middle-class and of Ashkenazi descent, we were swept away by the alchemy of identification with the indomitable spirit that came through this music. Many of us grew up on songs of freedom and justice—Soviet, Yiddish, American, Spanish, and Hebrew. That music shaped our aspirations. We knew that Theodorakis, a former Communist and heir to the anti-fascist partisan spirit of World War II, had been a political prisoner and was now, even as he played in Caesarea, in political exile. His music spoke to our own history—to the fighters of the ghettos, to our underground's fight against the British, and to the socialism that inspired our early pioneers.

Yet for me at least, something has changed since then. The inspiration that suffused these evenings has given way to another realization: absent from our shared elation at ideals of freedom and justice were the Palestinians to whose situation that music spoke most urgently. The Nakba was within living memory, the '67 war less than a decade old; Caesarea's Palestinian ruins were still in plain view, as yet barely reclaimed for tourism. Not surprisingly, in 1982, Theodorakis, who had previously composed the acclaimed "The Ballad of Mauthausen" in response to the Holocaust, composed the PLO hymn at Yasser Arafat's invitation.

I don't know why or when the irony of these occasions—the audience present and the audience absent—struck me, though I know it happened before I met Deborah. I felt it again in 2007 as I looked at the tourists streaming past the old village mosque. It concerned oblivion. I was thinking of the child I used to be, climbing the minaret, gazing from its high balcony across lands that were becoming ours, giving no thought to the people whose home it used to be.

"A minaret?" I remember an American friend recalling her visit to Caesaria. "Was there a minaret? No, I didn't see any."

There was no minaret in Tantura when my family went there for a day at the beach, and no derelict buildings like the ones I saw in Caesarea. The Tantura I knew shortly after the '48 war was just a beach safe for children: pristine sand, shallow little bays, and sparkling wavelets lapping at a few flat rocks at the water's edge. When I suggested to Deborah that we go there—sometime after we saw Caesarea—it was to be as a short reprieve from our Nakba searches. "No Nakba," I said. "Just sea and sand."

The illusion should have dissipated the moment I noticed that the name "Tantura" was not on the map. Nagging at me were also foggy memories of ruins rimming Tantura's sand and, years later, a television program where a history student, Teddy Katz, was being questioned about a massacre he claimed to have discovered in the course of his research. I'd suppressed all of that. Though it stood to reason that the Nakba would not have spared the place, I still hoped for a pleasant vacation. The map showed "Dor" in Tantura's place, including a beach resort. We could stay there overnight, I told Deborah.

There is no direct access to Dor from the coastal highway. You need to detour to the old coast road and then take a narrow, badly marked access road that leads, after a few kilometers, into a parking lot where drifts of sand half-cover the dead grass that peeks through creviced hard ground. This access road was the same one my family had taken more than five decades earlier, then unpaved, the rutted earth crunching under our wheels. It was also the dusty road Tantura's refugees trudged along in the opposite direction, in May of 1948, mostly women and children, survivors of a brutal attack by the elite IDF unit, the Alexandroni Brigade.

Were you to take this road to Dor now, as Deborah and I did in 2007, you wouldn't have guessed that the bleak landscape you were crossing was once a village. All that was left were dun weedy mounds that turned green during the short rainy season—seemingly natural land formations. But a blurry black-and-white home movie, now lost, told a different story. Shot with my father's 8 mm camera, it showed the barely recognizable human form that was me, filmed in Tantura during the early 1950s or perhaps even earlier. Taken at a distance and transposed later onto video, the image became almost indecipherable. There are smudgy chunks in the lower part of the frame where a tiny figure seems to be clambering, silhouetted against a murky gray sky. The terrain is obviously uneven. Sometimes the girl bends to hold onto an invisible support, sometimes she's upright, her arms extended for balance.

Those chunks were the remains of Palestinian homes. When my father filmed me feeling my way across them, I already knew that I was walking over ruins, or at least half-knew. Some masonry was still exposed.

By the time Deborah and I arrived there, planning to stay overnight in one of the resort's cabins, windblown soil and sand had covered the ruins, and the beach had been fenced off for paid use. The entrance gateway was stained with salty humidity and the rusting turnstile whined as it let us in. A lone ice cream vendor heaved his dented icebox over the turnstile, exiting behind a tired-looking woman who was shepherding three irritable children. The beach litter visible behind them had not been picked up for some time.

Yet despite this run-down feeling, something of the old beauty lingered. It was that hour of "between the suns," as it's called in poetic Hebrew, when the light turns limpid, suffusing everything with a golden pink glow that edges into mauves and blues. People are gone, birds settled in for the night, and the trash recedes from sight as the shadows deepen. Peace, it seemed, settled over the land.

That sense of peace did not last. Walking ahead of me toward the beach, Deborah suddenly stopped. She was staring at a strangely futuristic sight: a colony of small igloos, their rounded domes a brilliant white against the dark water. Our cabin would be among them, we realized, when another strange sight came into view: small, factory-made terracotta fawn statuettes standing spay-legged along the sandy paths that run between the igloos. Deborah, always irreverent, laughed at the bizarre scene. I was too astounded to laugh. Still, as darkness descended, the lulling whisper of the waves took over. The fawns and iridescent igloos melted into the darkness, as did the memory of the mounds on which I had walked half a century earlier. It is so easy to forget, or perhaps not notice at all, I thought.

Some fifteen hundred Palestinians had lived, fished, and farmed in Tantura, I learned later. It had two schools and more than two hundred houses. In a rare archival photograph taken by Beno Rothenberg—for years the only Nakba photograph in circulation—you can see a row of women and children leaving the village, carrying babies and bundles that will soon be too heavy for them. The situation seems benign: just women and children walking. There is no sign of the fighting in the photograph, no armed soldiers or prisoners, no blocked escape routes, and certainly no dead or wounded bodies. Casual viewers may not register the absence of men. They may not know that these women and children had just witnessed, or at least heard the sounds of a battle where two hundred or more of their menfolk—fathers, husbands, and brothers—were massacred.

Among us Israelis, what actually happened in Tantura was buried for decades. It would have probably remained this way were it not for the uproar that rose in 1998, when a newspaper reported Teddy Katz's academic research, where he documented Tantura's massacre, second in its brutality only to Deir Yassin's. Excoriated, intimidated, and threatened with legal action by members of the Alexandroni Brigade, and ejected by his own university, Katz was coerced into recanting, despite the 140 hours of taped testimonies he had accumulated, Jewish as well as Palestinian.

The televised interview of Katz, which I happened to see shortly after his findings became known, was ruthlessly aggressive and insolent. His veracity was assaulted, his intelligence derided, the facts shrugged off. I had no way to judge any of this at the time; in an earlier version of this account I remained cautious. Yet now, with Alon Schwarz's 2022 documentary, *Tantura*, the fact of a massacre can no longer be dismissed. Surviving veterans of the Alexandroni Brigade, men in their nineties, admit on film to the massacre. Not unlike Amos Kenan in his interview about Deir Yassin, these men are visibly uneasy about what they are saying, their discomfort finding refuge in trailing sentences, shrugs, and awkward laughter.

When Deborah and I first came to Dor, I had not yet seen Rothenberg's photograph, and Schwarz's documentary wasn't in preparation. But I already knew enough to register—and failed to register—that the destitute women and children I had seen as a child, penned behind barbed wire near the Palestinian village of Fureidis, were Tantura's refugees. Among them were girls my age and younger who for a few seconds returned my gaze as our car sped by. I remember my fascinated recoil from the misery that was there in full view. What they may have thought of us, neat and well-fed, never occurred to me. I now recall this scene in muddy browns and grays: an expanse of grimy tents and listless people meandering aimlessly on hard dusty ground, a scene of utter abjection. And every so often another image invades my resisting memory: flies creeping near the runny eyes, nostrils, and mouths of children standing by that barbed wire fence, impassive, not bothering to shoo the flies away.

None of this occurred to me when Deborah and I arrived at Dor. The next morning, though, as we strolled toward the beach, our eyes were drawn to a large building, oddly solitary, perched at the water's edge: massive proportions, grand vaulted arches, excellent masonry. Some fishing tackle was stored underneath the arches, and two small dinghies were beached nearby. Once again we found ourselves debating the forensics of architecture and the intricacies of Arab calligraphy. "Ottoman?" Deborah asked, removing the lens cap from her camera, about to photograph a beautifully carved keystone. "But maybe Crusader?" she added, noting the tall arches and the imposing scale of the building. The keystone, Khalidi writes, identifies this as the al-Yahya family home, dated 1882, but how to interpret this grandeur?

This inconclusive discussion was interrupted when another strange sight caught my eye: a *makaam*, a Muslim sheikh's shrine, standing on the resort's lawn, its convex dome made invisible among the igloos, as it gradually dawned on me. This is Sheikh al-Majrani's shrine, I later learned, for Israeli Jews a mere ornament within the resort's design. Legend has it that this holy tomb survived the Nakba when it caused the bulldozer's blades to break, resisting demolition.

When Deborah and I returned to that beach later that year—now on a photographic mission, not a vacation—we found pastel banners fluttering in the breeze and the air thrumming with soft drum sounds. Young people were streaming through the creaky turnstiles, carrying food, sleeping bags, and musical instruments. There was an abundance of sun-bleached dreadlocks and tie-dyed clothing as people set up pup tents and settled down to smoke weed and make music. "They're here for some 'Purple Festival,'" the woman at the ticket booth shrugged. Shrugging in return, we turned back toward the parking lot. We had only come for a few hours anyway.

On our way back to our car I wondered about those young people. They had all served in the army or were about to do so soon. Did they wonder about the Yahya family's home as they relaxed in its shade? Did they notice Sheikh al-Marjani's *makaam*? Most of them probably never heard of Teddy Katz. I, too, had forgotten about his research when I suggested to Deborah this visit.

In 2022, with a draft of this book about to be sent to publishers, I was stunned to see the subject line "Tantura" in my email: Alon Schwarz's documentary had just been screened at the Sundance Film Festival, to great acclaim. The film was not yet in distribution when Schwartz sent me a link to it, but the reviews were already out. Schwarz, I could see, was defying a long-held consensus of silence, and the film's account of the massacre was bound to be harrowing. "If you make this film you'll be destroyed, as I was," Teddy Katz, wheelchair-bound, warns him at the start of their first interview.

The film's weaving of archival war footage, reluctant testimonies, and assaults on Katz for daring to uncover this history, are unrelenting. The judge in this case saw none of Katz's tapes, the IDF held back relevant material, Katz's academic advisors withdrew their support, and the media fanned the flames of public condemnation. The Alexandroni veterans filmed by Schwartz were all in their nineties: their bodies failing, their memories lacerated, their reluctant confessions extracted "as if forced by the devil," dismaying in their tangled ambivalence. "I'd have mowed down all of them," says one veteran. "I didn't hear, that's for sure," says another, "No, I didn't see … It's not in our character," says a third.

Once again I'm thinking of Amos Kenan talking about Deir Yassin, "I don't remember … I don't know … didn't see … not exactly."

19. *"Yahrab Beitak"*

So here is another confession. During my teens, just a few years after the '48 war, I badgered my parents to get an Arab house as a weekend retreat. I had no idea what "get" might mean, no sense of how one acquired such houses, though I knew that some people did just that. Like any other war booty, from a brass coffee pot to swaths of arable land, these houses seemed to occupy a gray zone of ownership. I knew that the *Apotropos* ("custodian") Office of Abandoned Properties was in charge of real estate, though when and how property had been abandoned and moved into Jewish hands was invisible to me.

The Arab house I dreamt of would have been a squat stone building nestled on a hillside, like the ones I remember seeing in the village of Lifta, outside Jerusalem, before the '48 war, or like the refurbished ruins I'd since seen elsewhere. Our house, I argued, would make for a lovely escape from Tel Aviv. Shaded by pines and fruit trees, it would be perfumed by jasmine climbing over the doorway and brightened with potted geraniums. Almond blossoms would veil it come February, pomegranate buds would ripen into the fall, and the figs' sticky sweetness would mingle with the dusty smell of the crumbling dry earth during the long, hot but marvelously dry summer months.

"Why not?" I asked, more than once. After all, there were abandoned Arab houses all over the country.

"Because!" came the predictable answer, when anyone bothered to respond. Sometimes there'd be a bit more: "Too much work," "You'll be bored," "There's plenty to do right here in Tel Aviv," and finally "And where's the money coming from?"

These were all reasonable answers, except that they sidestepped the questions I didn't think to ask: How come these houses were empty? Who owned them? What did it mean that a romantic teenager could even dream of owning another family's home so casually? Did any of us pause to consider that a smooth, ever so slight depression worn into a stone threshold was made by generations of Palestinian feet? I never heard my parents discuss my callous request, though they may well have done so in private. Dad was always quiet and Mom would have sidestepped it with a joke. As for me, I accepted without question the widely shared, self-serving Jewish consensus: the Arabs attacked, lost, and fled; we suffered, won, and needed. Of course whatever they abandoned was ours, we reasoned.

The empty Palestinian housing stock was a boon to a young state suddenly flooded with thousands of traumatized and displaced persons. The phrase "the spoils of war" had no legal meaning for us. It was "need," not "loot," as we saw it. When I first visited my school friend Raya, who survived the Holocaust in hiding and then was detained in Cypress before finally arriving in Israel, I did not question her family's living in an abandoned Palestinian house in Jaffa. They were among the lucky ones.

Many buildings had official notices posted in entrance lobbies announcing their management by the *Apotropos* of those properties. On my way to visit my friend K'lillah, still in elementary school, I saw such a notice posted prominently by the stairwell. A few years later, by then a student at the Hebrew University, I passed by another such notice daily, posted at the entrance to the house where I'd rented a room. The word "abandoned" proved handy, obscuring both the suffering and the illegality of expulsion, while the mention of a government-appointed "custodian" reassured us about good management by a trusted caretaker of some unnamed "absentees." Like many others, I gave those announcements no thought, hardly noticing when they disappeared, tacitly accepting the shift of ownership into Jewish hands.

Whole villages, not just individual houses, were being swallowed by Tel Aviv: Abu Kabir, Kafr Salameh, Sheikh Muwanis, Summayl, al-Jamaseen, and more, and the same was happening throughout the country. It was rightful ownership, we told ourselves, historic, God-given, and practical. Though my own family did not share directly in this urgency—none of us were refugees, partisans, Holocaust survivors, or land-hungry revisionists—I never heard my parents comment about this collective national entitlement. It was accepted without question both within the *yishuv* and among the newly arrived who were clawing their way out of their history. The need to take possession rendered the "custodian" notices invisible.

Looking back at my teenage self I am struck not only by how unremarkable taking possession of Palestinian property seemed, but also by how privileged my fantasy of having a *second* home was when so many had lost their only one.

"How beautiful," I remember exclaiming when Deborah and I first chanced on the so-called "Castle" in Kerem Maharal (previously Palestinian Ijzim), near the bramble-choked building that used to be Ijzim's mosque. For some years an upmarket Israeli bed-and-breakfast, there was a touch of French Provence about it and a hint of a Hallmark biblical scene: a massive stone building, a blue-shuttered window high up where a potted geranium beckoned from its deep sill, wide arches below, and a peacock strolling near a stone patio. Though the very expensive artifice of the place repelled me, a spark of covetousness remained.

As I think of my fantasy Arab house and imagine the tourists enjoying a stay at Ijzim's "Castle," an old Palmach song, "The Reunion," worms its way back into my memory. Like several other songs of that era, it envisions a war-free future when Palmach veterans may meet and reminisce about a war that is now, in the song's imaginary present, over. "How goes it? What's new? Haven't seen you in ages!" the refrain goes. Mostly it's about the comradeship, yet two Arabic words stick out: "*yahrab beitak*," the men say in greeting as a kind of high five.

The words were just gibberish to me at the time, nonsense syllables that would delight a child. It was only years later, when I studied Arabic in high school, that I grasped their meaning. Ominous and threatening, at once a prediction and a curse, they translate as "Your house will be destroyed," but also as "May your house be destroyed," either way naturalized into the slang of '48 as a swagger. "For whenever a Palmachnik meets a comrade/ *yahrab beitak*! / And something stirs in the heart …"

For years, "*yahrab beitak*" was just an amusing snippet of a song I happened to remember and mostly forgot. Once I understood the words I still did not consider their use. Similarly, from 1949 onward I felt sad to see the abandoned village of Lifta, just outside Jerusalem, without thinking about what caused its dereliction. I saw no connection between our "sons" singing "*yahrab beitak*!" and the abandoned village. Only gradually did awareness creep in.

Lifta is now mostly demolished, but when I saw it before '48, on my way to visit my grandmother, this large Palestinian village seemed magical. I was always impatient to see it appear as we entered Jerusalem, and always craned to see it recede on our way back to Tel Aviv. I loved to see its old stone houses crowding companionably down the hillside. Their squat shape, thick walls, and small windows felt womb-like, much like my great-grandparents' home in Metula, while Lifta's domed roofs had a storybook aura of mystery for me, growing up in a city of straight angles. There was a rootedness about it that I was too young to name. I knew without knowing that the stones from which it was built had belonged to the land and had been cut and fitted into walls by people who lived on that land.

As a child, I also thrilled to see Lifta's two roadside cafés come into view just outside the village proper. Here men would sit on low rush stools, chatting, smoking hookahs, fingering their prayer beads, or leaning over a backgammon board. Passing the village at dusk, as faint lights would begin to flicker in its windows, I'd imagine its children being tucked into bed as I would be into mine. In images borrowed from my children's books, I'd meld Palestinian and European village life into one incongruous fantasy that had Arab women in long black dresses balancing water jugs on their heads and European women in billowing skirts sitting at spinning wheels. There'd be a man in black pantaloons and a kaffiyeh leading a donkey but also a girl in clogs and a Dutch bonnet chasing geese.

After '48, Lifta went dark. Its people had "left," I knew, even if I didn't yet know why or how. By the time Deborah and I walked into the demolished village—in 2006 and again in 2007 and 2008—almost all its houses were gone. The few houses still standing had large holes in their domed roofs, and the almonds I found still growing on a tree were shriveled and bitter. In some houses you could see signs of tenuous habitation by homeless people: rain-soaked newspapers disintegrating among discarded bottles and rusting cans, a stained mattress half-propped against a wall, flies buzzing above human feces. The only people I saw occupying Lifta were a group of Haredi squatters. One of them approached me to assert territorial claims when he saw Deborah,

Swimmers at Lifta's reservoir—orthodox and secular, male and female.

camera in hand, about to photograph the village reservoir. "No photos. It's a mikvah," he said, a ritual bath. There was no trace of ritual in the yelling, diving, and splashing of the boys fooling around in this pool.

The two Palestinian coffee shops I remember at the roadside are long gone. In December 1947 the Hagana attacked one of them, strafing its guests with machine gun fire while Lehi members of the Stern Gang, in a separate action, fired randomly into a passing bus. All that's left of the coffee shops is a slightly wider roadside shoulder where buses and hitchhikers now stop. What little is left of the village looks more bucolic than ever now that only a few houses remain of what used to be a crowded village. On nice days hikers can be seen, following a stream as they head away from the village. Every so often there is a report of city planners and real estate entrepreneurs submitting blueprints to develop what little remains of Lifta into an upscale suburb.

Though the romance of having an Arab house kept smoldering in me for a while, the first time I remember becoming uneasy about its seduction was in July of 1965. It was my first visit home since I'd left for the US five years earlier, and I was returning much changed.

On that muggy morning, as I leaned over the clammy guardrail of the Marseilles-to-Haifa car ferry that was docking in Haifa, I was thrilled to see my parents waving to me from the hot tarmac. Suitcase in hand and holding onto the rope banister of the swaying gangplank, I walked down, had my passport stamped, and flew toward them: hugs, kisses, exclamations, tearing eyes. Their suggestion that we detour to Nazareth on the way home was an added joy. Instead of the fumes and tensions of speeding to Tel Aviv on a crowded highway, we would drive along the secondary roads that hug the curves of the hills I loved best.

It had been a grueling trip home. I'd come the cheapest way possible: a cross-country bus from San Francisco to New York, an Icelandic Air flight via Reykjavik to some tertiary airport in France, a long bus ride to Paris, a train to Marseille, and finally the car ferry to Haifa. Ten days. And this after five years in the United States, where I worked and studied on almost no money and lost the marriage that had brought me there in the first place. Most importantly, this personal upheaval occurred in the midst of radical change in my new country: civil rights struggles and the Vietnam War most obviously, but also the counterculture, the rise of feminism, and many other calls for social justice, including the farmworkers' boycott, and Native American unrest, and news of liberation movements worldwide.

It was all trailing me as our car headed for Nazareth, for a while forgotten in my joy at being home. I was thrilled and touched by my parents' thought that lunch at Nazareth would make for a wonderful homecoming. Of course this Christian-Arab town couldn't possibly be "home," but they knew that its architecture and pace would touch off my affinity for a world we had known and loved before '48: the old stone buildings, the pushcarts piled high with skinny sesame bagels as they rattled on uneven flagstones, the smoke of grilled kebabs served with fresh cilantro at small rickety tables by a street's edge, and the aroma of thick cardamom-laced coffee served in tiny cups.

This was pure nostalgia, I rebuke myself now. Pure orientalism, as Edward Said would have called that spurious affection with which empires stake their ownership. In my fantasy, and perhaps in my parents' too, Nazareth stood for the "old days," when Palestine was Ottoman and Jewish life still meshed with local customs.

What on earth were we thinking as we strolled through Nazareth's marketplace, exclaiming over the freshness of produce? What memories did the people we passed carry from '48, or for that matter from yesterday or this morning? Many of them were refugees from neighboring villages and all of them were still under military rule. Of course the restaurant owner was happy to take our money, as was the man who sold me the wooden *ma'amool* pastry molds that for some years decorated my American kitchen, claiming an ethnicity that was not mine.

Today's Nazareth is hardly the Christian town I remember from that visit, and certainly not the town I remember from 1945 when, as a six- or seven-year-old, I first walked with my parents on its cobbled streets and stayed at the long-gone Galilee Hotel, at the heart of the old town. I still remember the cool flagstones of the dim corridor that led to my stark whitewashed room at that hotel, where two bound sticks hung above my narrow white bed and an earthenware water jug nestled in a deep-set alcove, covered with a spotless white cloth with a beaded lace edging. Like the lace-edged handkerchiefs and rosaries sold in the hotel's small gift shop, this was the handiwork of local nuns. I had no idea what the two bound sticks meant, but the whitewashed simplicity of the place and its reigning sweet silence had me wishing to be a nun.

While Lifta lies in ruins, today's Nazareth is a crowded city spreading into its adjacent hills. No longer just Christian, it has become a checkerboard of communities and a tangle of roads. Palestinian politics had changed too: in 1964, a year before my parents and I detoured from Haifa to Nazareth, the militant Fatah was formed, galvanizing Palestinian nationalism. Its call would have been heard by the man who sold me the pastry molds in 1965 and by the waiter who served us lunch, though not yet by me. All I remember about that visit is vague uneasiness; somehow, the fantasy of belonging to that world felt tarnished. That feeling, I now think, had to do with the political education I'd acquired in the United States, where the poverty and racism I saw in New York, the news of racial violence in the South, and realities of the Vietnam War translated into a new awareness about my own country too, even if I couldn't quite name it yet.

By 2008, as Deborah's and my time in Israel was ending, none of this opaqueness remained. Gradually, imperceptibly, my views had changed. That year found us once more in Nazareth, where we stopped briefly on the way to the Galilee. Passing by a bookshop in the old market, I noticed the familiar blue cover of Walid Khalidi's encyclopedic *All That Remains*, displayed prominently on a sidewalk stall. A recorded male voice was blaring into the street from inside the bookshop, its Arabic speech passionate, unstoppable. A diatribe? The book and the voice suggested as much. This massive census of demolished villages that was so hard for us to locate in English was readily available here for casual browsing. Seeing it in Arabic was a reminder: the book is above all theirs, not ours.

"Look, here's an entry on Saffuriya," I said to Deborah, chancing on it as I turned pages at random, showing off my scant knowledge of Arabic.

The store owner, pointedly unfriendly, his bulk filling the doorway, was eyeing us suspiciously. When I nodded toward him, he refused to meet my eyes. After all, why should he see me as an ally? His white skullcap suggested that he was Muslim, maybe radical given his close-cropped hair, trimmed beard, and the harangue blaring into the street. He could easily peg me as European, probably Israeli—secular and liberal given my jeans. That Deborah looked more like the Christian pilgrims who stream through Nazareth was no help. Everything about us asserted Israel's hated power. Unlike the Palestinian store owner who gave me a pen in Tarshiha during Zochrot's visit, this man allowed no common ground.

Unpleasant though it was, I hardly blame this bookseller. To him we were the enemy, casually invading his home in a country where "heritage tourism" had become a lively business. There were Circassian "heritage villages" advertised in the Galilee and "Bedouin hospitality tents" in the Negev. On Saturdays, Israeli Jews flock to Haifa's Wadi Nisnas to shop for hummus while others dine in Jaffa, dance at its clubs, and search its flea market for ethnic "finds" often made in India or the Philippines. You can have your photo taken on a bedecked camel on Mount Scopus overlooking minarets, steeples, domes, and rooftop solar water heaters, or shop for factory-made "oriental" souvenirs in the old city's market, at least on days when there are no "troubles," as an Irish-American woman once put it to me.

This nostalgia for borrowed authenticity rests on a tortured history of lost and found homelands, real and imagined, ours and theirs. Palestinian Eyn Khud became the romantic Jewish artists' village of Ein Hod, while now Israelis go to a new Palestinian Eyn Khud, until recently unrecognized and without water or electricity, in search of authentic Arab food. The springs and verdant terraces of the Palestinian village of Sattaf are now a national park billed as an example of biblical agriculture. The faculty club at Tel Aviv University was once a grand Palestinian home, and Safed's city museum is housed under the arched domes of a mosque, while its "Rimonim" hotel occupies a complex of refurbished Palestinian homes.

"Of course I know that we're living in an Arab house," a friend said one afternoon as we sipped coffee under the vaulted whitewashed ceiling of his Jaffa home. He already knew I was writing about the Nakba—an uncomfortable topic even for liberal Israelis, many of whom patronize Palestinian businesses as a matter of solidarity. Here lies the fault line between assimilation and separation, knowing an unwelcome truth and yet letting it be. I could see Jaffa's rooftops through the twin tall windows set deeply into my friend's thick stone wall, the blue Mediterranean sparkling in a gap between two nearby houses. Yes, I had to admit to myself, I would have loved to live there.

Unlike Nazareth, which was not bombed in '48, the old part of Jaffa— the ancient port city Jonah sailed from to meet his big fish—lay in ruins when I saw it in the early 1950s, before it was refurbished for Jewish use. We felt daring, my school friends and I, as we bicycled there one holiday morning. The almost impassable debris-choked alleys that greeted us had become Tel Aviv's temporary red-light district. Too ruined to house even our most destitute immigrants, it sheltered pimps, prostitutes, and drug dealers, their presence confirmed by used condoms and smashed bottles. Old Jaffa's perch on a cliff overlooking the ancient harbor saved its rich housing stock from bulldozers. Though zoned for artists and galleries, it was becoming an oriental theme park, as Deborah wryly noted.

In his memoir, *Strangers in the House*, Raja Shehadeh describes his grandparents' life as hotel owners in Jaffa before they fled to Ramallah in '48. It's a poignant account of a world lost, the scars of survival, and the spirit that nonetheless sustains people. Were any of the tables and armoires and crystal chandeliers that flooded Jaffa's flea market after '48 theirs, I wondered? And what became of the thousands who ended up not in Ramallah but destitute in refugee camps? One small detail in Shehadeh's book made me catch my breath: his grandmother used to go to a Jewish dressmaker named Batya, in Tel Aviv. Before '48, my mother told me, Batya had been famous as the best dressmaker in town. My paternal grandmother, too, used to have her dresses sewn by Batya.

I imagine my grandmother and old Mrs. Shehadeh waiting for their fittings in Batya's waiting room, seated side by side, leafing through magazines or fingering cloth samples. An unlikely pair, the orthodox Jewish woman from Cape Town and the cosmopolitan Arab hotel owner from Jaffa! Neither of them would have spoken Hebrew, and my grandmother didn't speak French, the language of the educated Near East, let alone Arabic. Would either of them have tried to converse in English, the colonial language of the British Mandate? Would they have even nodded hello to each other?

I remember also Jerusalem's Armenian shoe designer, Mr. Garabadian, whose name was sacred on my other grandmother's lips. His shoes were "like butter," she used to say, the only shoes her bunion-crippled feet could wear. Mr. Garabadian left for Paris in '48 and Batya lost her Palestinian clients. The proximity they created between Arab and Jew was probably feared or disliked by one side, often by both. Such ordinary urban opportunities were squandered even as Palestinians and Jews would shop in the same market, wait together at a bus stop, or shelter side by side in a doorway during a sudden downpour.

One afternoon Deborah and I stopped at Jaffa's Ali Baba café, facing Tel Aviv's lively beachfront from the top of Old Jaffa's cliff. It had been a *makaam*, a holy man's tomb, standing within what used to be a Muslim cemetery. Some deal to empty the cemetery must have been struck with its Waqf custodians, I supposed, looking out the window at the promenade that replaced it. The café's very name, Ali Baba, offended me with its colonizing *salaam* to Old Jaffa's callous orientalist renewal. Seeing Deborah's gaze meander over the café's vaulted ceilings, already anticipating what she might say about the place, I plunged into telling her about wanting my parents to get us an Arab house when I was young.

"A what?" she exclaimed before I finished the sentence. "How can you say 'get' after all we've seen?"

I flushed. Deborah had touched a raw nerve, but in making this confession I was making a point. It was not about an entitled, thoughtless adolescent but about a national fantasy that sought to redefine our sense of belonging, an urge for ownership that rested on a bogus illusion of home and origin.

20. Gales of Silence

At the end of our fourth summer in Israel, in 2008, Deborah and I were preparing to drive toward Jerusalem, maybe see Lifta one last time, when she suggested we first turn off to Beit Hakerem, the Jewish suburb where my grandmother had lived through much of the siege in '48. "It's on the way," she said, registering my reluctance. "We can easily stop there. Isn't it strange that we haven't done it yet?"

How to explain the paralyzing reluctance I felt? My pre-'48 days with my grandmother Savta were among the happiest in my childhood, and yet by the time Deborah and I began tracing the Nakba that sweetness was shattered. The Beit Hakerem of my childhood was gone. There was no room left for innocence: Lifta and Deir Yassin were both within walking distance of her house.

"Well, shall we?" Deborah persisted as she was preparing her camera bag while I, frozen, leaned against the door-jamb.

Something in her voice persuaded me. I'd kept so much of my childhood locked inside me, dreading the letdown of failing to convey it as fully as I wished. But I knew that time was running out. I agreed.

We mostly drove in silence, every so often pointing to places we already knew along the way: the cactus banks at the edge of Daniel, the Latroun monastery, the khan at Bab el-Wad, the derelict convoy vehicles, and the perch of what used to be Lifta's two coffee shops. Lost in reverie, I was only half seeing the familiar landscape.

Memories of my time with Savta, when I was four, five, and six years old, surfaced. The days, as I remembered them, were blissful, pinned in place by the reassuring patterns of daily living. The hammering we could hear from the quarry downhill would trace each day's passing hours, punctuated only rarely by cries of "*barroud, barroud,*" that warned of dynamite use. Somewhere down below us we could hear Arabic spoken, muffled by distance. Come summer, Palestinian village women would climb the steps down to my grandmother's patio. They'd arrive in twos or threes, graceful in their long embroidered black dresses, one hand steadying the woven fruit trays they'd balance on their heads. There would be the customary Arabic greetings of "*marhaba*" and "*t'fadalu,*" the offer of water, and a friendly chat in Arabic as we'd settle on the patio's stone floor. I'd sit by, fascinated, as Savta would select an apricot or a fig, gently pressing its flesh between her fingers to test its ripeness. A little pile of fruit would form, followed by the rites of bargaining, voices undulating between laughter and resistance.

Some afternoons Savta and I would sit at a small folding table on the patio near her rosemary shrubs and remove tiny stones from a pile of lentils spread on the table as we'd drink tea she'd serve Russian style, in glasses. Going to Café Raviv's afternoon tea dances was a special treat. Savta would struggle into her floral crepe dress, pin a small black hat to her thinning hair, and make me suffer the ordeal of having my snarled curls brushed and combed. We'd sit under the trees and watch men in suits and elegant women in hats and heels dance to a small live band as they might have done in Budapest, Paris, or Vienna. My ice cream would arrive in a silvered pedestal cup with a small blunt spoon, "a farmer's spoon" as I called it because it was squared off like the spade I'd seen in an illustrated children's book about our pioneers.

Lulled by the sun, the translucent mountain air, and the buzz of bees among the rosemary, it never occurred to me to wonder about the men in the quarry or the women who sold us their fruit. In the late afternoon, as a western breeze blew over the eroded hilltops, a heavy, pregnant moon would appear just below Savta's patio, silvering the rim of the Valley of the Crucifixion, I'd lie on the quilts spread on the top of the steamer trunk that was my bed, dozing off to the click-clack of Savta's orthopedic shoes as the din of cicadas rose to fill the darkness. Tomorrow, I assumed, would be no different.

It was only once Deborah and I pored over our maps that I realized that the men overheard at the quarry and the women who sold us the fruit must have walked over from nearby Lifta or Deir Yassin. Some of these men might have been sitting at the roadside café after work, fingering their prayer beads or smoking a hookah, when our soldiers strafed the place with machine gun fire. One of the women could have been the woman Nurith's husband, Amos, killed (or perhaps didn't kill) when he entered (or perhaps didn't enter) Deir Yassin, as he told Nurith in their interview.

Some version of these thoughts and recollections may have tugged at me when I first resisted seeing Savta's place. Yet deep down I wanted to relent, and did.

Entering Beit Hakerm's old main street, Hachalutz ("The Pioneer"), felt like a throwback to old times. The trees shading the street had grown taller and Café Raviv was gone, but the modest town hall and the small public garden nearby were unchanged, as were most of the houses that lined the street. The Gaon family's house, where Savta's semi-basement flat was tucked into the rocky hillside, also seemed unchanged, though once we drew closer I could see that it hadn't been occupied for some time. The windows were shuttered, the entrance patio was littered with debris, and the garden had gone to seed.

What we found as I led the way down the uneven rocks that served as steps to Savta's flat shocked me: shutters half-hanging off their hinges, brambles choking the dead rosemary, and, visible inside through dusty windows, the wreckage of abandoned construction. We could see assorted lumber, dry paint buckets, a torn paper bag of spilled nails, and a paint-splattered ladder leaning against one wall. There was also a good padlock on the door. Fairly recent, I noticed.

Hardest to take were the "*menscheles*" affixed to the wall. They were still in place, those tiny cast-iron man-shaped figures common in old houses, just torsos with heads wearing trilby hats, maybe five inches tall, meant to hold in place metal shutters that now barely hung on their hinges.

"We might as well head back," Deborah said after a long pause.

I nodded and started the steep climb up the treacherous steps, remembering how hard that climb used to be for Savta and how gingerly she'd step on the way down, turning her body sideways as each foot searched for a safe landing place.

So much in this history barely hangs on its hinges, I'm thinking now, remembering Amos's stillborn confession to Nurith: "I don't remember … I don't know … didn't see …," and "No! (I don't remember something—that is a weapon—in my hand), and your should know that I'm getting fed up with this interview … I didn't remember that I shot a woman, I didn't remember. But apparently I shot, apparently it was at a woman."

Amos's refusal to know the past belongs to all of us Israelis. My silence when Deborah and I visited Savta's home was, first, about a loss that occurs in the course of ordinary life: a grandmother dies, a house loses its tenants. But by 2008 my silence was also inseparable from other silences. It's safer to remain silent, I thought—to refuse to talk, to be afraid to talk, to not know how to talk, or to forget to talk—even when inwardly we scream. There are the thoughts and explanations my parents withheld from me, the learning that did not happen at school, the comments I did not hear in the streets, the facts omitted by the press and hourly broadcasts, the muteness of soldiers returning from combat, and the life stories not told by our immigrants and by the Palestinians whom we prefer not to hear. And there was my own muteness. In this noisy, voluble, opinionated, and contentious country, some things remain unspoken.

Yet as Deborah and I sought out traces of the Nakba, another kind of silence haunted us—that of the Palestinians whose voices seemed gone from this land. Mostly we were utterly alone as we walked through an empty field or scrambled among deserted ruins, only occasionally meeting a local Palestinian. At least I could talk with the shopkeeper at Tarshiha, though the bookseller in Nazareth remained hostile. At least my Druze neighbor at Shlomi felt he could speak to me, though even such conversations are strained. One never knows what the other might really be feeling. The walls that separate us are made of the myriad suspicions, prohibitions, and a very realistic distrust that is too dangerous to voice.

I felt that wall come up one day at the Haifa train station, when I asked a taxi driver to take me to an address in what I knew to be a Palestinian neighborhood. It must have been in 2014, when I was teaching at Tel Aviv University.

"You can't go there. No access," he said, sounding accusatory, as if I had no right to go to that address. A moody Jew, I thought. He didn't even return my hello when I first settled into his cab.

"I know cars can't go there," I said. "Just drop me off at the top of the stairs. I'll walk down from there."

At that, he pivoted to look me over and asked whom I was visiting, his voice friendly. Oh, it's his neighborhood, I realized, a Palestinian. I was no longer an unwelcome outsider. He smiled when I explained that I was joining women in a landscaping project, and said a warm goodbye as he stopped by those steps. Shaking hands, I felt grateful for his accepting me. I didn't dare ask whether he too felt grateful for this rare instance of coming together.

When I returned to Haifa a week or two later, I was taken on a tour of a Palestinian neighborhood by Marwa, an administrator of Palestinian youth activities and a friend of my cousin, whom I had met in Boston a few months earlier. Haifa, I already knew, was touted as Israel's model "mixed" city. It still had many ruins in view, but the Palestinian neighborhood of Wadi Nisnas had an air of well-being. Our tour ended at a Palestinian cultural center, housed in an elegant mansion whose spacious entrance lobby served as a gallery of local Palestinian art.

"This has been a controversial painting, " Marwa said as she paused by a painting that showed Haifa's bay, seen from up high. It was a view I'd seen countless times from my grandfather's house. The painting showed a dense mass of people filling a street that heads toward the bay, with its familiar jetty curving into an intensely blue sea.

"Yes, I know," I nodded. "The expulsion."

"How do you know?"

"Because I know Kanafani's novella 'Returning to Haifa.' I even taught it," I said, hoping to open a door for more discussion.

Marwa said nothing. The door remained shut. Though we'd formed a warm connection in Boston, we had stayed away from politics. Now, my mention of the story's author had us treading on dangerous ground. Ghassan Kanafani may have been a freedom fighter to the Palestinians, but to Israelis he was a terrorist "with blood on his hands," assassinated by a car bomb in Beirut in 1972.

Questions about what can be said and how to say it haunt this history. The Palestinian writer Mahmoud al-Asaad describes the fall of Haifa as hurling the city's Palestinians into a vortex of hallucinations, "a world of sudden signs and wails that descended from the skies, turning the world around us into a gale of silence." This silence, born of trauma, reverberates with sounds heard only when one chooses to hear them.

People often ask me whether Deborah and I interviewed Palestinians as part of our search for traces of the Nakba. "No," I answer awkwardly, knowing that it would have been a good thing to do. Some people do that, including the American photographer Skip Schiel, who pairs portraits of refugees with interviews and photographs of their lost villages. But this was not Deborah's and my goal. In our different way each of us has been giving voice to al-Asaad's "gale of silence," where absence reverberates with "signs and wails."

Painful though it is, such silence is a shelter, a holding in of breath that is a way of staying alive. Like Marwa, like the shopkeepers in Tarshiha and Nazareth, I avoid contact. It's a matter of trust. There's no telling what a conversation may stir up.

One day, perhaps in 2007, as I waited in line to copy some documents in my Tel Aviv neighborhood, I noticed a page being photographed by the man ahead of me. He looked to be in his mid- to late thirties, well dressed in good gray slacks and crisp buttoned shirt, perhaps a lawyer or bank employee, much like the other Jewish men you see in this affluent Ashkenazi neighborhood. The colored photograph emerging from the printer caught my attention. In it, a group of men, women, and children were walking under a freestanding stone arch, the masonry clearly Palestinian, probably the sole remnant of a large building. Deborah and I had seen countless such arches in various states of bare survival.

"What's this?" I asked, peering over his shoulder.

"The *Eid*," he said, not looking at me, discouraging further discussion, his face reddening.

I had "outed" him as Palestinian, I realized, mortified that my careless curiosity could have that effect. There's a certain familial ease among us Israeli Jews that we take for granted. In the bus, people often lean over strangers' shoulders to read the paper. This man looked like any other Jewish Israeli of his age and social class living or working in this affluent, liberal part of north Tel Aviv, and yet he wasn't. In a country where the very legal system is rigged against his ethnicity, my question was not innocuous.

It pleases me that I can't tell Arab and Jew apart. I like the historian Shlomo Sand's suggestion that the Palestinians are actually the descendants of

Jews who'd lived in the country all along, since the destruction of the Second Temple. Our genetic similarity gives me hope, though this stranger's blush proved the notion of kinship a sham.

"The photo came out very well," I said, making light of what we'd both left unsaid.

Among the things I did not say was another thought that flashed through my mind: The copy shop where we stood was on land that had previously belonged to the Palestinian village of Summayl, the village that used to face my home.

Few people passing through the section of Ibn Gabirol Street where that copy shop stood are likely to know that this busy stretch used to be Summayel. It is now crowded with shops, banks, eateries, and real estate agencies, including a stylish mall and tower and Tel Aviv's municipal headquarters. It was here, in 1995, that Prime Minister Yitzhak Rabin was assassinated by a young Israeli intent on derailing the Oslo peace initiative. Rabin had just left the stage at the end of an inspiring peace rally where thousands had assembled.

A modest memorial for Rabin—slabs of black marble and a perpetual flame—is sunken into the sidewalk where he fell, diagonally across the street from the copy shop. When I passed nearby in 2019, I noticed that the adjacent wall of the municipal parking area, where loving pro-Rabin graffiti and wishes for peace had been protected for years under plexiglass, had since been replaced by an innocuous mural of flowers. The square that saw mass demonstrations, Israel's annual Hebrew Book Fair, and popular entertainment, had been newly landscaped, with a portion of its paved area now a lawn with easy chairs. The voice of protest and civic passion had given way to the lulling murmur of well-being. Only a lone olive tree that had been transplanted into the Square continues its incongruous life there.

Passing this area almost daily for years, I'd seen its gradual transformation as both Summayl's fields and orchards and fallow city-owned lands became the pulsing heart of Israel's first modern Jewish city. For years after the '48 fighting ended, the air was heavy with the dust of construction, the smell of tar, and the grinding sounds of cement mixers. Most of Tel Aviv's major public buildings and many apartment blocks are now in this part of town. What pockets of nostalgia were preserved are farther south: Neveh Tzedek neighborhood, built on the sand dunes where in 1909 a handful of families had gathered for a lottery of the city's first building lots; an old railroad station that is now an exhibition hall, and a collection of Bauhaus buildings whose streamlined modernism earned Tel Aviv a UNESCO World Heritage recognition.

Our own house, built just two years before '48, was a tiny outpost of this new city. During those years of tense uncertainty, I saw Summayl's farmers plow, sow, and reap wheat in fields that almost reached our low fence. Sometimes they'd stop by for water or nod to my mother if she happened to be out weeding the garden. Some winter nights my father would be called to join them to extract a car from the muddy field that some hapless driver had mistaken for a road. One time two village men in white kaffiyehs and black pantaloons came to help us remove a snake that had found its way into our house.

When my sister recently asked me whether our house stood on stolen Palestinian land, it was a relief to reassure her that it didn't, at least not literally. The British rezoning Geddes plan, dated 1925, included transferring Summayl lands to Tel Aviv's municipality. Presumably our parents bought our lot from the city either before or shortly after World War II, though I still don't know how the people of Summayl felt about the rezoning. I have read that their families started migrating to neighboring Jammasin al-Gharbi as early as 1946 and that those who remained left in '47 or '48 (reports vary), apparently without struggle. One day, as if overnight, they were gone. All I remember is a strange new stillness hovering over Summayl. For a while I could still hear the jackals bay at night, and then they were silent too.

I also don't know when the current Mizrahi families were given the abandoned village houses. For decades after Jewish immigrants were settled in the abandoned village, little seemed to change on that rocky sandstone hill. Some crumbling houses were torn down; others acquired whitewashed plaster, pitched red roofs, and shuttered windows. A synagogue appeared, and a plant nursery. At some point part of the hill was sliced through and bulldozed to allow for new construction. Sheared off, the rest of the hill was left to rise above the street like a hunk of cake. What remained of the village, no longer recognizable as "Arab," clung to its cliff top, incongruously in the midst of modern Tel Aviv's real estate boom. On its tallest blank wall, a two-story house pitched at the hill's steep rise above Ibn Gabirol Street, someone painted a playful trompe l'oeil mural of a woman at a window above a laundry line where a pair of jeans, twenty feet long, flapped in the wind.

There was no easy access to this Jewish enclave, where Ibn Gabirol street's thoroughfare slices through its cliff. With major civic institutions and booming commerce nearby and real estate values soaring, this enclave's largely Mizrahi residents held on to their village houses with fierce determination. The fight was not only about land values. It was also about the right to one's home, colored by Israel's internal ethnic conflicts, with the enclave's residents knowing themselves to be among the country's most disenfranchised Jews, squeezed yet again by the Ashkenazi elite. Only in 2019 did I see this holdout being torn down, the leveled hill now slated for luxury development. Twelve or more years earlier, when Deborah and I first tried to enter from street level through the wooden steps that led up to it, we were met with snarling dogs, hostile faces peering from behind curtains, and "Keep Out" signs under large blue and white of Israeli flags.

There was nothing to keep six of us, a small gaggle of eleven-year-old boys and girls, with my five-year-old sister in tow, from entering Summayl shortly after the cease-fire of '49. The empty village beckoned with the promise of adventure. What remained of Palestine in this village hovered at a distance, mirage-like, beyond fields where deep gashes in the hardened clay threatened to swallow our sandaled feet. We were all on the lookout for snakes, jumpy when one of us set off the alarm: "Watch out! Here! Here!" and then, "Tricked you, tricked you," followed by shrieks of laughter.

By the time we reached the low rise of the village our nerves were jangled. A vague sense of menace lurked in the abandoned houses, some-thing "Arab" we didn't understand. Some joker whispered that the *debba* had been spotted roaming nearby—a mythical hyena or an Arab ogre, supposedly female, who'd lure Jewish children to teach them the language of beasts. The cramped buildings, musty with the lingering smell of fires burnt into their clay walls, seemed proof enough. Though nobody admitted it, we weren't eager to enter. Only a challenging "Hey, cowards!" got us to step in, my sister clutching at my shirt in fear. The rags we found, the torn blanket, a broken-down two-legged chair, all spoke of disaster that had better remain unmentioned.

At the brink of adolescence, my friends and I were all reading adventure stories: how the children of *Emil and the Detectives* caught a thief and how youngsters in *Children's Island* survived a plane crash on a desert island, about Tom Sawyer encountering Injun Joe during his spelunking adventure, and about how *Hasamba's* youngsters, ordinary Tel Aviv kids like us, helped the Hagana fight the British—all stories of brave children's encounters with shadowy, menacing "others." Scariest of all were *Treasure Island's* buccaneers, whose "black spot" death sentence seemed to lurk at every turn.

Entering Summayl, our little group was tense, expecting danger, wanting to be brave. What's there to worry about? Just some "Arabs" who had "run away," we told ourselves with false bravado. Playing hide-and-seek in the abandoned houses, leaping out of dark corners, slashing the air with blood-curdling roars, we made the village our hallucinatory playground. After sitting out air raids, walking in and out of sandbag barricades, and playing with unexploded shells, we reassured ourselves: what's there to fear in an old empty building?

I had just calmed my sister, trying to disengage her trembling hand, when a boy shrieked, "It's here, it's here! The Black Hand!"

For a moment we froze. Standing in the dark and not seeing was no comfort. The sound of the shriek was enough to invite panic, and not knowing what this supposed hand or its blackness foretold made it terrifying. To us, "the Black Hand" sounded very much like *Treasure Island's* "black spot," a decree of imminent death. Suddenly Summayl became dangerous, an islet cut off from the mainland of civil order and parental care.

It didn't take long for us to recover. Silhouetted against a bright doorway, that boy was doubled over with laughter, though the joke was lost on my sister. Terrified, she sprinted home across the fields in such a panic that I couldn't catch up with her till we reached our garden gate.

Nowadays my sister and I laugh about this incident. She remembers a stooped, elderly man walking through the abandoned village, wearing ordinary clothes and carrying a backpack of sorts. To her he was that dreaded Black Hand. I remember him too, though as carrying a briefcase, looking like a dowdy clerk. Either way, the only notable thing about this nondescript man was his being in Summayl at all. I don't know if anybody else noticed him or thought of him as the Black Hand; whatever menace we attached to that phrase was our own invention.

Though we did not know it, the menace of the Black Hand was not merely the stuff of children's stories. We all knew that we'd entered the alien territory of a Palestinian village. The boy who sounded the alarm must have heard "the Black Hand" mentioned somewhere. He may have heard somebody comment on Saffuriya's armed resistance to the Hagana, or about the role of Sheikh Izz ad-Din al-Qassam's Black Hand organization in the Arab Revolt. Shortly after we ventured into Summayl, members of the Azazme Bedouin tribe killed eleven Israelis at the Negev's "Scorpion Pass" under the name of "the Black Hand." The Qassam rockets that are nowadays shot by the al-Qassam Brigades from Gaza into Israel carry Sheikh Izz ad-Din's name.

Like all bogeymen, the panic stirred in us by the Black Hand touched on deeper, primal fears. Though we children knew nothing about the many avatars of the Black Hand, some of us may have heard ominous reports of a scary *debba*, always mentioned in a lowered voice, as if just saying her name would bring her out of the shadows. We could sense that something harsh and destructive lurked in the derelict buildings where we screamed and played hide-and-go-seek, especially as that "something" was unheard and unseen. Whatever its cause, the wretchedness we encountered in Summayl's ravaged houses embodied an uncanny threat that could reveal itself at any moment. Something was clearly out of kilter. We, children of the '48 war, sensed it.

21. A Taboon

Unlike the other sites Deborah and I got to see over our four years in Israel, including the derelict remains of some forty villages, Summayl's fields touched on my family's front gate. Here, within just a few city blocks, I saw Zionist reclamation in process, and this proximity made Summayl part of my life. I sensed the same tug of proximity when my friend Judd—a combat surgeon and a celebrated film director and professor—urged Deborah and me to join him on a trip to what used to be the Palestinian village of Aqir. The Aqir of Judd's childhood was next door to his grandparents' village of Ekron, later renamed Mazkeret Batya in memory of the Baron de Rothschild's wife. Judd remembered how the relations between the two villages were close. It was possible to envision a shared future.

Deborah and I were searching Israel's coastal plain when Judd suggested going there. By then, toward the end of 2007, she and I were finally hitting our stride. Each could just about predict what the other might say when we'd find, or not find, yet another evidence of Palestinian life. We were completing each other's sentences, mirroring each other's feelings. Fingers pointing. Eyes shaded against the sun. Feet scratched by thorns during the long dry season or stung by nettles after the early rains. Eyes meeting. Heads nodding. Dismay shared wordlessly.

Traveling with Judd wouldn't have the same easy understanding the two of us shared, yet of all my Israeli friends Judd was "a soul brother," the one who shared my feelings about the Nakba openly and most closely. "You must see Aqir," he said. "Its mere name brings back to me the scent of weeds and cooking fires. I used to go there with my grandfather," he added. 'There's one house still standing." This would be his trip too, a pilgrimage, like Amira's to the Palmach Museum.

Judd was over seventy, wiry, edgy, and determined. Permanently tanned and slightly freckled from years of exposure to Israel's harsh sun, his lean body poised as if ready to leap forward, Judd projected a restiveness that I had come to know as a mark of his distrust of complacent assurances, personal or communal. I saw it when we'd team-taught a course on Vietnam War films at Tel Aviv University, where his questioning and probing drew students beyond facile mouthing, egging them on into discussion and debate. For him, as for me, acknowledging the Nakba was an act of defiance, the proverbial "speaking truth to power."

Like me, Judd is a child of the first Aliyah—the early wave of East European Zionists who embraced farming as "redeeming the land of our fathers," a land they believed had been waiting for them, fallow, for centuries. He and I also shared roots in the early settlements—the *colonias*, as the early Yishuv called them—that the Baron de Rothschild strung along the spine of Palestine in the late nineteenth century, bound by my family's Metula in the far north and his family's Ekron as the southernmost Jewish outpost at the time.

These days, Israelis tend to be sentimental about those early Jewish settlements. Old farmers' homes and other old *yishuv* buildings often serve as country inns, quaint restaurants, gift shops, and museums. Like me and others of my generation or older, Judd had heard firsthand about the hardships Jewish settlers faced as they struggled to farm this unfamiliar land. Alien to the local language and culture, they drained swamps, cleared rocky lands, and survived fevers and snakebites. Yet by the time he and I were born, in the late 1930s, houses were solid, fields were plowed, and trees were bearing fruit. Though the Second World War was decimating Europe and the Israeli-Palestinian war of '48 was soon to follow, Judd and I grew up in what were for us, in British Mandate Palestine, easy times.

Was any of this on his mind that fall afternoon as we neared the flourishing Jewish neighborhood built on Aqir's lands? Was this why he suggested, rather unexpectedly, that we detour first to see Mazkeret Batya, as Ekron had been renamed? That original village, like Metula's main street for me, had been his family home but also a reminder, for him, of a time when good relations between Arabs and Jews promised, at least locally, a neighborly future.

The historic Jewish village we drove into that dreary fall afternoon hardly seemed to belong to Israel as we know it today. Preserved as a museum—"Zionism at its Apex," a YouTube video called it—the village seemed cut off from Israel's pulsing energy, from its construction sites and restless streams of traffic whizzing by on roads that always seem to have just been built or to be in the process of being widened and repaved. Frozen in time and utterly devoid of people, the village square lay before us in the gray light as if in a coma, its farmhouses resting heavily on the dark flat earth of the coastal lowlands. Other than the wisps of steam that curled upward from the damp earth, nothing seemed to move.

"Ekron was founded by the *Hovevei-Zion* movement in 1882" Judd said, suddenly sounding like a tour guide. I had never heard him speak this way before. Now he was packing in facts, dates, and numbers, none of which I remember. "Do you want to get out and look around?" he asked, a new urgency creeping into his voice. I could see that he wanted us to breathe his village air, let its smells waft around us, and feel its muddy, spongy earth underfoot.

It must have rained earlier that day, I half-registered as the wet chill penetrated my jacket. Here was yet another kind of knowing what my own childhood shared with his, I thought, as we stepped onto the waterlogged earth: mud! The *bassa* swamp where I lost a shoe in Herzelia, the cars stuck in the mud in front of our house in Tel Aviv, the houses I saw melt into mud on the way to the Negev, a photograph of a muddy field where three Palestinian men walked toward the camera. Judd and I grew up on the same coastal plain. His mud was the same mud I knew in front of our house, deeply rutted by the junk man's wagon or the creaking ice cart passing by.

Back in Judd's car, the history lesson continued. There were the Ottomans and the British, diseases and famine, locusts and the Arab Rebellion. Jews arrived, left, and returned. There were friendly relations with some Arabs but also tensions with others as Jewish immigration accelerated. It was a labyrinthine history of new beginnings that set in motion new displacements and more new beginnings. Everybody was from somewhere else and many did not stay put. "My father was born in … his parents immigrated to Palestine… he grew up in … he worked … he left … he studied … he returned … he married…" Yes, but what did this inventory *feel* like, I wondered, and why was I reluctant to ask?

Facts are the default line, not the way of the heart. My unspoken questions colluded with Judd's non-answers. We talked, he and I, as if facts were all that's needed while Deborah, in the back seat, stared out the window. She was a stranger to this conversation, while for Judd and me the mere mention of *Hovevei Zion* was enough to evoke a whole chapter of early Zionist history. We were joined by the emotional sinews of our grandparents' and great grandparents' struggles at the outer edges of their precarious foothold on this land.

There had to be profound anxiety not only about the new land into which those early settlers barely put roots but also about the Palestinian neighbors they did not understand, a language they did not know, smells they had never inhaled, and thoughts of loved ones lost or abandoned in the miasmas of pogroms, way before the Holocaust. There were also droughts, unemployment, and hunger, tuberculosis and malaria. There were too many tombstones for young women who died in childbirth and for solitary men who will forever be nameless. Still, some of these settlers did get to know their Arab neighbors, teach themselves to speak Arabic, and share acts of kindness. Unlike Metula, which had been under repeated Arab attack by dispossessed Druze, local Bedouins, and Syrian militias, Ekron was able to exist peacefully near Aqir.

None of this was talked about as we turned from Mazkeret Batya, heading away from the history Israel works to preserve toward the history it does its best to negate. Now, decades after the Nakba, Judd's tiny old Renault 4 was ferrying us toward the modern suburb that has since spread over Aqir's lands.

It was disconcerting, this re-entry into contemporary Israel. While Mazkeret Batya seemed embalmed, Aqir was nowhere to be seen. Instead we found ourselves threading our way through a crisp Jewish neighborhood that bore no relation to either place. The air had cleared, and signs of a well-lived life were everywhere: in the whitewashed, newly built stucco houses, the lovingly tended gardens, and the red-tiled pitched roofs that peeked above lush canopies of trees. Even the ceaseless vibration of cars rushing on the nearby highway was reassuring. Israel was alive with the traffic coursing through its veins.

Judd drove slowly, looking to the right and left in search of a landmark, some telltale sign that would lead to the Arab house he was intent on showing us was the only Palestinian house remaining. We could hear a radio faintly through a half-open window of a house we were passing, where a curtain swelled in the late afternoon breeze. In another house, a woman was shushing a baby. Two boys were bouncing a ball on the street's cooling asphalt, and we could smell onions frying somewhere nearby. In this pleasant neighborhood there wasn't a trace of either the sepia memories of Mazkeret Batya or the tragedy of Aqir.

And yet for all that, and perhaps because of that, all three of us were keenly aware that the streets on which we traveled had been paved over leveled homes. About that, too, we said nothing. Our quest was simply to locate and photograph a building, though we knew that this seemingly simple task rested on much that was unvoiced.

We were silent as Judd navigated his car through the winding, tree-shaded streets of this new Jewish neighborhood, where all the houses were of the same age and all the streets looked alike as they twisted and doubled back on themselves in elegant flourishes of town planning. Swerving and turning right and then left, the search seemed to go on forever.

"Damn!" Judd eventually said, straining toward the windshield, hoping for better visibility. "All the landmarks are gone."

Meandering through twisting roads, I lost sense of where we were heading. The search seemed to go on forever, and I could see that Judd was losing patience.

"Some town planning!" he said. We all fell quiet, letting his anger hang in the air. It was so different when we first set out from Tel Aviv, as Judd spoke about his childhood in Ekron and Aqir.

His grandfather, he had told us two hours earlier, on the way out of Tel Aviv, used to take him along when he went to Aqir to buy watermelons and sheep's cheese or to sell the new Shamouti oranges that Jewish farmers began cultivating.

"So what was it like in Aqir?" I finally asked.

I could see his fingers relaxing on the steering wheel, and his voice began to lose its impatient edge. Such friendly people, he told us. The men and his grandfather greeting each other with gracious old-world formality: "*Al-salam aleykum*" he'd say, "*Wa-aleykum al-salam*," they'd reply. To Judd, who knew only some Arabic, it sounded like poetry. He told us that the farmers would invite his grandfather to sit on a rush stool, offer him sweet tea in a small glass, joke with him, and talk about crops and weather and village news. Sometimes there would be a happy exclamation or a head shaking sadly—news of a wedding or somebody's passing, his grandfather would explain to his young grandson, standing nearby and trying to make sense of the voices.

He was fascinated by the sounds of their conversation, Judd went on. On days when he'd see some boys kicking a ball in in the dusty street, he'd join them. They'd giggle at his formal greeting of *al-salam aleykum*, as he'd seen the old men do. He was just beginning to pick up some Arabic. Mostly he'd wave his arms and shout in Hebrew "*kan, kan*" to have the ball passed on to him, or "*hon, hon*" in Arabic ("here, here"). But even without Arabic he could feel an old man's affection when he patted his head and called him *ibni* ("my son").

Ibni! I am thinking now, remembering the Arab women who'd walk down the treacherous steps to my grandmother's patio with baskets of figs on their heads, and the one who called me "*habibti*." In a few years, I thought as I listened to Judd's story, that affection would turn to anger, grief, and maybe even hate.

"But what I remember most," Judd continued, "are the smells of the village: the smell of dung fire, burning thorns and wood, wild za'atar, ripe figs. They remained lodged in the clay bricks of their homes long after they'd left."

"Left," I thought. That's how we all referred to the Nakba. Not "expelled," "forced out," or "cleansed." Just a departure: "left."

A heavy silence settled in the car as Deborah and I watched Judd navigate the streets in search of a house that may have just been an illusion or, most likely, torn down years ago. Judd clutched the steering wheel tightly, as if to make the building step forward by his sheer determination. There had been such warmth in his voice when he described Aqir. For him Aqir was still the place where an Arab man might pat a Jewish child and call him *ibni*.

Still silent, looking out of the car window at houses that could not possibly be Palestinian, I was losing hope of ever seeing the one remaining village house Judd was grimly determined to find, when we saw three teenage boys idly tracing figure eights with their bicycles—one hand on the handlebars or no hands at all. Leaning out of his window, Judd asked them if they knew of an Arab house nearby. They didn't, surprised that such a possibility would even exist. I suggested giving up, but Judd shook his head, jaw clenched, his hands tightening on the steering wheel.

It was late afternoon when he suddenly jerked forward, slammed on the brakes, pointed to a small, nondescript stucco building tucked in a yard at the end of a short alley. "There it is!" he exclaimed.

There was nothing identifiably "Arab" about it. Just an ordinary stucco box-like structure, whitewashed and with the usual pitched red roof—a Jewish structure. This street was no different from others; the house we were staring at was not different either.

"This is it," Judd said as we scrambled out of his car, pointing toward what turned out to be a lean-to attached to a Jewish home.

This one-room structure could have easily passed for an ordinary addition to any Israeli house of 1970s vintage. Except for a ladder leaning against a stained white wall and an empty light socket dangling from the ceiling, the place was empty, clearly not in use. And yet I sensed, perhaps because Judd singled it out, that there was something ineffably different about the walls, where a barely perceptible unevenness seemed to swell the plaster.

Judd was already motioning for Deborah and me to come close to a small patch of wall where the plaster had come loose, an ordinary gash that I wouldn't have noticed. Here, the crumbling plaster revealed not the usual cinderblocks of Israeli construction, but alternating layers of sticks and pebbly mud. "Arab era," an archaeologist might say.

We stood staring at the wall, shaken. The skies had cleared but it was getting dark and a chilly wind was rising. Soon we wouldn't be able to see much, and any moment somebody might come to ask what we were doing there, trespassing on private property.

Is that all, I wondered? But Judd was already a few feet away, walking across a paved path toward a smaller building, this one free standing. We followed, ducking under the low opening that led into this one-room building. In the gathering darkness it was hard at first to identify the few objects lying on the packed mud floor: a rusty old hoe, obviously not used for decades, and a dented and tarnished metal jug, also "Arab era," of a kind not found in a Jewish home.

Judd was turning the hoe in his hands when I noticed a large shadowy bulge at the far corner of the room.

"Look! It's a *taboon*, an adobe baking oven!" I exclaimed, pointing. It was built into the corner, rounded, like a Native American clay oven.

We stood there, speechless. The outside of the *taboon* still had dark smoke marks on it. One could feel the presence of the women who had cooked there, women who, if they were lucky, had ended up in a refugee camp near Ramallah. It could have been an older woman, her legs swollen after years of childbearing and housework, bending to take out the loaves, or a younger one, still lithe, a toddler holding on to her dress. I imagined them in long black everyday dresses—their embroidery perhaps frayed but still beautiful—talking to one another in subdued voices.

I thought of my grandmother as we bent to exit through the small door. She would have known women like the ones who baked bread in this *taboon*. In her young days, still in Metula, she might have met women from Lebanon's neighboring Marjayoun. I thought of her buying apricots and figs from such women before the war, patting a child on the head: "*Ibnek*? Your son? How old?" I can see these women in their world as vividly as Judd can still see his grandfather talking with a man wearing a kaffiyeh scarf—the man who laid his hand on Judd's young head and called him "*ibni*." Our worlds could have overlapped. One of these women might have called me "*binti*, my daughter."

By the time we walked out of that free-standing kitchen, bending single file through its low arched doorway, what little remained of twilight was fast giving way to darkness. In the lingering blue-gray light I saw Judd approach the lean-to's outer wall and press his palms against it. Leaning forward, he brought his face close to the smooth adobe skin of the wall and breathed its scent.

"This is the smell I remember," he said.

Though we were losing the light, Deborah took a photograph of this moment: Judd is awash in blue shadows. He is inhaling—taking into his being—the life that continues to cling to that Palestinian house. It is a moment of ineffable longing, where the pain of all that was lost keeps alive the possibility of restitution.

22. Bir'im

Our time in Aqir differed from others mostly in its details, I now think. The arch of a doorway, the smell lingering in a wall, the smoke staining a clay oven … they are, like so much else Deborah and I had seen, variations on a theme. Now back in my American home in 2020, with my writing nearing completion, I am awed by the cumulative weight of the Nakba as we came to see it, but also as I have sensed and gradually got to understand it from 1947 to this day. Included are not only memories but intimate tactile reminders: the floor tile fragments and bullet casings Deborah lugged back to the United States, her burnt Kewpie doll and my plaster star, our laminated map segments, her archive of more than two thousand photographs taken between 2005 and 2008, and a CD that reached me in Boston only after Deborah and I had stopped our search—a recording of my time in yet another Palestinian village, Bir'im, when I joined a tour group of Scottish visitors.

That tour was not my first time in Bir'im, now Israeli Baram. Deborah and I had first gone there in 2006, our first year of searching deliberately for villages demolished during the Nakba. Together with another Galilee village, Iqrit, Bir'im had been in the news for many years. In this instance there was no fighting. The residents were asked to evacuate temporarily, assured that the evacuation would be brief, "just to let the army secure the border with Lebanon." They complied, and yet they were never allowed to return. There have been mass demonstrations and many lawsuits, ongoing since 1951, all the way up to the Supreme Court, all decided in Bir'im's favor, to no avail.

It was easy to locate Kibbutz Baram on the map and thus to guess where we'd find Bir'im. The windswept promontory that is now the Israeli national forest of Baram was another clue. During the long drive up north I told Deborah what I knew of this Christian community's determined efforts to regain their village. Much of the village lands has since been given to neighboring Jewish Dovev and Baram, the rest turned by the JNF into a park that includes an ancient synagogue as well as what's left of Bir'im's Palestinian houses and church. Worship in the church is allowed only on special occasions: at Christmas and Easter and for marriages, baptisms, and funerals.

Knowing this history, we imagined ourselves prepared for the visit, but we weren't. Something about the silent emptiness of the place felt eerie, despite the warm afternoon. Maybe it was the contrast between the expectations set by the large parking lot and the total absence of cars, except for the park ranger's. Bir'im felt like a ghost village. There were more half-standing houses in full view than we'd expected, broken down and half-buried in thistles and dead grasses, but still identifiable as houses. We could see them as soon as we stepped out of our car.

Deborah, anxious to photograph while the light was good, headed abruptly toward the ruins before I finished paying for admission.

With nothing to do but wait, I sat on the wide stone steps that led into the park, taking in the silence: no distant cars laboring uphill, no feet crunching on gravel, no voices. Other than a lizard that scampered to hide under a rock, all was peaceful. High above the pines' canopy, two diminutive military jets, inaudible at that distance, were slicing white curlicues into the sky.

I'd opened my notebook, planning to write, when a woman's voice broke the silence.

"Shalom," she said as she approached—khaki uniform, JNF badge, a friendly smile. A young Israeli park ranger, maybe thirty years old. "If you need to use the washroom you'd better use it now. I'll be locking up soon," she said.

"I'm OK," I smiled back. "Just waiting for my photographer friend. Down there," I gestured toward the ruins, sensing that this woman wanted to chat.

Smoothing her military-looking khaki skirt, she hesitated for a moment and sat down next to me.

"Where are you from?" I asked as I closed my notebook.

"From Jish" she said, adding the Hebrew name, "Gush Halav," after a pause.

Jish! I registered, tensing. That's the *Arab* name for her Israeli-Palestinian village. She, a Palestinian, felt she needed to translate it into the newly revived Hebrew name. Were it not for her using "Jish" I'd have never guessed she's Palestinian. Her khaki uniform, her Ashkenazi Hebrew accent, even her short haircut—everything about her pegged her as "one of us."

"Is Jish where your family's from?" I asked, using the Arabic name to signal my ease with her Palestinian identity.

"Oh no," she said. "We're from here, from Bir'im."

This rattled me. How was I, obviously an Israeli Jew, to respond to *that*, sitting as we were in sight of her village ruins? Knowing Bir'im's history—the expulsion, the legal struggle, the residents' determination to return—what could I say? The ruins Deborah went to photograph could have been her family's home. She could have so easily seen me as the enemy.

Neither of us mentioned this history. Ours was the uncomfortable silence I'd come to know—when Marwa avoided talking about Haifa's Nakba painting or when I'd inadvertently "outed" the Palestinian man who was printing the *Eid* photograph in Tel Aviv.

"Are you married?" I asked instead. "Children?"

"Yes, two," she smiled. "One's a year old, and I have a four-year-old boy. My husband works in Haifa," she added, explaining that there wasn't any work for men nearby. In the park she could choose her own hours, and her mother helped with the kids.

I nodded, working mother to working mother, a bond we could share.

Maybe she understood my silence regarding Bir'im, for as she got up to leave, she told me that many of the people in Jish are from Bir'im. "My uncle wrote a book about Bir'im. You can buy it in the grocery store, in the center of Jish."

I nodded and waved as she walked off, pleased that she no longer used the Hebrew name Gush Halav, but also aware of all that we'd left unspoken.

By the time Deborah emerged, the sun was about to begin its descent.

"I saw the park ranger," I told her. "She told me that her family's from here and that her uncle had written a book about Bir'i. It's available in his grocery, nearby in Gush Halav—Jish in Arabic," I added, meeting her eyes.

I was still thinking about the conundrum of Israeli place names when we came to a large sign installed near the steps leading into the park, written in Israel's three official languages: Hebrew, English, and Arabic. Put up by the JNF, it informed visitors that Baram had been home to a prosperous Jewish community centuries ago, as the remains of its elegant synagogue attest. The sign had no mention of the Palestinian village that had existed on this mountaintop for centuries, its church facing the synagogue nearby, the village ruins in full view.

The synagogue was as impressive as the park's brochures promised. What remained of it towered above us, with its massive pillars, beautifully carved capitals, and ornate stone rafters looming against a distant horizon. We approached it silently, almost reverently, crossing the spacious clearing that made the approach all the more imposing. The trees that fringed the clearing partly screened the modest church, though its bell tower peeked above the pines. The disintegrating Palestinian houses were to be ignored, the trees instructed, even if the cracked walls, caving roofs, and weeds taking root in the mortar spoke with another voice.

Standing there quietly, I mused about the Jewish grandeur to which these monumental fragments attested. I could imagine the skill, muscle, and wealth it took to erect this edifice on the crest of a remote Galilee hilltop. Its mere endurance inspired awe. Carved into its ravaged glory was a people's history of loss and nostalgia, where Jewish past splendor lingers only as a faint afterimage, long gone and yet refusing to vanish.

For Bir'im's Palestinian residents, the imposing remains of Baram's ancient synagogue are bound to mean something different. A year later I'd hear a local man guiding Scottish visitors suggest that it may not have been a synagogue at all. It could have been a Roman temple, built to include all worshipers, as it had no religious symbols, only carvings of grapes and a laurel wreath. But even during our first visit here, I could see that for Bir'im's Palestinians the temple would seem a relic from somebody else's distant past, belonging to a history that preceded their own. For them it would be impressive but irrelevant, maybe even an irritant, a triumphal symbol of a Jewish drama venerated while their own houses lay in ruins.

This is what made my conversation with the park ranger so guarded, sitting together on the stone steps leading into the park. I was acutely aware of what kept us apart. It's a question of ownership, resting on an essential notion of homeland: Palestinian "Bir'im" or Jewish "Baram"? "Jish" or "Gush Halav"? A temple or a synagogue?

I had lost all sense of time when a car engine broke the spell. A car door slammed, then another. A child, petulant, was demanding something, and an emphatic male voice answered. We turned toward the trees that separated the church from the synagogue.

The voices belonged to a small family: a mother, father, and two children, speaking loudly as they approached the synagogue. A few photos were snapped: boy and girl straddling a fallen column, Mom standing near a pillar, a grinning Dad with a kid posed on top of a carved capital. Other than the church, where the boy climbed to ring the bell, they never seemed to notice the village ruins. They were barely gone when another Israeli group arrived, some twelve youths tramping single file through the ruins, their canteens clinking against backpack hardware—a scout troop, or perhaps "*Gadna*" or youth movement members, led by a young man barely older than his charges. Ordering them to pause, he lectured them briefly about Bir'im's contested status and the dangers of Palestinians reclaiming their homes: " … border … infiltrators … Lebanon … no choice …"

"What was that all about?" Deborah asked once they left.

"Oh, the usual. Expulsion was necessary. Something about an existential threat. At least he didn't pretend the village didn't exist."

"That's more than that other family did," she scoffed.

The events of the afternoon were getting to me: the Palestinian woman from Jish, the Israeli family's casual disrespect, the complacent history lesson, the callous bell-ringing, and the JNF sign disregarding centuries of Palestinian presence. It felt good to know that Deborah felt something of the same.

Bir'im's ruins were intact enough to let us imagine the life that had been lived there. Fragments of houses were close enough to one another to give us the sense of a village: a free-standing wall with a doorway that led to rubble, a courtyard where a self-sown fig tree broke the paving, a house whose beams no longer supported a roof, and the afternoon sun streaming in through twin windows, high up on what was left of somebody's second floor, illuminating a void that was once a room. I could imagine a woman calling a neighbor, children playing in a courtyard, or a donkey's hooves clomping on the cobblestones of narrow alleys that had become impassable, choked by stones and scrub.

One of these alleys brought us back to the village church, recently whitewashed by Bir'im's exiles, now living in Haifa, Jish, and Lebanon. Deborah was off to photograph yet again while I stood by the church, feeling the chill of the descending evening. The sanctuary's windows were shuttered, and a large padlock had been placed on the front door. But people had obviously been here to paint the church, and a plastic chair had been left standing on the flat roof, where someone could climb to ring the bell and enjoy the view. In a nearby clearing I saw the remains of a campfire with some ten or twelve stones arranged in a circle. People keep coming here, I thought. They were not about to give up.

"Hey, come here!" I suddenly heard Deborah call to me from under an open archway.

I had not noticed this building earlier, its cavernous interior sheltering under wide arches. Entering it, I saw that almost all the large stones that made up the interior walls of its two rooms had inscriptions in Arabic: letters and numbers drawn thickly in shiny black paint on the uneven surfaces, with a sure hand, breathtakingly beautiful.

"This is no ordinary graffiti," I half-whispered, awed by the writing that crowded in from all sides.

"Amazing! Like an artwork in a museum or a gallery," Deborah said. "Or a memorial."

Summoning the Arabic I had studied fifty years earlier, I read out to her names and numbers: George Abu Nimr 1954, Mazen Rouhani 1942, Elias Rouhani 1972, Emil Mansour 1965, Yusef Abu'l Hadi 1938 … written as high up on the wall as a hand could reach, a name to each stone. The paint glistened, black against the ripples of pale hand-hewn masonry. The cursive Arabic letters bent, rose, and flattened on the uneven surfaces, subtly form-shifting from wide, brush strokes to delicately tapering lines.

Time seemed measured only by the names I was reading as I moved from stone to stone. Their sheer number conveyed urgency, a determination to bring them into perpetuity. A year later I'd hear the Scottish visitors' guide, Anis Chacour, explain that this had been the village school.

By the time we finally emerged from that building, the shadows had lengthened and the western horizon was turning a pale pink. Though it was getting chilly, we paused to reread the JNF sign on our way to the parking lot. Its etched Hebrew, English, and Arabic texts were identical except for one small detail I had not noticed earlier. In the Arabic version, someone had scratched out the word "Jewish" used to describe ancient Baram, replacing it with the handwritten word "Arab," and someone else scratched out the word "Arab" but failed to insert "Jewish" in its place. This wasn't idle doodling. It took effort to scrape the original etched "Jewish" and then, for the next person, to scrape handwritten Arabic language "Arab" that had replaced it, leaving the space blank. Did it mean that that the second person did not know enough Arabic to re-insert "Jewish" in the Arabic text? Or was it enough to simply walk away, having cleansed the word "Arab"?

The argument is not going to end any time soon, I thought, remembering how, just a few minutes earlier, as we were leaving the school, I made Deborah pause by the church door. "Did you see that?" I said, pointing to a large rectangular cornerstone to the right of its padlocked door. Even in the dimming light one could still make out the large yellow block letters painted on it. It was the word "FREEDOM," written in English, addressed to all who pass by.

A year later we returned to Bir'im, this time arriving earlier in order to give Deborah more time to photograph. Once again the place was silent—just the call of an odd bird and the whir of grasshoppers. The only two cars in the parking lot were a park ranger's and an old passenger van. Maybe I'd have the place to myself, I thought as Deborah walked off, hefting her tripod over her shoulder. But as I walked uphill, past the now-familiar JNF sign, a small cluster of tourists came into view. Of course, I thought. That van! Some eight men and women, probably European, middle-aged, were listening to an older man who was gesturing toward the village, their gaze following his pointing hand. One man was aiming a small box toward the speaker—a recorder, I later discovered.

These attentive, neatly dressed people looked more like the pilgrims and missionaries one might come across in Nazareth, Bethlehem, or Jerusalem than like hikers to a remote mountaintop in the Upper Galilee. Their guide, as I supposed the older man to be, also seemed out of place in his casual shirt, slacks, and now dusty city shoes. Clearly I am not one of them, I felt, as I hovered a few feet away, trying to hear what was being said, painfully aware that I was Israeli.

"… and it's only by stealth that we manage to repair the church," the guide was saying. "That's how we repaired the roof. A little at a time, so the Israelis wouldn't notice."

I was both relieved and uneasy to realize that he was speaking in English: it meant that I could understand what was being said, except that his Arabic accent worried me. How would he feel about me, with my Hebrew accent, I wondered, as he told these outsiders about the destruction done by my people? It was the same jolt I felt the previous year when I learned that the park ranger's family came from Bir'im. She and I had skirted the matter, but now the village history was clearly the topic. Straining to hear what was being said and already knowing what *could* be said, I felt a familiar anxiety press on my chest. Here, in full view, were the consequences of our "silver platter," Bir'im's mute ruins exposing the lie of "a land without people." But this time the ruins weren't mute. The man guiding the group was giving the village its voice.

Shaken by this awareness, I took refuge in resentment as I surveyed the group. They reminded me of the European missionaries who accosted me as a child, before '48, gentiles who thrust pocket-size New Testaments into my unwilling hands. Who were they to pass judgment, given all that we, Jews, suffered for centuries at their hands?

It didn't take long for somebody in the group to notice me and for the rest to follow his gaze. One of them, holding a small recorder and taking notes on a clipboard, invited me to join them. "I'm Donnie," he said, explaining that they were from Scotland on a bicycle ride from Nazareth to Jerusalem to raise funds for Nazareth's Scottish hospital. His handshake was firm, his eyes direct, his face friendly—not a trace of the missionary condescension I expected. Joining the group, I only saw welcoming faces.

'I'm from Boston … but originally from here, Israel," I said, answering the predictable questions. "And no, I'm not alone. I am with an American photographer," I said, gesturing in the direction where I'd seen Deborah clamber downhill. I explained that we were doing a story about Bir'im, and that we knew about the expulsion and the court cases.

I was not altogether wrong to label them as Christian pilgrims. They'd been invited to tour Bir'im because of their church's contact with Bir'im's Melkite community, including Haifa's Bishop Chacour. The bishop's relative, a lawyer called Anis Chacour, was the man leading the tour. Inevitably, they wanted to know more about me and their questions began to feel like cross-examination, much as Eitan's were when I first met him at Zochrot. An unspoken question had to be answered: Is she one of "us" or one of "them"? After all, what's an Israeli Jew doing in a place known as a political flashpoint for debates about the Nakba and the Palestinians' "right of return"?

Words tumbled out of me as I tried to explain the work Deborah and I were doing. It was the first time I found myself talking to strangers about it, and the effort left me shaken. It felt like a confession, a giving voice to the unspeakable.

"*Aideh*, let's go," Anis finally said, bending to pick up a fallen tree limb that would serve him as walking stick. "This was the Suleif family's home," he said, leading us into a derelict courtyard. "They're now in Jish. Here," he said, gesturing at a gaping hole in the wall, "was the entrance, and here, to the side, they did their cooking."

Peering through a gap that had been a doorway, we could see the remains of what used to be rooms—broken-down walls, crumbling plaster, garbage, and Hebrew graffiti.

"Awful!" whispered a woman leaning toward me. "How could the Jews do that?" I bent, pretending to adjust a sandal, an alarm bell sounding in my mind. It *was* awful, but "the Jews"? Let's not confuse "Jews" and "Israelis," I wanted to say, but that would need some explaining. She and I are on the same side, yet her not knowing the difference could so easily be seen as anti-Semitism, tarring all Jews with one brush.

There was no time for discussion. Anis was already pausing by another house. Every house we passed had been home to a family with grandparents and uncles and aunts, some on the mother's side and some on the father's, families that shared alleys and married into one another, all of them living close by. Every house was a repository of a genealogy and stories that were woven into its neighbors' stories and genealogies. There was the house Anis's great-grandfather had built when he was summoned to leave the neighboring village of Khurfeish to repair Bir'im's church; the house where Anis's school friend Anton lived; somebody else's house where you could still see the old cistern in the courtyard—each house invoked as if to repopulate the ruins with names like those Deborah and I had seen inscribed inside the schoolhouse.

The contrast between the village as we saw it and Anis's memories was powerful, the dismay unrelenting. We kept passing roofs that gaped, cisterns clogged with rubble, walls that were barely standing, and views of newly forested vistas. Whatever we still saw standing, Anis explained, was standing only because of these houses' proximity to the church. Most of the village had been leveled.

Modern Israel is so near, I thought, as my eyes followed a car weaving in and out of the dark green forest heading for Israeli Dovev or kibbutz Baram. Beyond them was Lebanon, mysterious, unknown. The tour was almost over, I realized, as Bir'im's church came into view. Solid, cared for, intact, it felt defiant, determined to last. Walking over to the door, I could see the yellow block letters of the word "FREEDOM" still visible on the church's cornerstone.

Annis explained that the church bell, sent from Lebanon, was made with contributions from Bir'im's exiles. The Israelis had stolen the original bell. "They also told us to put all our belongings in the church," he added, as he pulled a massive key out of a leather pouch. "They said that our things would be safe till we return, but of course everything was stolen."

These Christian visitors must be indignant about the ban on using the church, I thought, looking at them as we entered the church single file. Hushed, we stood inside, taking in the spare interior: a pale stone altar, a pristine lace-trimmed cloth over it, windows deep-set in thick walls, simple wooden chairs.

Stepping over a threshold worn to marble-smoothness by countless feet, we left the church, momentarily blinded by the sun. Donnie had just turned off his recorder and Anis was putting his key back in its pouch when Deborah emerged, dusty and disheveled, weighted down by her camera and tripod. Surprised to see me with this group of strangers clustered by the church, she froze for a minute before walking toward us. I knew what would come next: people would ask her the same questions they already asked me, and Anis would welcome her with a reassuring "*marhaba*." But now there was no time.

Anis's family had prepared a picnic. The smoke of grilling kebabs was already rising into the air.

It was a relief to see her walk toward us. Too much guilt and anger swirled inside me during the tour. I needed an understanding glance, a word to reassure me that the comment about "the Jews" had no malice in it. None of it was possible at that moment. It was time for fellowship and then goodbyes. We'll talk later, we told one another wordlessly.

On our way back to the parking lot, words poured out of me: "Exiting that church, I'd crossed more than a stone threshold," I heard myself say, hesitating, searching for words. "Something about Anis, a Palestinian who's about my age and remembers Bir'im and the Nakba. Our stories are so mixed together," I went on, remembering the Scottish people's warm acceptance but also my own belonging to the people who expelled my hosts. "I couldn't quite be part of this group," I said.

"But you don't represent Israel," she said. "You only represent yourself. You *were* one of the group when you told them what we are doing. That takes courage."

I still pulled back from her. Looking at her straight silvery hair that still had some gold in it, her gray-blue eyes, her thin straight nose and high cheekbones half-hidden under her cap, she, too, seemed one of "them," not one of "us." No, I'm being unfair, I corrected myself as I looked again at the face I knew so intimately. She's a person, much as I am, as are the people with whom I had just spent several deeply moving hours.

"You're right," I said, touching her cheek lightly by way of thanks. "But my history is part of the story too—not only the Nakba but the suffering that created Zionism in the first place. Maybe the 'threshold' I said I'd crossed has to do with trust. I do feel what separates us, but I can also see what keeps us together—me, these well-meaning people from Scotland, and Mr. Chacour."

Though I didn't realize it, we had paused by the JNF sign where the fight over homelands could still be seen, scratched into its metal: "Jewish" written in Arabic had been erased, "Arab" had been inserted, and yet another person had scratched the "Arab," leaving a blank space in its place.

"You know," I said, "as the group was entering the church, I left them for a minute to check the cornerstone. The word 'FREEDOM' is still there."

23. Thresholds

*T*hough we did not know it at the time, the summer of 2008 turned out to be Deborah's last time in Israel. Not long after that, she moved to New York and we parted ways. Though I couldn't have predicted that ending, my mother's death after a long decline and my father's slow death just two years earlier prefigured it, anchored as it was in the emptying and sale of our family flat in Tel Aviv—a lifetime of memories gone. A vortex of grieving followed, as these losses melded into a shapeless mass of pain: my family, my home, my life partner, my innocence. For two years Deborah and I didn't talk to each other, our Nakba work at a standstill. We were each reconstituting our own lives, she in New York and I in Boston. Yet out of this grief new life emerged.

Our tracing the Nakba—so arduous and dispiriting—was not what drew us apart. If anything, the pain at witnessing that catastrophe drew us closer. A shared sense of the Nakba's injustice kept us going as we pored over maps, charted routes, and packed and unpacked our bags. That it was dispiriting only strengthened our resolve. We'd come a long way from that first conversation in a Washington hotel, in 1993, when I recoiled from her wish to photograph Israel's cactus bushes, and we'd come a long way, too, from her need for guidance. We knew each other's elation when a discovery would follow a difficult search and shared the crushing dismay into which that elation would dissolve. For Deborah uncovering proof of the Nakba became a forensic obsession, each site of agony needing to be scrutinized and recorded. For me, the search for Palestine inside Israel was forever mired in contradictions that wouldn't let go: to see or not to see, or as trauma therapists put it, to fight or to flee.

One could say that after we separated, I fled. Though I kept returning to Israel with some regularity, nine years would pass before I could face seeing the Nakba's ravaged lands again. But I also fought; freed from the collaboration, I began writing, reclaiming the raw material of our work and turning it into words. By 2014, when my friend Jacoby offered to accompany me as I retrace my earlier searches, I was able to accept her offer. Traveling with her would be easy. A warmly effusive Jewish American who had lived in Israel, an informed and assertive activist, she'd be the right companion. The gnawing worry of "Is she really getting it?" that I sometimes felt with Deborah would be gone.

The old worry about planning the trip and charting access would also be gone. I already knew where to find Sheikh Shahada's shrine in Ein Ghazzal. It would no longer be by accident that we would veer into the Gilboa's scenic road. It would be easy to find the dirt road that leads to Hittin's ancient mosque, or the right point on the road from which to view Saffuriya's forested hill. At each of these places it felt as if time had stood still—the sheep crossing the narrow bridge in Akbara, the bird calls in Hittin, the giant cactuses still lining the paths in Saffuriya.

Bir'im, too, seemed unchanged—the ruins right next to the parking lot, the steps that guided tourists toward the synagogue, the church spire that continued to peek above the pines, all there. Only the old JNF sign was different. A new one had been installed; the argument scratched over the old sign's surface suspended. And this time the place was not deserted. A group of youngsters, fourteen- or fifteen-year-old boys and girls, were seated on a low wall, listening to an animated lecture by a wiry old man in sandals and khaki shorts—a familiar type, I thought. A kibbutznik.

Holding a sheaf of documents, his gestures suggested a well-worn but still passionately felt lecture about love of country and the pioneering spirit that made Israeli statehood possible. But something was not quite right. Though he looked like a kibbutznik, this man was lecturing in English, and his accent was guttural, not the typical Ashkenazi kibbutz accent of his generation. To my amazement, I soon realized that he was actually talking about the Nakba—the broken promise that the evacuation would be temporary, the freezing winter days spent in the open, the petitions and court cases. There are documents, he said, showing his young audience the inventory of possessions his own family had compiled before leaving them in the church for safekeeping—just as Anis Chacour had told us back in 2007.

A Palestinian! Not a kibbutznik after all. But why lecture in English?

The presentation done, he packed his documents in a worn leather portfolio and walked away, leaving the discussion to the two teachers who'd been standing to the side. When one of them took his place in front of the class, I approached the other, a woman in her thirties. She seemed Israeli; her loose khaki pants and long braid again suggesting a kibbutznik, though I no longer trusted myself to tell.

"*Slikha*," I said in Hebrew, hesitating to barge in. "Excuse me … I was wondering, who is this group?"

"And who are *you*?" she asked.

Of course she wouldn't be quick to trust me. The lecture was about Bir'im's destruction, given by a Palestinian who was exposing its injustice. The whole topic was a minefield, especially here, where proof of the Nakba was so obvious. Why should she expect me, a chance Israeli, to welcome this lecture? Whatever she'd say might end up in a shouting match. I understood that. My own initial impulse had also been to avoid the group because I'd assumed that the speaker was offering yet again the standard Israeli "no choice" narrative.

I reviewed for her our good-faith credentials: Jacoby, a long-time American activist, who had lived in Israel and was headed to the Occupied Territories; I, a retired professor and editorial member of *Radical Teacher* magazine, now writing about the Nakba.

"So all right," the teacher said. "This is a Democratic School class, here to learn about the Nakba."

This didn't surprise me. I already knew about these independent, progressive elementary and high schools; a cousin of mine taught in one. But why in English?

"It's a mixed German and Israeli class," she explained. "We're studying the Holocaust and the Nakba."

"Together? In one course?"

"Yes, the whole year." They'd just been to Kibbutz Lohamei Hageta'ot, she added, to visit its museum about the Jewish ghetto fighters' resistance.

I had seen the museum, but what struck me was that the school was teaching the two catastrophes in tandem, and to the German and Jewish youths who were heirs to these catastrophes. I was about to comment on this challenge when the other teacher summoned her colleague. It was time for their class to leave.

Strange to be here without Deborah, I thought, as Jacoby and I stepped carefully through Bir'im's familiar rubble and scrub-filled pathways. The abandoned houses were unchanged, frozen in their state of partial collapse, waiting to be rebuilt. The caved-in roofs, the jagged walls, and the fallen masonry were all as they had been. The gangly, self-sown fig trees, now taller, were still here too, reaching for light through gaping roofs. The yellow block letters spelling "FREEDOM" on the church's cornerstone were slightly faded but still legible. In the adjacent schoolhouse, where Bir'im children's summer camp was held annually, the lower rows of names and dates painted on the masonry were now covered by lumpy gray mortar spread to reinforce the building, but the names inscribed higher up still formed a clearly legible band along the walls.

"This is so moving," Jacoby murmured.

Moving, yes, but also melancholy, I thought, sensing a nip in the air and October's slight graying of the light. Deborah would not be seeing Bir'im again, and I too was not likely to return. I felt a sense of an ending as Jacoby and I headed for the parking lot. This visit, my third, was a pilgrimage.

No, not an ending, I told myself, thinking of Sheikh Shahada's tomb in Ein Ghazal, maintained with such devotion. Bir'im is a site of resistance, struggle, and hope. Its sons and daughters would continue to come to repair the school, repaint the church, and clear brush from its alleys; the voices of children would continue to ring here during their summer camp; the church would welcome its people when they returned to commemorate life's changes; and people like Anis Chacour would continue to guide visitors and tell Bir'im's story. They would not give up on returning home. "We still legally own the place," Anis had said. "There's always hope."

In March 2020, as the corona virus was killing untold numbers of people, I finally picked up a small, flat cardboard box, sealed and by now tattered. It had been lying on my desk for years, postmarked Inverness 2007—a recording of the Scottish tour Anis Chacour had led, as I knew all along. For twelve years I held back, not wanting to hear those voices, avoiding the ache I feel whenever the Nakba comes up, shame about what an Israeli colleague called "the original sin" of the state's founding, and grief about utopian dreams gone awry. This sense of the fundamental wrongness of the Nakba did not let go, but my knowing that the CD was a live recording of our time together, so vividly immediate, made me all the more reluctant to hear it.

Only once I began writing this last chapter did I finally cut through the sealing tape, and even then my fingers hesitated. To my relief, hearing those living voices filled me with happiness. There were the Scottish visitors, animated, interested, and concerned. There was Anis with his wealth of information and ready laughter, with some of his relatives chiming in. And there was Donnie MacLean welcoming me into the group and me talking too. For one short afternoon we had been a community, sharing Bir'im's determined resilience.

The recording confirmed what I remembered of our tour of the village as I listened to Anis describing village life once again: the animals, the plants, the courtyards and water cisterns. Family homes built close together— parents, grandparents, uncles and aunts. Anton's home nearby and, near it, the house of a doctor who'd left for the United States but asked to be buried in Bir'im's church, near its bishops. As a part-time cobbler, Anis's father knew all the neighboring villages' gossip, passed on while people waited for their shoes to be repaired. His great-grandfather, a skilled stonemason, moved there a hundred and fifty years before my visit, just a few years before my own great-grandparents would settle in Metula. There had been one thousand people living in Bir'im before the Nakba, he said, all of them linked by kinship, maternal and paternal, including a long line of Chacour bishops, almost all of them now in Jish, Haifa, and Lebanon.

In '48, at age ten, as I sat through air raids in Tel Aviv, eight-year-old Anis walked five kilometers to Lebanon.

Anis's recorded voice was just describing the volunteers who have been coming to repair the church surreptitiously, despite government prohibition, when a tiny skip in the soundtrack interrupted him. Suddenly my own voice came on. I had assumed that that part will be off-record, but there I was, answering questions about who I was and what I was doing there. The questions, I noticed, were curious, not suspicious. Missing was the reflexive barrier of distrust that rises among us, Israelis and Palestinians, the second we register that the other is an "other." I hadn't heard myself speak for years, and was shaken to hear my voice sounding sad and passionate. "Bir'im is not alone," I heard myself say as I described Deborah's and my work. "There are many other villages like it. Too many. You see another village, and another, and another. It's heartbreaking," my voice trailed off.

Tears stung my throat when I heard myself saying these words, thinking of all that had happened between 2005, when Deborah first came to Israel, and 2020, when I finally made myself listen to this recording. The tears were not about me any more than this book is about me. They are about us—Israelis, Palestinians, and whoever may be reading this account. They are about possibilities squandered—for peace, for coexistence, for ordinary human fellowship.

The story *Tracing Homelands* tells is circumscribed, carefully kept within the '48 armistice Green Line border. It stays close to what I know best, though always shadowed the brutal realities of exiled Palestinian life under Israeli rule in Gaza, the West Bank, and the seemingly quiet Golan. Implicit is the fact that neither the graffiti calling for "TRANSFER" that Deborah and I saw scrawled on walls and billboards, nor the word "HARRUS" stamped on old mandatory maps, is a thing of the past, even if an altered vocabulary and newly devised laws and policies cover up this reality.

Nor is the word "FREEDOM outdated," written as it is at the entrance to Bir'im's church and spoken on many lips. Place names may be changed and localities demolished, but the Palestinians' will to survive—to resist, to embrace dignity, and to win justice—is still there. It is a will to live we Jews know all too well, inextricable from our own history of near-annihilation. Marked by the ravages of a turbulent regional history—Palestinian, Pan-Arab, Jewish, and Western—this will to live is jostled by discordant aspirations: humanist, egalitarian, and freedom-seeking, but also nationalist, ethnocentric, colonialist, and authoritarian.

My own love of my homeland, and that of many others, was marked by this heritage. It engendered a devotion I embraced for years and abandoned only gradually and with great anguish once I began to register the devastating ethical and geopolitical consequences that were born of that history. This slow change cannot be traced to the accidental detour Deborah and

I took in 2005, on the way to what we still thought of as Beit Shean, not Beissan. It cannot be traced back to that afternoon in Washington, DC, in 1993, when I first told her about cactuses marking sites of Palestinian villages. It is a story whose beginnings are many, with roots and capillaries reaching into the dark recesses of history in relays of causes and effects.

There is no easy way to chart these causes and effects, where each cause has earlier causes and webs of subsequent effects. The Nakba that looks back to Kishinev and Auschwitz and further back is also a harbinger of the ongoing destruction we see now in the Occupied Territories and Gaza, with a future yet to be determined. It is a story that to date has no closure. In the meantime, the following anecdote, also concerning Bir'im, may serve as a provisional coda.

In 2007 Deborah and I detoured to Jish on our way home, hoping to buy the book about Bir'im that the park ranger had mentioned to me. Though night had fallen, the small village grocery was still lit by a dim lamp, its iron grate already half-lowered over the entrance. The owner, a tired-looking stocky man in his late fifties, was dragging in the heavy hemp bags full of rice and lentils that in daytime stand by the door. He barely nodded to my Hebrew shalom and, when I asked to buy his book about Bir'im, he pulled a slim booklet out of a small stack and handed it to me wordlessly. Back home, when I could finally see the book in lamplight, it turned out to be in Arabic, not meant for outsiders.

The booklet is now in my American home, propped up by its neighboring volumes, line after line of sinuous Arabic print still waiting for a translator. The few people I knew to ask to translate it didn't have time. Now, in 2020, as I think about an Arabic book I cannot read, I am reminded of walking up the cobbled street in Tarshiha, frustrated by a pen that wouldn't write. It also occurs to me that I have been referring to language repeatedly in this account, sometimes as a bridge and often as a barrier. Place names double on themselves, endlessly mirroring, negating, and replacing one another across this narrow strip of land that each side claims as its homeland. Accents, translations, and legibility haunt this story. Words are printed, stamped, chiseled, scratched, drawn, faded, denied, and erased. They keep appearing, unbidden, all of them clues. Beyond what they say are the who, where, and why of the telling. They are all runes, markings in languages we have yet to learn if we are ever to listen, hear, and come together.

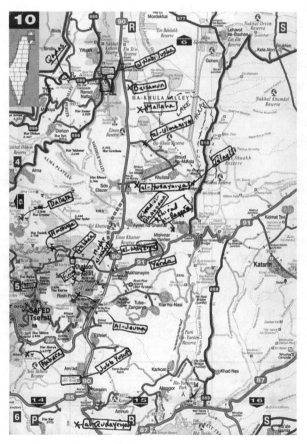

An annotated page from Linda and Deborah's
road atlas, 2008

Afterword

*H*istory is hurtling forward even as I write this "Afterword." New information keeps surfacing, amplifying, qualifying, and clamoring to be known. New laws, new illegal settlements, new settler violence, new surveillance, new silence. The film "Tantura," released just as I was sending out my manuscript, confirmed what until then was only a contested allegation: the '48 massacre of Tantura's Palestinians by the Alexandroni brigade actually did happen. I now know that the Dor parking lot where I'd parked covers a mass grave. I learned about it just in time to rewrite that section of *Tracing Homelands* but not in time to correct an earlier version, published in *Consequences* magazine. Other facts surfaced later and continue to surface: the arson my mother prophesied; accelerating home demolitions and evictions on both sides of the Green Line border; IDF carnage in Gaza and routine killing in the occupied West Bank, children included; and now, as this book goes to press, Israel voted into power the most extreme right-wing government in its history.

"How did we get to this point?" I hear people ask, meaning the recent elections, since news of the Occupied Territories, Gaza, and the Golan barely gets reported. "Connect the dots," I want to answer, and sometimes do. The history *Tracing Homelands'* fragmented and layered account tells is a direct response to this question, at once looking back to points of origin and looking ahead to a still unknown future. That this account concerns a history unfolding almost entirely inside the Green Line 1949 cease-fire border does not evade this question. Its scrutiny of Israel's founding years uncovers the seeds of the present: the vengeful "Song of the Houligans" calling for blood and fire, the nationalist propping up of the myths of Masada and Tel Hai, the corrosive intra-Jewish as well as anti-"Arab" racism, and the bravado of *"yahrab Beitak."* These are all dots available for connecting.

As a memoir, *Tracing Homelands* necessarily concerns the history I happened to be born into and an Israel demarcated by the old Cease Fire border of '49, in place until the '67 war. But the events my early life touched on have further implications. Pointing toward the Occupied West Bank, Gaza, and the Golan, they trace a direct line from the Nakba of '48 to the Naksa of '67 and beyond them. As an account of a festering Israeli-Palestinian strife, they expose substrata of politics where different and unequal tangles of injuries and desperation shape ideology and drive the bitter fighting that lacerates this land. While at stake are territorial claims to lands each side sees as inalienably theirs, these claims invoke needs far beyond any land's practical use. The land as homeland is the crux of the matter—a place of origin, the core of self. It is a motherland, sheltering and bountiful, familiar, comforting, and intimately known. At once a place and an idea for which people on either side have been willing to die.

This primal sense of a homeland permeated my young life. I understand the willingness to die for it, Palestinian as well as Jewish-Israeli. I understand but distrust its spell, seeing its damage. This distrust propels *Tracing Homelands'* exploration of the profound sense of existential injury that fused Zionist slogans of blood, fire, and revenge into Israel's relentless and ever-expanding hold over Palestinian lives and lands. While these slogans are rooted in historic Jewish anguish, the evidence on the ground and events currently underway speak to Palestinian current anguish, perpetuated daily. Both histories are seeded in traumas that can't be erased, and they help us understand how we got from one point to the next. But the notion of "both" mustn't obscure the profound harm done now, and done unequally. There is no computing suffering, no equivalence of pain. What matters now is not the weighing of pain but its consequences.

Inevitably, *Tracing Homelands'* first person narrative concerns my own Jewish-Israeli part in this history. The Palestinian experience is mostly implicit in this telling, a mark of the chasm separating us, known by me mostly in its rubble, rarely in person. My own narrative is about what I knew as a child bystander-participant in this momentous history, and about what I learned, unlearned, questioned, and revised as an adult regarding our presence on this land. It entailed a slow and painfully reluctant peeling away of layers of the myths, convictions, and obfuscations that sustain Israel's geo-political aspirations. In so doing, I came to know my own roots in Israel's early settler-colonialism and to look squarely at its increasingly brutal chokehold over Palestinians' daily lives.

The anguish that went into probing this history is indeed personal, but the dots *Tracing Homelands* connects are political, pointing toward a future yet to be decided. Crucial to this future is the role outside powers may or may not wish to play in it—those who have been keeping the Israeli-Palestinian "conflict," as it is blandly called, simmering as a proxy war to serve their own geo-political aspirations. That is, shadowing the tangled narratives of our two peoples are partners deftly dealing out of sight: Mandatory Britain and France early on, and now the United States, Russia, the Arab "world," and Iran, among others. For them, as well as for the Israelis and the Palestinians, it is never a situation of "no choice."

Acknowledgements

Tracing Homelands came into being in Lady Borton's memoir workshops, held for several inspiring summers at the William Joiner Centre (now Institute) for the Study of War and its Social Consequences, at the University of Massachusetts Boston. Other mentors include Thomas Daley, Dorian Fox, and especially Alysia Abbott at Boston's Grub Street, and Joan Wickersham and the late Richard McCann at Provincetown's Fine Arts Work Center. I am deeply grateful to each of them, and to Alex Johnson, Cat Parnell, and Laura Tillem for astute editorial help.

Several residencies offered safe-havens and financial support: The Vermont Studio Center, Santa Fe's Women's International Study Center, Santa Fe's Art Institute, and (unofficially) Rosalind Brackenbury and Allen Meece's "Osprey Nest" in Key West. I am grateful, too, to the following periodicals for publishing early chapters from *Tracing Homelands*: *Jewish Currents*, *Nowhere*, *Consequence*, Harvard's Divinity School's *Bulletin*, and the *Massachusetts Review*. A generous artist grant from the Massachusetts Cultural Council sustained me just when I needed it most. People who helped my work on the ground, in Israel, are Deborah Bright, Eitan Bronstein Aparicio, Nurith Gertz, Judd Neeman, Amira Ofer, Donnie McLean, Anis Chacour, Susan Jacoby, and members of Zochrot—all essential to this work.

While I cannot name here all the many wonderful friends who read drafts and cheered me on with trust and commitment, I hope you know how much I appreciate your being at my side. Donna Luff, Joseph Fox, and Jan Jacobson offered invaluable advice as they work-shopped the book with me, chapter by chapter. Skip Schiel, a.k.a *Ein el-Nour*, shared photos, information, and heart. Louise Dunlap's writing about settler-colonialism in Napa CA was an inspiring "soul-sister" to my own writing all along the way. Fred Sinclair gave me the gift of time and knowledge reading the entire manuscript, and Susan Jacoby edited early drafts with a keen eye. I think with sadness of Barbara Hammer, Lois Rudnick, Louis Kampf, Richard Ohmann, and Saul Slapikoff, who followed this project closely but did not live to see it done.

These acknowledgements would not be complete without warm thanks to Michel Moushabeck and his wonderful colleagues at Interlink , including David Klein for keen editing and Pam Fontes-May for thoughtful guidance and design. Most importantly, heartfelt thanks go to Deborah Bright, without whose forensic intelligence and commitment my search for traces of the Nakba would have never happened, and to Martha Collins, brilliant poet and friend, whose editorial acumen and unstinting gift of time and trust gave my manuscript its final shape.

Finally, I thank Naomi Brussel for reminding me of the enduring courage needed in struggle, and my son, Jeremiah, for an understanding that goes beyond words.